AL
DAVIS
TO
WIN

AL DAVIS TO WIN

A FIRSTHAND ACCOUNT OF SILVER & BLACK GREATNESS

DENNIS RANAHAN

Only one for me, Pam.

Dennis Ranahan served as personal assistant to Al Davis in the 1970s, a job he remembers fondly in this joyful memoir about Davis and the Raiders. Ranahan was innocent, and this book reads like Huck Finn meets Al Davis—the collision of innocence and experience. Davis comes across as utterly demanding, monomaniacal, cruel, kind, insensitive, sensitive, brilliant and dense. And totally unknowable. There is a late-night scene at a Doggie Diner in Oakland where Davis lectures Ranahan on the difference between "right" and "best." It could be straight out of Plato. The book provides new insights—some surprising—into John Madden, George Blanda, Ken Stabler and others. This book gives a deep inside look at Davis at the height of his powers and his charisma and into a memorable epoch of the Raiders, deeper than other books on the subject.

~ Lowell Cohn, author and sports columnist

Table of Contents

Table of Contents

Foreword

I MET AL DAVIS BEFORE I GOT TO PLAY FOR HIM. When I began playing center for the Raiders in the 1960s, I used to finish the season and head back to my home in Wisconsin for the Christmas holidays. I'd work there until spring practice started for my old college team, the University of Miami, when the coaches would invite me to work with the players. One year, this assistant coach from San Diego Chargers, Al Davis, showed up and took over the practice. What balls this guy has, I thought, as he stepped in front of the team's coaches to have the receivers run his drill or take over the defensive practice, asking the kids to try it his way.

He wasn't asking permission to assert himself in the practices; he was getting done what he wanted to get done. He was evaluating the players as well as coaching them. No one got in his way as he fulfilled his agenda.

I first had an opportunity to be coached by him—and the head coach at the time in San Diego, Sid Gilman—when I was named to the AFL All-Star team. I wanted to be taught the right way to do things, to have a design to accomplish on the field. In those few days, I learned more about the game with Davis and Gilman than the whole season playing in Oakland.

My football life changed forever when Davis was named the Raiders head coach in 1963. He brought in a brand of football I wanted. He taught us the right techniques to block and taught receivers how to run patterns. I recall walking into our first meeting under his leadership, and two important words were written on the blackboard for the squad: "Pride and Poise."

I know the Raiders have had a number of slogans since—Commitment to Excellence, Pro Football's Winningest Organization, and Just Win Baby—but those first two words, Pride and Poise, were the two that always drove me. As a player, in business, and as a man. I soon learned what they meant and how they were earned.

I couldn't get enough of his coaching. He believed in doing things right, and perfection took a level of commitment and discipline that challenged us every day. In the middle of the night, I would wake with thoughts of what was the right block on a particular play, where the tight end would be, and I would have to check the playbook to make sure I knew how to best do my job on the field. My wife Sally would see me fumbling in the dark and ask me what I was doing, and I would just tell her to go back to sleep because I needed to check something in my playbook.

That level of attention to detail didn't exist before Coach Davis came to the team. We were just going through the motions; he gave purpose to everything we did and taught us that greatness comes from design. We executed it, understood what we needed to do to win, and did it all with pride and poise.

That first year, 1963, we beat the San Diego Chargers twice, his old team and the squad many considered the best in the AFL. Beating them in Oakland was great, but winning in San Diego, at Balboa Stadium, was the most emotional moment I had ever experienced on a football field. This is tough for me to admit, but Al Davis and I hugged each other on the field after that win, unable to talk, with tears in our eyes. That burst of happiness I will never forget. He had pure joy etched on his face, and it was a feeling that I will always carry in my heart.

I used the top of my helmet to block, and that would often cause a stinger in my neck, forcing me down for the mandatory eight counts. During one game in 1963, I got a pretty bad one that forced me to drop to one knee to try to clear the hit's effects. Before I was even able to rise, Davis was marching onto the field, yelling at me not to come out of the game because then our opponent would think they had us whipped.

That call to action, his belief that I could do it and needed to do it, forced me to overcome the pain in favor of the goal to win. It was the essence of his program. It pushed me to start 210 straight games and play in 308 through a series of injuries.

One day after John Madden was named coach, Al was on me pretty good at practice. He chewed me out unmercifully, and when I got back to the locker room after practice, I stayed by the door to confront him. I asked him why he said all that stuff to me. "Did I offend you? I thought I could offend you," he said, "because I thought you were strong enough to take it."

I commented back, indicating I was a human; perhaps he didn't know that. He just put his head down and walked away.

Even that exchange made me want to do more for him and our team.

He was loyal to his players, and we returned his loyalty. That extended beyond just the Raiders. When we were on the East Coast for a game, he would sometimes call me to join him in his suite to meet some of the players he coached at the Citadel or as a younger man in the army. These guys loved him and were loyal to him; he considered me a part of this fraternity.

He always told me that we weren't going to go into battle with one bazooka but with all cannons and bazookas blaring. He applied that approach to the football field, negotiations, business, and life.

In 1975, I knew I was going to retire; still, I wanted to give it one last shot to see how my knees responded to my most recent offseason surgery. We were playing the San Francisco 49ers in our final home preseason game. I started, made all my blocks, and played as well as I ever had on a 13-play opening drive, resulting in a touchdown.

After snapping for the successful extra point, though, I walked off the field knowing I was done. I had given it all and was headed home to Sally and the kids. I raised my helmet to say goodbye to the game while saluting Sally in the stands. I told her with that gesture that I was coming home, babe.

Al knew I was considering retirement. We had talked about it during that summer camp in Santa Rosa. When I came off the field and took myself out of the game, he knew I was done playing center for the Raiders, but he still wanted me in the organization. "You come work for me in the office. You'll become our business manager," Davis offered.

My move into the front office was emotional. The first time I heard the stadium public-address system announce, "At center, number 50, Dave Dalby," I missed not being out there. Our second regular season game after I retired was in Baltimore, against the Colts, and Dalby took a hit on his knee that sent him limping to the sideline. Davis was sitting behind me in the owner's box, and as the medical crew worked with Dalby, he tapped me on the back, "Can you go next week if he's hurt?"

I could and nodded back to him. "I can still go; I'm ready," I repeated.

By this time, I didn't have any cruciate ligaments left in my knees, but I could have just taped them up and got back into action.

Fortunately, the injury to Dalby proved not to be severe, and he didn't miss any games.

I found that working for Coach Davis as a player or in the front office required the same discipline, attention to detail, and respect that everything we did mattered toward our objective of winning. We didn't prepare to win; we expected to win. We expected to be successful . . . that's the way the Raiders were.

I had known Tom Grimes from Miami when he was a cub reporter and realized his challenges as public relations director. He not only had Davis to please, but was getting constant assignments from Al LoCasale and John Madden. When Dennis Ranahan joined him, I'll tell you, those guys really hustled. Denny was young, energetic, and always in service to the team and Mr. Davis. Still, Al would never be satisfied, and he chewed out Dennis and all the front office workers the same way he would challenge players on the field.

While I was playing on the field, Dennis used to sit with Mr. Davis on Sundays and run notes to coaches during games. After he was gone, I took over doing that.

After a few years in a full-time capacity running the team's business affairs with LoCasale, I wanted to do other things. Sometimes Davis would return to the office around 5:30 after meeting with the coaches at the practice field, and before going upstairs, would stop by my office to tell me he wanted to meet me. He'd ask how long I was planning on being around, and I would say I was planning on getting out of here in an hour or so. Knowing I wanted to catch my son's football practice, he would say, "Oh, I'm going to need you for longer than that."

I'd sit in my office, working on other projects while waiting to be summoned upstairs to his office, and when the call didn't come, I would finally call him. It might be after 8:30 now, I'd missed Jimmy's practice and dinner with the family, and I'd tell him I was still down-stairs waiting for him.

He tossed it off, saying he no longer needed to meet.

I realized that if I were ever going to get control of my own life, I would need to break away from the Raiders and get away from his dominating influence on me. He kept coming after me when I bought my ranch and moved to Auburn, California—calling for advice on play-ers and coaches, wanting my opinion on things related to the team and the organization. He told me he wanted me around and that I should sit with him during the games again. He offered me a retainer to fly to Los Angeles when the Raiders played there. When the possibility for them to move back was in play, he had me represent the team in negotiations with Sacramento and Oakland.

He wanted the pride and poise he had instilled in the organization to guide the future greatness of the Raiders. I wanted to do all I could to repay him for all he had done for me. Everything I've accomplished in my business life has revolved around the principles and focus he taught me. Those that don't respect and honor the loyalty and generous nature of the man, simply don't know Al Davis.

He was a man that those in need could count on for a lifeline. Even with someone he had professional disagreements, when they were in real need—a sick relative or serious financial setback—he would come to their aid without any fanfare. Some of his recipients didn't even know how he ever found out about their situation, but he was there for them.

He won't be coming around that corner in the Raiders office any-more, but I still cherish the memories of when he did.

I feel his pride and poise.

~ JIM OTTO

Jim Otto played 15 seasons for the Oakland Raiders, and one of the last things he contributed to the football world was the foreword for this book. He finished it not long before he died on May 19, 2024.

He was 86 years old, and while he sacrificed his body for his sport, his mind remained sharp. Otto did not suffer the ill effects with brain trauma that has come to light in more recent years. The man that many consider the greatest center in professional football history had plenty of operations . . . mostly on his knees. Enough procedures to fill every day of any calendar month. Those battle wounds were absorbed in pursuit of Al Davis' driving force in search of wins. By today's standards, much of the punishment Otto endured would be banned by the rules.

The man had a clearer understanding of what needed to be done to win as any athlete Al Davis had the opportunity to coach. Davis didn't often show his favoritism, but he confided with me one afternoon, "The gold standard for excellence that exemplifies the Silver and Black is Jim Otto."

Jim was married to Sally for over 60 years, and their family includes enough grandchildren to fill a park.

He was likable from so many angles, while he died on a Sunday, we remember all the Sundays he lived while becoming one of the most beloved athletes in history.

— — — — — —

Prologue

"**Y**A FUCKED THAT UP," Al Davis said over his shoulder to Mike Taylor, his longtime public relations representative with both the Los Angeles and Oakland Raiders.

It might just have been a benign comment on a Tuesday afternoon from a boss to an employee. There was no threat of physical violence behind the remark. But Davis didn't utter it in the privacy of his office; rather, at a press conference on January 18, 2011, introducing Hue Jackson as the Raiders new head coach. Jackson was the team's eleventh head coach since the Raiders enjoyed their best success under John Madden and Tom Flores in a 21-year span beginning in 1963. Five successive coaches have been dismissed with losing marks.

Jackson delivered his opening statement and answered questions. Then the assembled media began exiting the room, yet Davis was not done.

"Wait one moment," the Raiders owner said like a spoiled child at a party that was breaking up before he had his fill of fun.

The media awkwardly ran into each other as some hesitated. Eventually, all returned to their seats to watch the second half of the Davis-called press conference.

Now that Davis had presented Jackson as the Raiders new man, he wanted to throw his former head coach publicly under the bus. When the media began leaving before he had a chance was when the "Ya fucked that up" remark was made, with cameras running at a live televised news conference.

In a rambling message that had become common in Davis' latter years with the Raiders, the onetime genius of football jumped from point to point while discrediting Tom Cable on nearly every front. He amplified accusations of Cable being a wife beater, said the team was forced to fly women to service the coach the night before games, and that his dismissed coach had brought wrath onto the organization.

It was a scathing indictment against a man who had been sitting to Davis' right only a couple of years earlier, just where Hue Jackson was today and declared to be the leader who would bring the Raiders back to greatness.

Before the press conference was even complete, I got a call in my office from a friend who was watching; he said, "The league ought to take the team away from this clown. Do you see him?"

Davis was a mere shadow of the man he once was. He appeared at the press conference with bandages on his head that were not large enough to conceal all his scabs. His hands were wracked with arthritis that made his fingers jet in all different directions, leaving them useless to turn the pages of notes on the table in front of him. He indeed looks like a real-life version of Mr. Burns, the animated character on *The Simpsons*.

I took no pleasure in seeing Davis crumble in stature. Once again, he was diminishing his once-proud reputation. For me, it felt like watching a loved one surrender to the effects of Alzheimer's.

After the press conference, my son Kevin, now 30, came to my office with Adam, his friend since grade school. Adam showed no respect for Davis' legacy. He didn't know what the man had accomplished prior to the dwindling success of the team after their return to Oakland following 13 seasons in Los Angeles.

"The Raiders will never be any good while that guy is in charge," Adam muttered.

Kevin, a Raiders fan all his life, wanted me to offer Adam a different picture of Davis, of his prime.

"Dad, tell him about the man," Kevin said while pulling a chair in front of my desk and straddling it with his elbows on the seat back.

That day, I spent the better part of the afternoon reliving some moments I had the opportunity of spending with Mr. Davis during the 1970s. Now I'd like to share with a larger audience some defining moments spent with Al Davis and told to Adam that afternoon.

— — — — — —

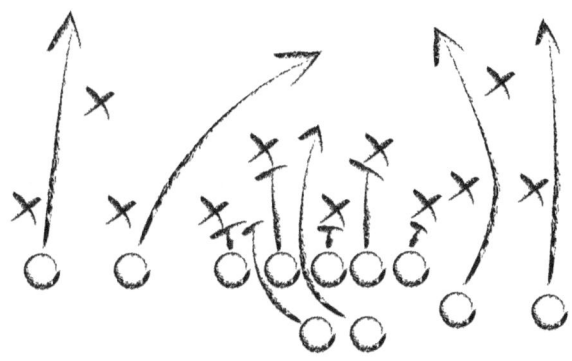

Chapter 1

Immaculate Reception

THE OAKLAND RAIDERS VERSUS PITTSBURGH STEELERS playoff game was already late in the second quarter when my girlfriend, Pam, who, along with her East Bay family, was an avid Raiders fan, arrived at my parents' home in San Bruno. We spent only a moment together before she headed to San Carlos with my dad, and I set course in the opposite direction for Candlestick Park. The San Francisco 49ers were hosting the Dallas Cowboys in the National Football Conference play-offs opening round, and the game was blacked out locally. At my dad's favorite bar in San Carlos, near his office, he and Pam were going to watch the end of the Raiders game and all of the 49ers contest on the establishment's out-of-town television feed.

While I didn't have a ticket to the game, I'd figured out long ago ways to crack the Candlestick gates. All I had to do was join a crowd of people and then point forward or backward to indicate someone else was holding my ticket.

I was hurrying through the parking lot at Candlestick when cheers cascaded through the smoke and smell of barbeques. Tailgaters were reacting to transistor radios tuned to Bill King's play-by-play description of the Raiders battle against the Steelers.

Raiders quarterback Ken Stabler had dashed 30 yards for their only score of the day after he relieved an ineffective Daryle Lamonica in the fourth quarter. *"Now Blanda lines up for the all-important extra point,"* King announced as veteran kicker George Blanda looked set to covert the kick that would give the Raiders a one-point lead. *"It's good!"*

A guy in a 49ers T-shirt flipped an empty beer bottle into a garbage bag by his opened station wagon tailgate. "They are the luckiest sons of bitches in the world," he said in obvious disdain for the Raiders success. "I just hope we get some luck today, too," he added.

I assumed the Raiders would triumph as I climbed the asphalt hill leading to the 49ers gate on the stadium's south side. I had slipped through that same entrance the week before to watch the 49ers beat the Vikings.

This time I wasn't so lucky.

"Everyone, hold your own ticket," the security guards were yelling as I approached the gate. They were ordering fathers to hand tickets to daughters and sons. An elderly woman was stopped at the gate, and the man behind her holding a pair of tickets was forced to hand one to her so she could enter.

I made one attempt, casually walking in, but the gatekeeper stopped me. He brushed off my finger-pointing and said sternly, "Have whoever you are pointing to give you your ticket."

"Bob," I said over my shoulder, "give me my ticket."

I held my hand back, like I expected to get it filled, but none came. I turned, as if expecting to see "Bob" behind me, and when no one responded to my call, I said, "Where did he go? I hope he isn't already in the game with my ticket."

The ticket taker wasn't buying my act for a second. "Step aside," he said, guarding the turnstile. "Next," he shouted.

Defeated, I emerged from the throng around the gate to hear someone say, "The Steelers won!"

In Pittsburgh, pandemonium had broken out at Three Rivers Stadium. Steelers rookie running back Franco Harris had crossed the goal line with a deflected pass. No one was talking about Oakland's luck any longer.

Pittsburgh quarterback Terry Bradshaw had avoided the Raiders rush on fourth down and snapped a pass over the middle intended for John "Frenchy" Fuqua. The Steelers running back was covered by Raiders defensive back Jack Tatum, and the two players converged on the ball at midfield. Their collision forced the ball to tumble loose, headed for the Three Rivers Stadium's artificial turf. Oakland players began a winning celebration, and the Pittsburgh crowd collectively slumped in apparent defeat.

Harris grabbed the ball inches above the ground and hurtled down the left sideline. Oakland defender Jimmy Warren failed on the Raiders last chance to stop him short of the end zone. Harris scored a 60-yard go-ahead touchdown with only seconds left on the game clock. The Raiders celebration shifted to stunned disbelief. The Steelers fans burst into a delirious celebration over their team's first-ever postseason victory.

Three hours later, the San Francisco fans were dealt a blow nearly as stunning. San Francisco led the Cowboys all day after Vic Washington returned the opening kickoff for a touchdown. But Roger Staubach relieved an ineffective Craig Morton and engineered three late-scoring drives, capped by a Ron Sellers catch in the end zone, providing the visitors a 30–28 win. I had an opportunity to watch it because a friend miraculously showed up at the gate with an extra ticket that got me a great seat to watch the action.

I was still talking about those dramatic games the following March when I was interviewed by Tom Grimes, the Oakland Raiders director of public relations. He had come to the campus at San Jose State to select a summer intern for his staff. The program was designed for students between their junior and senior years of college, but I had negotiated with the school to serve my internship after my senior year for my final three credits toward graduation. I did that for two reasons. First, I needed the money I had earned working in San Francisco the previous summer to finance my senior year. Second, I had talked to friends who had served internships with good companies, including San Francisco Giants and the 49ers. They were offered full-time positions after their internships but couldn't accept them because they had to go back and finish their final year of college. I figured, once in the workplace, I wanted to stay there.

The internship with the Oakland Raiders was not posted, but by sheer luck, I was sitting in my advisor's office when he took a call from Grimes to confirm the campus visit.

"I want to interview for that position," I announced.

"You should sign up for a few others just in case that one doesn't work out." My advisor pushed across the desk a list of businesses scheduled to hire an intern for the summer.

"No," I said flatly, "I want the Raiders spot. That's where I'm going to focus my efforts."

"Better have some backups," he reiterated. "You need those three units to complete your degree."

Even though I didn't take his advice, I realized on the morning of the interview why the position wasn't posted. The only other candidate, Eric Cullenward, had already been promised the summer internship position. He had a connection with Grimes because his father was a staff writer with the *San Francisco Examiner*.

Still, Grimes arranged to interview us together. Cullenward brought a portfolio full of promotions he had done with the music department at San Jose. It was very impressive, and while Grimes was paging through his presentation, I acknowledged his excellent work before shifting the subject from music to football.

I said, "The loss to the Steelers must have been a crushing experience."

Grimes looked up from Eric's work and acknowledged, "It was a quiet plane ride home."

"I was at Candlestick that day. What a blow to Bay Area sports on both counts, huh?"

He nodded in agreement. "We were getting scores of the 49ers game on the plane ride. We were shocked they suffered a similar fate on the same day."

I was excited to talk about professional football with someone who really worked in the sport, and I pursued our connection. "Should motivate both teams to succeed this year, though, wouldn't you think?"

"I like our chances," Grimes said, seemingly agreeing with my assessment. He turned his attention to Eric. "You like sports?"

"Golf is my favorite," was his quick reply.

Grimes paused and eyed the two of us, making some calculations. "You know what? I think we'll go with two interns this year."

He pulled out a small calendar and announced the first intern job would start on June 4. It would be focused mostly on preparation for the upcoming season with editorial work on the media guide and *Pro! Magazine*. The second internship would start in mid-July after training camp opened and the players reported.

He offered me the choice between the first or second date. I jumped on the first one without hesitation, and Eric seemed pleased that he wouldn't have to be around until the players reported. I knew all about football. Learning how a team prepared for the upcoming season sounded like heaven. That was exactly where I wanted to spend my summer—and a lot more than that, if I proved invaluable enough.

The Raiders offices were located at 7811 Oakport Street, across the freeway from the Oakland/Alameda County Coliseum. The public relations department was downstairs in a room ringed on two walls by clipboards hanging on hooks with press releases from all 26 NFL teams. Two desks faced each other in the office with a chair between them, and that's where Al LoCasale was sitting, my first day on the job. While showing me the 1972 media guide, he advised me to read the bios of everyone to know whom I would be working for in the organization.

"When is the new media guide coming out?" LoCasale asked Grimes.

Grimes frowned; even to me, it sounded like LoCasale was delivering an indictment on the guide's progress rather than a genuine interest in its completion date. LoCasale was Al Davis' executive assistant, officially his right-hand man. Davis ran the offices upstairs, and LoCasale oversaw the downstairs operation of the Raiders organization.

"It will be out before the first preseason game—when we know what players to include," Grimes replied in a soft but defiant voice as

LoCasale left the office. Then he told me, "In fact, there is something you can do right now to help our little old media guide come out on time." He handed me the galleys he had been proofreading and told me the directions to Cardinal Company, the printer we worked with across San Francisco Bay.

Before I left, still uncertain about how the place was run, I asked Grimes if I should fulfill LoCasale's instructions first.

"You'll have plenty of time to read bios and meet the people that work here," Grimes said, not looking up. He was drawing a map for the Raiders printers. "Right now, get these over to Mr. Emery at Cardinal Company."

The commute to San Francisco was a breeze. The Raiders offices were located minutes from the freeway entrance, and Cardinal Company was right off the Fifth Street exit, just across the Bay Bridge. I drove there and back in just over an hour.

When I got back, Ken LaRue was sitting in the chair previously occupied by LoCasale. Grimes introduced us as Mr. Ranahan and Mr. LaRue, to which Ken replied, "You don't need to call me Mr., but always call Mr. Davis, Mr." Then he added, smiling at Grimes, "LoCasale would like everyone to call him Mr., but the only one you really have to worry about is Mr. Davis."

The front entrance of the Raiders offices led into a foyer laid with white marble. Along one wall was a nine-foot-long, chromed-framed glass case that displayed Raiders novelties. The team colors were used exclusively throughout the headquarters. Two staircases on either end of the building were guarded by secretaries. The stairway was clearly marked for employees only, and any breach was met with an instant request to stop. At the top of the stairs was a pair of secretary desks posted in front of the two most important football offices in the facility, Ron Wolf's player personnel department and Al Davis' corner office. Through his windows, he had a view of the Oakland Coliseum.

At the opposite end of the second floor was John Madden's corner office, which had no window. A room the coaches used adjoined Madden's space, and halfway down the hall was a conference room with cushioned silver armchairs around a 12-foot black slate table. The conference room was available to whichever department needed extra space for current projects but was mostly devoted to coaching and team personnel functions. At one end was a projector screen where coaches would study both NFL opponents and college prospects on black-and-white 8mm film.

Since Ron Wolf was constantly scouting college players, his office had a large area designed like a library, with metallic shelves holding different colored binders organized by conference, college, and position. Each college prospect had at least four reports from different sources, mostly from coaches and scouts, although one quarterback from Penn State also had a series of recommendations from his mother.

Within the first week of my 1973 internship with the Raiders, I was working with Wolf, filing reports received in the mail. His outspoken candor was a breath of fresh air in an organization managed by a demanding boss, creating a tense environment. Many observers thought Ron was the man inside the organization most responsible for the excellence Davis had established with the Raiders. Wolf's personnel department consistently drafted athletes contributing to the Raiders ongoing success. That very year punter Ray Guy had been a controversial number-one selection. He was the first special teams player ever to be selected in the first round and would soon reward Wolf's gamble handsomely.

I hadn't yet met my boss, but my curiosity about Al Davis sharply enhanced when Wolf counseled me, "There is no use trying to hide anything from him because he is going to know. Don't worry about screwing up. He'll catch you doing that." He paused to let that point sink in. "Just focus on solutions. Ultimately, that's all he really cares about."

— — — — — —

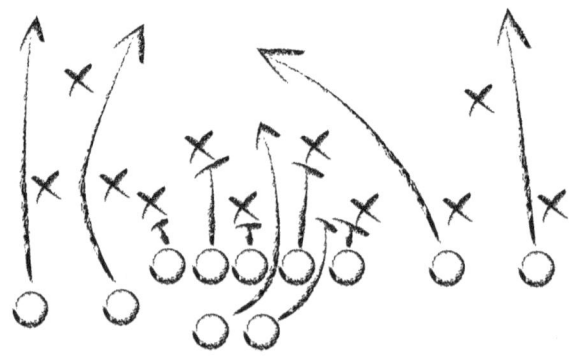

Chapter 2

Open Doors

ONE DAY, I CAME IN THE SIDE DOOR after lunch and saw five employees in states of shock, laughter, and concern gathered around one secretary's desk. My first thought was a mouse was loose in the office. Ken LaRue was standing there cleaning his pipe and shaking his head in disbelief. Grimes was sitting at his desk with his hands behind his head, enjoying the uproar.

When I asked Kris what was going on, she said, "I told him he couldn't go upstairs."

"Told who?"

"I didn't know it was him." She had only joined the Raiders front office a short time before, but she knew one of her primary duties was to make sure nobody went up those back stairs. "Some guy flies in the back door with greased-back hair and starts up the stairs," Kris said in defense of what she'd done. "I jumped from my chair and told him to stop right there."

I had a pretty good idea who she'd stopped. "What did he do?"

"He stopped."

I burst out laughing. I couldn't help it.

Kris wasn't happy with my response and told me it wasn't funny.

"He asked if he could help me, and I said, 'You can by coming right back down these stairs,'" Kris stated while showing the gesture she used with a pointed finger.

"'No,' he said, 'I don't think you understand. I'm Al Davis.'"

"Did you believe him?"

Kris solemnly replied, "I knew it had to be him when he said that. He wasn't asking me to believe him; he was telling me he was Al Davis. He also said, 'I own the place.'"

"Was he mad?"

"I don't know; that was the last thing he said."

"He isn't mad," LaRue assured her. "I think it's funny."

"I'd go with hilarious," Grimes shouted from his desk.

"Well, it's been nice working here," Kris said glumly.

Twenty minutes later, LoCasale came down the hallway from his office and suggested to Kris, "It's okay to let Mr. Davis up those stairs."

He didn't wait for a response and came to where Grimes and I were sitting in the public relations office.

"So, Mr. Wolf has a proposition for your young intern here," LoCasale announced. "He wants to know if you'd be willing to have him spend the last two weeks of his internship working at training camp."

"Well," Grimes responded without raising his eyes off the stat sheet on his desk, "we have Nelson's kid starting his internship on July 16, and we had him penciled in for camp work."

Wolf entered the room himself. "This would be the 'Joe Driver' spot; would you be interested?" Before I could answer, he added, "This would be a paid position, and you'd live with us in Santa Rosa and drive players back and forth from the airport." Wolf turned his attention to Grimes. "Can we have your guy?"

"Well, what does young Mr. Ranahan want to do?" Grimes posed to me.

"I'd like to go to camp."

That settled the matter. LoCasale took me to his office to fill out tax information and hiring forms. I was being hired for an eight-week position that paid $600 plus room, board, car, and gas. I was going to be driving players and was alerted to the fact that sometimes I would be driving Mr. Davis.

The El Rancho Tropicana, one of the largest hotels in Santa Rosa, is located in the heart of the Sonoma Valley wine country. The property owners had built two grass football fields to lure the Raiders to their facility for their annual summer training camp. The fields included a locker room with all the essentials, plus a weight and training room. The living facilities at the hotel were three rows of connected rooms. The players were housed in the middle of the three buildings, while the Raiders staff and media occupied the first building. The third building was reserved for hotel guests and featured the nicest suites on the property. Davis had a suite in building three.

"Just drive like your driving instructor was sitting next to you," Ken Bishop advised while giving me a piece of paper with Davis' room number. Bishop was Tom Grimes' assistant. "Nobody is supposed to know what room he is in, so keep this hush-hush."

Bishop, an avid San Francisco Giants baseball fan, had hundreds of batter-by-batter scorecards compiled while sitting at Candlestick Park or listening on the radio. Jim Barr was pitching for the Giants this afternoon, and Bishop marked a satisfied K next to a batter in the fifth inning before wishing me the best of luck.

I was finally going to meet Al Davis.

I was supposed to drive him to the airport so he could catch a 6:05 p.m. PSA flight to Los Angeles. His departure was scheduled out of Oakland, and he had asked me to show up at his room ten minutes before four.

I stopped at the number 314 on the door and took a deep breath before knocking.

I heard from inside the room a question, "Who's there?"

"I'm Dennis, sir. I'm here to drive you to the Oakland Airport."

The door opened six inches; I could only see his head looking sideways out the door. "Are you a good driver?"

My response was like a private reporting to a general on presentation day: "Yes, sir."

"Then come in," he offered while walking away from the widening door crack.

He was naked, just out of the shower, and left a trail of water as he headed to the back bedroom. I let myself in and surveyed the room, which was dominated by a massive set of weights and a workout bench that must have challenged the strength of the hotel floor.

A few minutes passed before he emerged from the back room, holding a shirt and asking me, "Is this shirt black?"

I wasn't sure what he meant. The shirt was obviously black. What was the test here? I wondered. I had been warned to listen to what he said. Everything meant something, and I needed to pay attention.

I confirmed that his shirt was black.

"Just put those bags in the trunk; the keys are right here. Have you ever driven a Cadillac?" he asked before wandering off, not waiting for an answer.

Davis was dressing like he was going out on a date. The room reeked of cologne while he buttoned a black fishnet shirt, which he wore with a pair of white embroidered slacks. No socks and a pair of loose-fitting loafers completed his ensemble.

He pointed to his car keys, perched on top of his black overnight bag, and asked me to take the bag, a briefcase, and a shirt he pulled from his closet.

"Put these in the car," Davis requested.

I dutifully followed instructions, and after hanging his shirt on the hanger in the back of his new Cadillac Fleetwood, I opened the trunk. After placing the other two items in the storage compartment, I had second thoughts. Would it be smarter to leave his briefcase in the car in case he had something he wanted to work on during the hour-long ride to the airport?

My question was left waiting a long time. It was a hot day to be standing in the sun, but I stayed in place until the door of Room 314 opened. He said with amusement, "What happened to you? I thought you went without me."

I apologized for not being where he wanted me and then asked if he wanted his briefcase in the car or trunk.

"In the car," he said while inspecting how I hung his shirt. "Is that going to be all right if I open my window?"

I didn't answer right away because I was mesmerized by the trunk. It was doing something I had never seen a car do before, closing itself the final inch or so with some motorized feature.

Finally, I responded. "I think it would be all right, but I'll move it to my side just to be safe," I said while rehanging it. I hustled back to open Mr. Davis' door, but he said impatiently, "Fuck my door. We've got to get going. You're going to make me miss my plane."

Like a Keystone Kop, I hurried around to my side of the car and assumed my place behind the wheel of the state-of-the-art automobile. It was completely different from what I was used to driving, a 1968 Volkswagen Bug.

I turned the ignition and cringed at that horrible sound when someone engaged the starter of an already running car. I remembered too late that I had started the car earlier to turn on the air-conditioning.

Davis let that ride, but he then asked, "What's that sound?" He was referring to a beep-beep I thought was coming because he had not fastened his seat belt.

"You need to fasten your seat belt, sir," I said. When he pulled the belt straight in front of him without the noise stopping, I suggested, "You need to buckle it."

"It's not my belt," Davis snapped. "You've still got the emergency brake on."

By now, I was in total panic. I was unable to find the release despite looking around at every possible place I thought it could be.

"Come on," Davis said, looking up from the papers he had pulled from his briefcase. "You are going to make me miss my flight!"

Flustered, I abandoned my search for the brake release and jammed the Caddy into reverse. To my great relief, the brake disengaged automatically when the car was taken out of park. Still, the annoying sound of the car warning system persisted, and now we both knew it was Davis' unfastened seat belt.

As he clicked it, the sound stopped. Then he looked up from his papers and asked, "Do I make you nervous?"

I answered that he didn't, but I respected and wanted to serve him well.

"Then get me to the airport on time."

When I pulled his Cadillac into the curb position at the Oakland Airport, he had 15 minutes left to make his PSA flight. Plenty of time. As he pulled himself out of the car, I asked if he wanted me to wait to make sure his flight was on time.

"I'll be fine, young man," he said while eyeing the shirt hanging in the back seat behind me. "I don't really need that," he added. Then he turned his attention back to me. "You've got four hours to do whatever you want. I'm coming back on the 9:00 p.m. flight. Pick me up then."

Four hours was enough time to drive across the Bay Bridge and visit home to bring Mom and Dad up-to-date on my work with the Raiders. When I parked Davis' black Cadillac in front of my parents' home on Crestmoor Drive in San Bruno, Dad was out front watering the lawn.

"That's what they've got you driving?" Dad asked with a smile. Turning off the water, he came to take a closer look at the Caddy.

"This is Mr. Davis' car," I explained. "I just dropped him off at the Oakland Airport and have a few hours before I pick him up tonight. He is in Los Angeles, going to meet with Bob Brown's attorney."

"Who's Bob Brown?" Dad queried.

"An offensive lineman."

"Well, come on inside," he said. "We'll get you something to eat. Are you hungry?"

"Starving," I reported.

I had a feeling of accomplishment following him into the house. I had met my boss, and I liked him.

– – – – – –

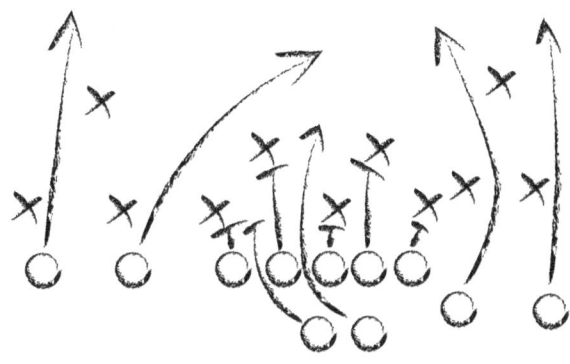

Chapter 3

Ten Years
Earlier

Aʟ Dᴀᴠɪs' sᴛᴏʀʏ ᴡɪᴛʜ ᴛʜᴇ Rᴀɪᴅᴇʀs started 10 years before I met him. In 1963, he was 33 when hired by Wayne Valley. In a sign of those early days in the AFL, the two men concluded their first negotiation by flipping a coin in the parking lot behind an East Bay restaurant to determine if the Raiders new coach and general manager would be paid $25,000 or $35,000 for his first season in Oakland.

The coin flip was called heads by Davis; coming up tails was of little consequence to him anyway. What he wanted had already been secured in the negotiations. A half-hour earlier, Davis had gained 2.4-percent ownership of the struggling third-year franchise, along with the voting power of a general partner and the opportunity to purchase additional shares of the team when they became available.

Davis also had complete authority over the football operations, including all personnel decisions. Control was a lot more important to him than his annual salary. Davis came from a well-to-do family that made their money in New York's garment district, and his wife, Carole, possessed a long-established fortune.

Valley also got what he wanted in the negotiations: a bright young innovative football mind with a ruthless reputation for doing whatever it took to win. Prior to joining the Raiders, Davis had served three seasons on the Los Angeles/San Diego Chargers staff under legendary coach Sid Gilman.

The Oakland Raiders had been a charter member of the American Football League, which began play in 1960. The Oakland franchise was originally supposed to be located in Minnesota, a deal that fell through when the older and more established National Football League induced Max Winter and Bill Boyer, owners of the AFL franchise, to opt instead for an NFL team in Minnesota. The NFL agreement was approved on January 28, 1960, for the Vikings to begin playing in Minnesota in 1961. The unexpected loss of the Winter/Boyer ownership group left the infant league scrambling to find a new site and financing for their suddenly orphaned eighth franchise.

East Bay businessman Y. Charles Soda led an investor group that included F. Wayne Valley, Ed McGah, Robert Osborne, and three others to relocate the franchise in Oakland. In 1961, Valley, McGah, and Osborne bought out their partners in the ownership of the Raiders. A year later, Valley and McGah acquired controlling interests in the franchise, and Valley became the managing general partner. Meetings of the Oakland investor group during early Raiders history included constant infusions of more capital to establish the fledging franchise. After three disappointing campaigns, the promise of success was more elusive than ever. Then Valley heard of this bright young offensive mind working with Gilman in San Diego.

The two met and became fast business partners.

Valley, a fiercely competitive businessman with a reputation for being cutthroat, was personally accomplished in sports. At Oregon State, he had starred on both offense and defense at fullback and line-backer on highly ranked Beaver teams of the 1930s; later, he earned his business degree from the University of Oregon. Davis also had on-field credentials, playing both center field on the baseball team and briefly on the football roster at Syracuse. But where Davis truly excelled was the strategic side of the game. His opinions on how to exploit defenses with an attack that stretched a secondary deep were widely regarded as the most innovative of his day.

Valley needed to turn around a team that had compiled 6–8, 2–12, and 1–13 regular season records while hemorrhaging money along with decreasing fan interest. The Raiders almost folded after their first season, but Buffalo Bills owner Ralph Wilson lent Valley $400,000 to keep the franchise afloat. For his part, Davis wanted the independence to develop his own kind of team, one that featured a vertical passing game and an intimidating, hard-charging defense.

The investors were still willing to finance the operation, but dramatic improvements in team play both on the field and in the front office had to be achieved, and the growth of fan interest needed to follow.

Davis said he could deliver all three . . . and did.

In his first season, Oakland's record jumped to 10–4, and Davis was named AFL Coach of the Year. Perhaps even more importantly, he established East Bay as a home base for the Raiders. Prior to his arrival, the team had played its first three seasons in three different locations. After playing their 1960 home games at Kezar Stadium in San Francisco, in 1961, the Raiders called Candlestick Park home. The Raiders staged their first East Bay campaign in 1962, when they hosted their home games at Frank Youell Field, a stadium Davis declared their permanent site until a new facility in the East Bay could be built for the developing franchise.

"You can't grow community pride in Oakland if you're playing your home games across the Bay," Davis said.

While Kezar Stadium routinely hosted more than 50,000 fans for San Francisco 49ers games in 1960, the Raiders seldom drew as many as 10,000 fans. The following season, at Candlestick Park, Raiders attendance declined to less than 7,000 per game. In their first season at quaint and much smaller Frank Youell Field, the Raiders enjoyed their best attendance, although many tickets were given away so crowds could be announced at 12,000 per home Sunday.

Davis put an end to the giveaway tickets when he arrived. He told his employees, "Never give away what you are trying to sell. You've just got to make the product worth buying."

Davis declared that the greatness of the Raiders would begin with the best organization in sports. He was committed to offering bright people the right tools and an environment to succeed. One of his first hires was Ron Wolf.

Ron was hired to reorganize the Raiders player personnel department. He proceeded to put together everything the team needed for their 1964 training camp in Santa Rosa. In particular, Wolf negotiated an additional practice field behind the El Rancho Hotel, where the Raiders set up camp for seven weeks each summer. Ron and equipment manager Dick Romanski also upgraded the weight room at camp, adding a new machine that promised to build calf muscles without straining the knees. Trainer George Anderson added a better medical table in his workspace, and the team dining area was enlarged.

Davis didn't wait long to flash his mercurial leadership style. On May 26, 1964, he asked Wolf, "Where are the spring reports?"

The question caught Wolf off guard. The 1963 NFL draft had already been conducted before Wolf joined the Raiders, and this was the first time spring reports had been discussed. He looked down at his desk in the Raiders offices on Franklin Street to gather his thoughts. Spring reports, he thought, what are spring reports?

"You do know what the spring reports are, don't ya?" Davis drawled in an accent that was a combination of Southern gentleman and New Jersey thug.

"Sir?"

"Ya fucking say that like you fucking don't know what the fuck we are here to do?"

Davis slammed down a folder full of contracts and information Ron had given him only moments before. The folder's papers gushed across Ron's desk, and most of them crashed up against the wall behind and spilled out onto the floor.

Ron had served as an intelligence expert in the army, so he knew all about conflicts. His steady, deliberate demeanor was a calming influence on all those around him. When caught in a situation like this, Ron evaluated and determined the best effective action, a skill he developed while stationed in West Berlin. While the team owner glared down, he replied honestly, "I don't know what spring reports are."

Davis shook his head with a look of utter disappointment and then went back on the attack. "It's your fucking job to know what spring reports are. What if they are the most important fucking thing to have us win? Would you want to know what the fuck they are then?"

"I want to know what the fuck they are now," Wolf said in a rejoinder that almost got a smile from Davis.

Wolf had completed his army service duty in 1960 and began compiling stats on college football players in that same year. Ron's work had been focused on players in their college years; he had never considered getting an updated height, weight, and running times in the 40- and 60-yard dashes during the college offseason.

"Ya see," Davis said, now in a more instructive tone, "if we know more, have more on each player than anyone else, we have an edge."

Ron agreed with a nod of his head.

"So," Davis said, "maybe spring reports are the most fucking important thing for us to win, do you understand?"

This time Ron was not so fast to agree, hoping that no response would end Davis' rant.

"Ya don't understand what I mean. Do you?" As Ron started to answer, Davis didn't give him a chance. "You've got a fucking decision to make here. Are you willing to really do all that is required to be great?" He paused, assessing his employee. "I'm not telling you that you have to. I'm just saying that is what is required to be here. To be a Raider."

"I didn't know what spring reports were," Wolf said calmly.

"It's not about the fucking reports," Davis said in a voice that filled the room. "It's about fucking doing whatever it fucking takes to be great!"

After two more seasons on the Raiders sidelines, in 1964 and 1965, campaigns that generated a combined 13–12–3 record, Davis was named AFL Commissioner on April 8, 1966. He turned the coaching duties over to John Rauch, who had earned All-American honors while playing quarterback at Georgia and was the second overall selection in the 1949 NFL draft. He was a good choice to carry on the offensive and defensive schemes that Davis had developed because he served all three years on Davis' staff in Oakland. The two had even been on the same staff at Army as assistant coaches in 1959.

Rauch would be inheriting a lot more fans. Davis was a driving force behind the construction of the $30-million Oakland/Alameda County Coliseum, which broke ground on February 1, 1965. His ability to influence outcomes in his favor was utilized on an even bigger stage when it came to league business in 1966.

"You win negotiations when you dominate the subject and stay with your objective to succeed longer than your opponent is willing," Davis advised American Football League owners before they named him AFL commissioner.

He took one employee along from the Oakland Raiders—Ron Wolf. "Listen," Davis explained to him at a restaurant in Oakland, "what we've got here is an opportunity to contribute to more than just a team. We can affect professional football overall."

Wolf did not want to leave the area. His wife, Virginia, had just given birth to their second daughter, Celli, and with a two-year-old and new baby in his home, Ron didn't want to uproot his family.

"Don't move the family," Davis said. "Just come to Houston. We'll get you a nice apartment. You're on the road all the time, anyway. You can get home when scouting in the Bay Area, and you can decide if you want to have Virginia and the kids move to Houston after we see how it goes. Don't move them now, though. We may be headed to New York soon enough."

At 36, Davis became the youngest league commissioner in professional sports. He was hired to facilitate a merger between the two leagues and devised a plan that the AFL owners embraced.

The NFL had recognition on its side, a more established fan base, and higher revenues from broadcasting rights. It gave them a position of power over the AFL in negotiations.

Still, Davis found a way to turn an edge against the NFL with his resources, which included deep pockets of the Hunt and Hilton families. While Lamar Hunt owned the Kansas City Chiefs, Baron Hilton had a major financial stake in the Los Angeles/San Diego Chargers.

The strategy Davis enacted was simple: Entice the best NFL players with contracts offering money the NFL couldn't or wouldn't dare match. The money was more than the targeted players deserved but worth every penny to the AFL if it forced the established NFL powers to the bargaining table in earnest. The AFL also lured stars out of college to choose the AFL over the NFL, household names such as quarterback Joe Namath of the New York Jets and Otis Taylor in Kansas City.

Davis' plan to bring the older league to its knees at the negotiating table worked; he enjoyed the fight so much that he didn't want it to end. Davis was convinced his fellow AFL owners were willing to surrender too much in the negotiations based on the perceived NFL strengths.

"We have the better product," Davis would argue in league meetings. Soon the original objective to negotiate a merger between the two leagues shifted for Davis. Instead of working toward a collective bargaining agreement to merge the two leagues, Davis lobbied to have the AFL take the NFL head-to-head. He wanted the battle to establish his league as the most profitable and respected in the world . . . and he wanted to run it.

"To win a negotiation, all you need to do is dominate the talks until the other side surrenders," Davis advised.

The misaligned objectives created three sides to the football negotiations in the spring of 1966: the NFL versus the AFL and Al Davis.

The AFL owners didn't want to give up the negotiating advantage
Davis had created, but they were not interested in a prolonged bidding
war over players and markets. The opposing objectives between Davis
and the majority of AFL and NFL owners prompted Hunt to organize
secret meetings with NFL powers spearheaded by Dallas Cowboys
General Manager Tex Schramm. That group hammered out an agreement without involving Davis.

These sessions produced the framework for one league and two
conferences. This plan would start with the AFL and NFL meeting in
an annual championship game beginning in January 1967 and blossom
into an alignment of one league with two conferences, the American
and National, for the 1970 season.

Pete Rozelle was chosen to oversee the combined leagues when the
merger was completed in 1970. Davis was informed of the agreement
and offered AFL presidency until the dissolution of the position before
the 1970 season. Offended at being left out of the talks that prompted the
merger, Davis declined the position and resigned as AFL commissioner.

Davis returned to the Raiders in the summer of '66, bitter over the
way he had been used by his fellow owners, and he carried from that
time forth a deep-seated hatred of Rozelle. The man who would not
hesitate to bend any rule in order to gain an advantage returned to the
Oakland Raiders with the added motivation of revenge.

With John Rauch already entrenched as head coach, Davis returned
as the team's principal owner and brought Ron Wolf back to Oakland.
Yet Davis had not given up his love for sideline tactics. Rauch suddenly
had another assistant coach, the team's owner, which blurred the lines
of authority between players and staff.

Davis' substantial influence would dominate the Raiders play on the field, even trump the head coach in the eyes of players and media. The formula worked on the scoreboard in 1967 and 1968, as the Raiders won back-to-back AFL Western Division titles while compiling a combined 25–3 regular season record.

Oakland capped their 1967 AFL season with a 40–7 championship win over the Houston Oilers to advance to the second AFL/NFL Championship Game against Vince Lombardi and his World Champion Green Bay Packers. "It is more difficult to maintain excellence than it is first to achieve," Davis said after the Raiders won their first AFL title.

In the '60s, Lombardi's Packers had dominated the NFL's most physical division, the Western Conference Central, while capturing six division titles and back-to-back Super Bowl wins, including the upcoming 33–14 triumph over the Raiders in Super Bowl II.

In Oakland, Rauch had guided the Raiders to the best regular season professional football records in 1967 and 1968. He was living up to standards of excellence on a near par with Lombardi, but he was not getting credit from the media or fans.

And he was miserable. Rauch was the head coach, but Davis ran the show.

Neither of the Raiders successful regular seasons in the following two years ended with a playoff win. They were outscored 27–23 by the New York Jets to end their 1968 campaign. Two weeks later, Joe Namath and the Jets pulled the biggest upset in NFL history, winning the American Football League their first victory in Super Bowl III, a 16–7 decision over the Baltimore Colts.

Davis had wanted to be the first to beat the NFL, and the fact that the Jets made history after beating the Raiders further splintered the fragile relationship between Davis and Rauch.

Four days after the Jets' Super Bowl triumph, Rauch accepted the head coaching spot with the Buffalo Bills, giving up the team with the best record in the AFL for the one with the worst.

Davis promptly hired the 32-year-old John Madden, who had served as linebacker coach on Rauch's staff the previous two seasons. Madden took the job knowing that he would be initially viewed as the coach assigned to implement Davis' orders. But, for those that knew him, Madden was also recognized as a teacher who could connect with his players effectively and engagingly.

This was a partnership custom-made for success. For the next decade, the Davis/Madden tandem won more games than any team in football. When Madden retired in 1979, he had the highest winning percentage of any coach and was the only one to win 100 games in his first ten seasons.

- - - - - -

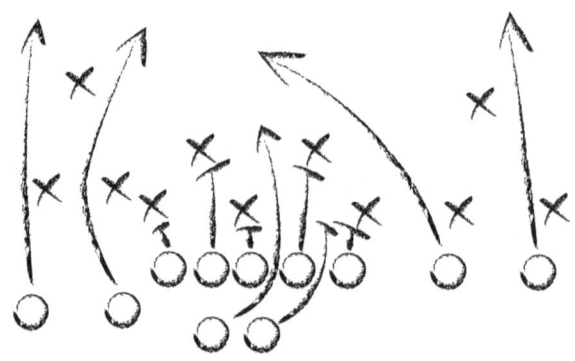

Chapter 4

18th Green

THREE PLAYERS THAT THE RAIDERS DRAFTED in 1973 arrived late to summer camp because of their participation in the annual College All-Star Game—a match between college all-stars and the reigning NFL champion. One of these all-stars was a 12th-round draft selection out of Alabama, Jim Krapf. He didn't know it yet, but he had a lot to learn.

"Hey, boy," Krapf said to me while leaning back in his chair. I was propping the door to the large room open with my elbow and knee while rolling in a 16mm projector and a 14-inch metal canister that held the 1972 Raiders highlight film. John Madden had asked me to set up the projector in the room the Raiders used to eat their meals at training camp.

"Get me a soda?" he said.

Though annoyed, I was ready to accommodate his request, but before I could respond, Krapf received a shot to the back of his head from the guy sitting directly behind him.

"Who do you think you are, rookie?" Ken Stabler said. "You don't get to order Dennis around."

I was surprised Stabler had remembered my name. We had just met for a couple of minutes the day before when I brought the projector into the quarterback meeting, where Stabler, Daryle Lamonica, and George Blanda were joined by a couple of rookies and Coach Madden. He had asked me then if I was this year's "highway Joe."

"Dennis was here before you, and he'll probably be here after you're gone, so you don't go ordering him around," Stabler said in his Alabama drawl. "He isn't your servant; he's my friend. So, 'my friend' and I would like a soda, and you are just the guy to get it for us." Stabler turned to me. "Dennis, what will you have, Coke or root beer?"

I was still a little stunned and said a root beer was fine.

Krapf trooped off to get us both sodas. He dropped mine off on the table next to the projector I was threading and handed Stabler his cup as he leaned back in his folding chair. But Stabler was not finished. Before Krapf could retake his seat, he had another demand of the rookie.

"You know what I like with my soda?" he said. "Don't go sittin' down there, boy, because what I like with my soda involves you. What I like with my soda is my good old Alabama fight song. Ever hear the Crimson Tide fight song, Dennis?"

I shrugged my shoulders with a smile, and Kenny said, "Well, you're gonna hear it tonight. You do know our fight song, don't you, Krapf?"

"I know it," he said reluctantly.

"Well then, let's hear it!"

Krapf began to sing softly, at a halting pace, and Stabler quickly objected to the feeble effort. "Does that sound like a good rendition of my fight song?" Stabler asked Pete Banaszak, the veteran Oakland running back, who was sitting next to him.

"Sounds like he doesn't mean it," Banaszak commented.

"Up on the chair and with some energy. I want you to give me a rendition of our Alabama song that we can all be proud of," Stabler demanded.

A louder and more up-tempo version had just begun when the glass door to the meeting room swung open. John Madden took a quick measure of the scene. He was here to indoctrinate the rookies with the Raiders highlight film while Stabler was conducting his own initiation.

"Can he sing?" Coach Madden said innocently, nodding toward the back of the room where Stabler, Banaszak, Fred Biletnikoff, and Tony Cline were clumped.

"I think he needs a little work," Stabler replied.

A rougher note came into Madden's voice. "Then you'll have to work with him after hours because right now, I want all of you to watch this film of last year's season that ended in Pittsburgh." He had no trouble capturing his players' attention with that announcement. "Those of you that contributed to last year's team are invited to enjoy its successes and rededicate yourselves to what you need to do this year in order to win it all this season. For you rookies, this is the standard you need to aspire to be a member of the Raiders."

Madden motioned for me to start the film. After clicking it on, I took a sip of the soda that had been brought to me. I have to say—I really enjoyed that root beer.

Krapf had learned only his first lesson from an Oakland quarterback, however. Before long, he would have some further schooling from an older, more wily one.

The following Sunday evening, I returned to Santa Rosa after dropping Al Davis off at the Oakland airport and went to the coffee shop to get some dinner.

I could see from my counter seat three booths occupied by Raiders. In the booth closest to the front of the restaurant sat Stabler and Banaszak. Biletnikoff sat by himself in the middle booth with his back up against the wall, knee bent, and foot flat on the bench seat. He was talking to linebacker Phil Villapiano, who sat in the next booth with Bob Moore, a Raiders tight end out of Stanford.

The vitality in the room picked up noticeably when George Blanda entered and ordered a coffee from the waitress in an upbeat voice. He took a seat across from Biletnikoff.

"Have a good day?" Freddie asked the veteran Oakland kicker and quarterback.

"They couldn't beat me today," Blanda scoffed. He'd obviously had a profitable trip to the track.

"Good day, George?" Phil Villapiano chimed in.

Bob Moore laughed out loud for all to hear, "George wins at everything!"

The comment caught the ear of rookie Krapf, sitting at the counter catty-corner to my stool.

"You win at everything?" he asked.

"I hold my own," Blanda said modestly, taking his first sip of coffee.

"Does that include golf?"

Blanda ignored the rookie, not lifting his eyes from his coffee cup.

Was a rookie challenging George Blanda?

Biletnikoff gave George a wide smile as if to suggest he should accept whatever challenge was in the offing.

"Would you be willing to put up what you won at the track today on a round of golf?" Krapf proposed.

Everyone in the coffee shop was suddenly a lot more interested in the challenge. Blanda himself, though, wanted no part of it.

Then Villapiano started egging him on. "The kid says he can beat you. You're going to let him leave here thinking he can beat you?"

"He can think whatever he wants," George said, pretending to be bored.

"How much did you win?" Krapf asked.

"If I were to play golf, I would want to make at least twice what I earned at the track today," Blanda said without looking at Krapf. "I don't think you have that kind of money to put up on a round of golf."

Turns out he did.

Krapf came from a family of substantial wealth, which showed on the first tee. A group of Raider players and friends took advantage of an off Tuesday to travel to the best course in the area to watch Blanda and Krapf play each other for more than twice what I was earning for my entire summer of work with the Raiders.

For Blanda and Krapf, the money was secondary to the competition. Krapf opened with a drive, showing all the signs of a man talented in the game. He had somehow time to play golf in addition to attending school, earning a collegiate wrestling championship, and playing football.

His skill caught everyone by surprise, and the anticipation of a Blanda win began eroding from that very first hole, which Krapf birdied and Blanda parred. During the next 17 holes, Krapf's lead swelled to as many as four strokes, although Blanda fought back. At the end, Krapf stood on the 18th green, needing only a putt of less than three feet to win the match by one stroke.

What a huge disappointment for most of the gallery that had followed the two golfers. Biletnikoff was chain-smoking while standing on the fringe of the 18th green. His shoulders were slumped in anticipation of this cocky rookie beating the Raiders most clutch performer. Villapiano and Marv Hubbard, Raiders running back, looked at each other in disbelief. How could a rookie beat the Raiders grand old man?

Everyone had given up on Blanda's chances that day except George himself.

As Krapf addressed the ball, Blanda interrupted. "This is truly amazing that you have a putt here that no one has ever made, but you only have to make it in order to beat me."

Blanda strolled toward the ball and cup, held his hands apart the length of the putt, and said, "This is all that is between you and doing something that no one has ever done, beat me. And you being a rookie makes it all that much more impressive. I think the event, you making a putt that has never been made, deserves more. How about we double the bet?" Blanda proposed to the surprised rookie.

"You want to double the bet now with me just needing this putt?" Krapf clarified.

"That's right," George said. "Because no one has ever made that putt, and if you do, I want it to be worth your while. Is an extra fifteen hundred dollars worth your while?"

Krapf didn't know what to say. All he needed to do was make that short putt. It was the same putt he had lined up before Blanda had interrupted his play. Why did it look so much more challenging now that the Raiders veteran kicker had just doubled the stakes?

"Okay," Krapf said in a less sure voice. "We're on for three grand."

In just a few moments, Blanda had shifted the energy on that green. Krapf's putt was no longer assured, and the new stakes had rattled the rookie just enough that his putt rimmed out. That forced a sudden-death overtime.

George walked back to the first tee with renewed enthusiasm. His competitive edge over the suddenly outwitted rookie continued. Blanda's next tee shot was true and long, while Krapf's chances sailed far right into the trees.

The rookie's losses multiplied two days later when word came he was among that day's cuts from training camp.

One of my duties was being the "Turk," a title given to the person who would knock on a player's door and advise him that the coach wanted to see him and that he should bring his playbook. It was a solemn event indicating that an athlete was being released; I did it with compassion for the disappointed player.

Yet that day, the knock on Krapf's door was quick and upbeat. So were my words after he answered the door. "The coach wants to see you," I said with a hint of satisfaction and, in a biting manner, added, "bring your playbook."

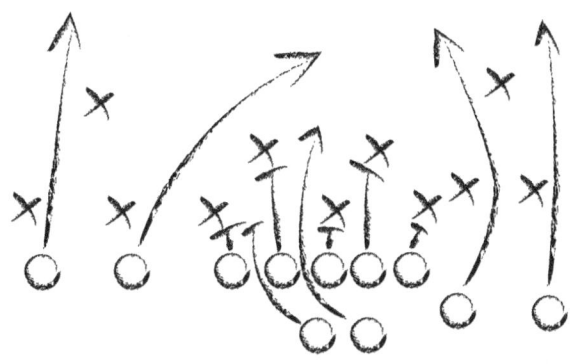

Chapter 5

Ball!

IN THE CAFETERIA OF THE HOTEL COMPLEX where we were staying, a partition that pulled halfway out from the wall separated areas designated for players from those reserved for staff, media, and training camp visitors. One of the room's walls was all glass, which allowed a clear view of anyone entering from the housing and practice field side of the complex. A swimming pool was outside the window, and when it was cleaned, the smell of chlorine would drift into the cafeteria, especially on a hot Santa Rosa afternoon.

Jimmy, a 14-year-old camp worker, was spending lunch with me. As we ate, he avidly watched the parade of Oakland players descending on the cafeteria between their morning and afternoon practices. This was Jimmy's third year of working at the Raiders training camp. The prior two summers he had been content to pick up towels in the locker room, but he was moving up in the ranks, he told me. This afternoon he was going to get to work on the field during practice.

He was a fan through and through. He told me how he used to peek through cracks in the fence to watch the Raiders practice while growing up in nearby Sebastopol. He was so excited now he'd be helping out on the field with his heroes.

Less than 90 minutes later, John Madden assumed his standard position for a Raiders shell offensive drill, eight yards behind the center with a group of quarterbacks and running backs gathered around him. Flanked out on each side of a formation that included offensive and defensive linemen were packs of Oakland wide receivers. Fred Biletnikoff joined Mike Siani on the far side, and Cliff Branch was a pass catcher on the near side. They were being guarded by some of the best defensive backs in football: Willie Brown, Jack Tatum, and George Atkinson.

I was standing off to the side in a group that included player personnel director Ron Wolf and Jack Smith, a writer from the *San Francisco Chronicle*. Wolf was pointing out the attributes he looked for in great receivers, such as Joe Wylie, a rookie from Oklahoma.

Ten yards away, Jimmy was standing in-bounds, part of the rotation that kept a new ball in play. The four-person relay began with Steve Sweeney, a rookie from Cal, retrieving the passed balls, whether caught or incomplete. As he flipped them to receivers coach Tom Flores, he announced what the offensive play was and what coverage the defense used.

What Flores may not have noticed, but I did, was the impression he was making on the young man next in line for those passed footballs. Jimmy was grabbing passes from Flores and underhanding them to Paul Roach, the Raiders running back coach, standing in the group next to Madden.

Jimmy was playing the biggest game of his life.

This was not just any set of receivers and quarterbacks; this was the cream of the NFL crop. Daryle Lamonica, Ken Stabler, and George Blanda were tossing strike after strike to a receiving corps led by Biletnikoff, Siani, and Branch.

One play was particularly eye-popping. Fred Biletnikoff left his feet at the final split-second available to grab a pass out of the reach of nearly every other receiver on the planet. Most plays on the practice field are taken in stride, but this one caught the attention of all those who saw it. It even generated an impromptu round of shouts and clapping of hands.

"Ball!" Madden yelled.

My eyes fell on Jimmy, who was still watching the corner of the end zone where Biletnikoff had made the catch.

He missed his cue. He was still holding the ball Flores had passed him, neglecting to forward it to Roach.

"Ball!" Madden yelled at decibels clearly higher than his previous bark.

But for Jimmy, the cry didn't register for a moment. He stood there open-mouthed, not believing what one of his heroes had just done.

"Ball!" Madden bellowed so loud that it prompted many, including Flores, to yell out Jimmy's name.

At last, Jimmy shook off his amazement and quickly tossed the ball to Roach. Yet his recovery was not quick enough for the Raiders head coach.

"What are you doing over there," Madden yelled while directing everyone's attention at Jimmy, "playing with your prick?"

The comment gained a smattering of laughs, and Madden's shoulders jiggled up and down in laughter as he turned in a circle to make sure everyone appreciated his comment. Meanwhile, Jimmy was left red-faced with humiliation.

Among the men I was standing with, the response was different.

"Why did he have to do that?" Wolf softly said while shaking his head in disgust.

"Because he's a bully," Smith replied.

Practice returned to its usual rhythm, but the thrill of helping out Raiders was lost for Jimmy. At an age when boys are so self-conscious, he has been humiliated. I could see dejection in his body language. His catches from Flores and passes to Roach didn't miss another beat for the rest of the drill, but his wide-eyed enthusiasm was gone. A few minutes later, when the drill ended, and the team headed to grab a drink of water, Jimmy slipped out of camp without another word.

Once equipment manager Dick Romanski, who had hired Jimmy to work on his summer crew, noticed he was missing, he called Jimmy's house to ensure he was okay and had made it home safely.

He had made it home, but whether he was okay was left unanswered because Jimmy never stepped foot in the Raiders camp again.

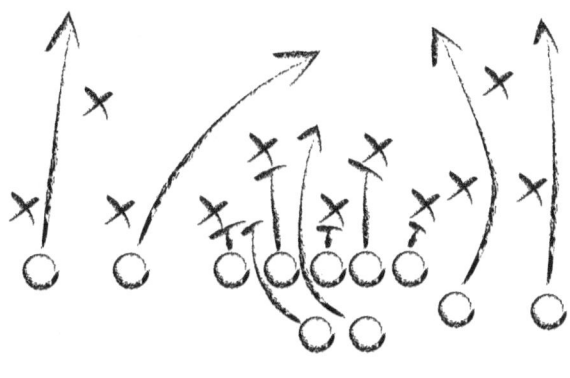

Chapter 6

Winning Lesson

THE HUB OF THE RAIDERS SUMMER TRAINING CAMP was the office located in what otherwise would have been a suite for motel guests. Down a short hallway was John Madden's office, equipped with merely a metal desk and an oversized swivel chair. Ken Bishop, the assistant director of public relations, occupied the larger office.

The extra space was certainly needed. Bishop used every inch on his desk for various projects, which included typed game plans and cut-out newspaper stories from various cities on the Raiders and other related information he thought Al Davis or the coaches might be interested in seeing. He had two phones on his desk, the one provided by the motel and another with five buttons below the dial installed by the Raiders. Three were used for incoming calls, one was blank, and the fifth was a red button used to put an incoming call on hold. A duplicate five-button phone was placed on the round table near the sliding glass door that had been set up as a workspace for me.

It was that phone I answered at 9:24 one morning with my standard greeting: "This is the Oakland Raiders; can I help you?"

"This is George Allen. I was wondering if your boss was around."

He spoke in a friendly, engaging manner, but I reacted with shock. For a moment, I was suspended between being a camp worker and a star-struck fan. George Allen was head coach of the NFC Champion Washington Redskins, a man I had admired greatly ever since watching him coach his Los Angeles Rams to consistent wins over my hometown 49ers.

He had brought together a number of NFL veterans in Washington to create the team affectionately known as the "over-the-hill gang." His strategy of trading draft choices for veterans had turned the Redskins from a doormat to conference champions in short order. Now he was asking if I could get my boss on the line.

"You mean Mr. Davis?" I asked politely.

"Do you have any other bosses?" Allen asked with a smile in his voice.

I explained that Mr. Davis was on the practice field, but I could get him if he wanted me to.

"Do you think you could do that?"

"Yes, sir."

"You don't have to call me sir," Allen said, still in a cheery tone.

Another "yes sir" was out before I registered his request, and I then hit the red button to put George Allen on hold. I paused to make double sure the blinking light didn't click off when I hung up the receiver, a problem that had happened several times the previous week.

I told Ken Bishop that George Allen was on hold on line two and not to disconnect him. He acknowledged me vaguely while taking a puff from his cigarette and continuing a conversation on his phone. Before I began my sprint to the practice field, I pointed at Bishop again to make sure: Don't lose line two. I didn't want to hang up on George Allen!

Once outside, I trotted down the asphalt path to the Raiders practice field. I came to the fence designed to keep out unwanted visitors, and with a move worthy of high scores in a gymnastics competition, I leaped up to unhitch the lock on the opposite side of the fence; the gate swung open. I spotted Davis through the uncommonly thick Sonoma Valley fog between the two practice fields.

On the near gridiron, most of the Raiders in camp had congregated in the far end zone. Davis was standing at midfield wearing a gray sweat suit with his hands clasped behind his back. His attention was focused solely on the players. I was used to such intense concentration; however, I was certain nothing mattered more than alerting him in a timely manner that George Allen was on the phone.

I darted across the field to reach the opposite side. As I got closer, he turned an intimidating glare on me. Still, once he knew George Allen was on the phone, he would appreciate my taking the shortcut.

As I began to speak, he interrupted with a forceful growl, "Dennis, what are we here to do?"

I started to explain about George Allen, but Davis stopped me short again. "Dennis," he repeated, "what are we here to do?"

The question seemed obvious, but I answered, "Uh, we are here to prepare for the season."

"No," he said flatly. "What are we here to do?"

"We're here to learn the plays, get the timing down."

"No!" Davis said in a forceful voice. "Dennis, think," he said, "what are we here to do?"

I was standing on a practice field with Al Davis on a cold morning in Santa Rosa, and he was asking me a philosophical question.

"Win," I answered triumphantly.

"Right," he said, ever the coach. "Everything we do needs to be geared toward what needs to be done to win. Did your running across that field help us win?"

The question was an accusation. Was I doing something that detracted from our winning?

"How did running across the field contribute to our team? Our players? The Raiders?" Davis said, now that he had my full attention. "When you run across the field, it looks like something is out of control, that we are in a crisis." A storm was gathering behind his eyes.

"I don't care if the fucking field house is on fire. When you come here to tell me something on the field, you walk," he said. "Our players will think something is wrong if you run across the field, and their attention will be distracted from what they need to do in order to get ready to accomplish our goal."

To illustrate his point, he instructed me to look at the players positioned in the end zone. Sure enough, at least half of them were sneaking a peek at Davis and me.

"Now just stand here, calm and relaxed, to let the players know that the Raiders organization is running smoothly," Davis ordered.

As I did, the glances melted away. Within seconds all the attention had turned from us and back onto their coaches.

Davis calmly said, "So, what did you want to tell me?"

"George Allen is on line two," I said calmly.

He did not respond.

I waited for long moments. Finally, taking a guess, I asked, "Do you want me to tell Coach Allen that you can't come to the phone?"

"Who is George calling?" Davis asked sternly.

"You, sir."

"Then why the fuck would I want you picking up the phone and talking to him?"

My response did not include any intelligible words, just a grunt of embarrassment. I waited a few seconds more in the stony silence and then decided to get lost. My mission to let Mr. Davis know that George Allen was on the phone had been successfully completed. In a controlled walk, down the sideline and around, I headed back toward the practice field gate. Once I closed the gate behind me, though, I raced back to the Raiders summer camp office.

I understood what Davis wanted to teach me. My haste had detracted from our sole objective: winning. Yet I felt uneasy leaving George Allen on hold that long. I stood over the blinking hold button, wondering if the fabled coach had really waited all this time.

Finally, the back door opened, and Davis strode into the main office space. He walked the length of the room toward the courtyard side of the office. His movements were slow and controlled as he pulled a white paper cup from the cylinder hooked to the water cooler and drank it down. He took the time to pour himself a second mini cup. He had filled the cup a third time before he looked at the blinking light on the phone and asked if that was Coach Allen.

I nodded, although I was not certain now if Allen would have waited that long on hold without someone acknowledging Davis was on his way. With the filled water cup in his hand, Davis headed for Madden's office; I followed.

"Would you hand me a pen?" Davis requested as he settled into Madden's chair.

I handed Davis a pen, and he said to me, "Do you think he waited?"

I shrugged my shoulders. "I hope he did."

"If he's still on that phone, who do you think is winning our nego-tiations?" Davis asked, still allowing the light to blink.

"If George Allen was willing to wait that long, you clearly have his attention in your current negotiations."

"He'll be there," Davis said with the first smile I'd seen from him that day. "Dennis," he directed, "close the door."

I stepped back and pulled the door shut, my eyes still riveted on that blinking light.

Davis shook his head in apparent amazement and then told me in precise terms, "No, Dennis, close the door with you on the other side."

As I turned to open the door, Davis pushed the blinking button and acknowledged George Allen with a robust greeting: "George, how ya doin'?" I looked back with relief that Allen had waited, and Davis gave me a confident smile that reassured me the current negotiations were going the Raiders way.

- - - - - -

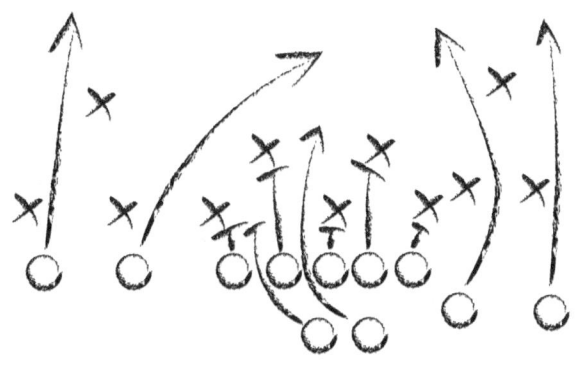

Chapter 7

There Is No
Job

My official title at training camp was camp driver, and that fit pretty well. On most days, I made at least two trips between the practice facility in Santa Rosa, the Raiders office, and the nearby airport in Oakland, a round trip of 130 miles. Daily weekday stops at the office were required to pick up the mail, while trips to the airport most often included passengers, either cut players on their way out of town or newly acquired athletes on their way in.

The person I drove most was Mr. Davis, and on those trips, we drove his black Cadillac Fleetwood without license plates. Beginning with our first ride from Santa Rosa, Davis assured me no cop was ever going to bother me as long as I was driving his car.

As it turned out, Ken Bishop's initial advice to me—"Drive like your driving instructor was sitting next to you"—couldn't have been further from the mark. I had constant deadlines, and the place I made up time was on the road. That black Cad without the plates was given a workout that summer.

If Davis wasn't the passenger, I would drive the Dodge Polaris provided by the Raiders to transport players or other camp visitors. Removing a player from camp needed to be done on a synchronized schedule. Raiders policy called for a cut player to be guarded from talking to any now-former teammates on his way out of Santa Rosa. That's why the "Turk" went to retrieve a player for the final visit with Madden.

Everything changed for a man after that knock on his door. Like a Roman centurion, I would escort the player to Madden's office. From behind his desk, Madden would tell an athlete to have a seat while taking the Raiders playbook out of his hands. While that conversation took place, I returned to the player's room, collected his personal belongings and put them in the car trunk.

Madden never let a player out of camp without a final visit. He had a skillful way of letting players go, acknowledging their accomplishments, and truly wishing them the best. In some cases, he even mentioned the possibility of bringing an athlete back for another chance to make the Raiders roster. At other times, he was saying goodbye to a veteran that had gone to war with the Raiders in past seasons. Most of the time, though, the Raiders had drafted or signed the player as a free agent; he was a long shot to stick with the team once camp broke. Behind closed doors, those players were characterized as "camp meat."

Madden always had the right words to say, allowing a cut player to leave with dignity and hope for the future intact. That was good for me because once a player was cut, I was the only Raiders employee that would see them again. When the meeting broke, a player would step outside Madden's office, and I would be holding the door that led into the waiting car.

"What about my stuff?" players would ask before they sat in the passenger seat. I let them know it was already packed and in the trunk. Then I whisked them away, leaving behind their dreams of making the Oakland Raiders final roster.

The Oakland airport was my most common stop, even if a player's arrival or departure required a flight from San Francisco. In that case, we would use a helicopter service to shuttle between the two airports. That's because driving through San Francisco could be such a nightmare. Putting a player on a flight that was leaving in less than an hour from the time we pulled out of the Raiders training facility was accomplished on a couple of occasions but required wild driving. I can't say I minded that so much.

The Polaris I drove that summer was provided by a local sponsor, Hayward Dodge, and it ran smooth, without shimmy, at speeds approaching triple digits. But it also carried the risk of attracting a California highway patrolman and suffering the consequences of a speeding ticket and increased insurance rates on my already tight budget.

That was not a problem, though, when I was driving Mr. Davis in his black Cad with no license plates. We could literally go as fast as we wanted in that car, and no CHP would pull us over.

"It's okay," Davis would say as we broke 80 with a patrol car right in view.

Sure enough, the guy wasn't bothering the black Cad with no license plates. Who would stop the owner of the Oakland Raiders?

On a Sunday afternoon in August, after we had hosted the Minnesota Vikings at the University of California stadium in Berkeley the day before, the coaches, along with Ron Wolf and Davis, huddled to make a crucial cut one week before breaking camp.

Releasing the needed number of veterans and promising rookies was an agonizing process. This was no place to make a mistake. No one wanted to allow an impact player to pass to another team and have future success. Stories like that were legends. In one of the worst examples, the Pittsburgh Steelers cut John Unitas before he went on to lead the Baltimore Colts to their championships and establish himself as the best quarterback in the game during an 18-year NFL career.

The Raiders success in personnel decisions was earned by an effective balance between three men with a great eye for talent, knew what they needed on the field, and had the ability to act on their intuition. The lynchpin in this process was Ron Wolf, who understood his role was making only recommendations despite working with firsthand knowledge of the players being considered.

Wolf also could admit a mistake and move on to what worked best next. That afternoon, as highly as Wolf had touted Joe Wylie, a rookie receiver out of Oklahoma, he was in agreement that the kid had to be released.

Davis had just completed that grueling process when he sent me to drive him to his home in Piedmont. Five minutes into the trip, he fell asleep with the stats he was reading still in his hand. We merged onto US 101, just minutes from the Raiders training site, and soon the four guys driving in the middle lane were pointing at him. Davis was so zonked out, he appeared to be dead. A corpse in a black Cadillac.

All four of them were roaring with laughter while the guy sitting behind the driver was hanging out the window, pretending to be dead himself.

It didn't matter if I slowed down or sped up; they paced me. This went on until the exit I took for the Richmond/San Rafael Bridge. Davis remained comatose until I took the Oakland Avenue exit off the freeway.

Davis was not asleep one week later during our next drive together to his home. Training camp had closed prior to the Raiders meeting the Bills in Buffalo for the sixth game on their 1973 preseason schedule. As I pulled the Caddy away from Room 314 for the last time, I was fully aware that the contract I had gotten from Wolf to work that summer would be completed at the end of the drive.

Davis was in a more talkative mood than I had seen all summer. He quizzed me on my time with the Raiders and seemed pleased when I confirmed to him that the most-asked question of me, when someone learned I was working with the Raiders, was, "What is he like?"

"What do you tell them?" Davis prodded.

"I tell them how much I respect you and enjoy working for you."

He was very pleased with that answer. "So, are you going back to school?"

I explained to him that the internship represented my final college units toward graduation. Then I floated my big idea: I was hoping to continue with the team.

"Why would you think that was a possibility?" Davis asked sharply and, before I could respond, added, "There is no job."

I came right back with my pitch. I told him that just the possibility of working with the Raiders had kept me from looking anywhere else. "If a job did present itself, I didn't want any conflicts."

"There is no job," he repeated as we pulled up in front of his Piedmont Hills home.

I didn't verbally respond but instead merely went about my usual business. Popping the trunk exposed Davis' two pieces of luggage, a black briefcase and an oversized silver bag with a Raiders shield. The bag was as bold as the front grille on a fifties Cadillac. As I reached for it, Davis moved in front of me and grabbed it instead. "I'll take that tonight," he said while jerking the overstuffed silver bag out of the trunk.

He was thinking about our conversation, though. He liked people that showed true commitment. As he started toward his house, he turned and said, "Maybe we can work something out. Call me on Monday."

I didn't get in the car until his outside gate closed; I saw the front door open and then shut. For what could well be the last time, I got behind the wheel of his black Cadillac and headed for the Raiders offices on Oakport Street. As I pulled into the parking space, with his name on the wheel block, I was buoyed by the realization that my time with the Raiders didn't have to end . . . but might just be beginning.

Even though it was only a preseason game, I was glad the Raiders beat the Buffalo Bills. That would put him in a better mood. On Monday, I called Mr. Davis. Rosemary Butt, his secretary, explained he wasn't available right now but assured me she would pass my message along to him.

On Tuesday, I called again. This time Rosemary responded not with a hello but with a message from Davis, who must have been standing at her desk. I'd heard him tell her to tell me to call back on Thursday but then abruptly asked for her to give him the phone.

"Dennis," Davis said, "I'm still looking into a couple of things here; I'll get back to you on Thursday."

I don't think he heard me say "Okay" before he hung up the phone.

I wished I knew what time Thursday. I waited in agony until 2:30 and then decided to call because I knew the Raiders were leaving for Minnesota the next day. If I missed him, he would be out of town until Monday. "He isn't here right now," I learned from Rosemary, but she anticipated he would return to the office in less than 30 minutes. She also cautioned me that he would only be in the office for about an hour before heading over to the practice field for his afternoon workout and Thursday night meeting with the coaches.

Rosemary then stopped herself. "He's coming down the hallway now." I overheard her tell him I was on the phone.

Davis picked it up. "Dennis," he said in a way that conveyed he didn't have a lot of time, "if I was to bring you in to work with the coaches and still help Tommy out in the PR department from time to time, what would you think about that?"

I quickly agreed to do whatever I could, wherever he wanted me, in order to work for the Raiders. He then shifted the topic to money. It was a subject I had given much thought to before our conversation. I knew what my monthly expenses were, and if I shared a house with friends in San Jose, I could limit my rent costs and get by on $600 a month.

I didn't want to give in to the minimum number I would need to survive, so I told Mr. Davis my situation and cost of living and said I could do it for $650 a month. I don't know why I said $650 because I had thought I was going to ask for $750 to start, but in the heat of the moment, not wanting to lose this opportunity, I already trimmed my opening proposal.

It didn't matter anyway because Davis said emphatically, "Oh no, we're not even in the same ballpark. I was thinking more in the line of a hundred bills a week."

I didn't know how I was going to survive on $400 a month. I didn't respond right away, digesting the thought of trying to live on that amount of money.

"Tell you what I'm going to do," Davis offered. "I'll give you that hundred bills a week in an expense check so you don't have to pay taxes."

That, I knew, was a bad deal. The last thing I wanted was to start a professional relationship with the Oakland Raiders with a possible tax liability.

"No, sir," I said, swallowing deeply, "I'll take the money with taxes taken out."

On Monday, I was sitting at the desk across from Tom Grimes' before he arrived at work. The team had lost their opener in Minnesota and landed late Sunday night at the Oakland Airport. He arrived a little past ten and was surprised to see me. After taking his seat at his desk, he said, "We are still trying to work something out, but nothing is done yet."

It was my turn to be surprised. Obviously, Davis had not shared the news that I had been hired. Minutes later, when LoCasale came into the office, he, too, was surprised to see me. He grumbled about the fact that no one had told him.

"I'm supposed to know these things," LoCasale said. "Did you know anything about this?" he asked Grimes.

"I was not aware." Grimes turned his attention to me. "Did Mr. Davis say exactly what you were hired to do?"

For a moment, I wondered how this was all going to work out or even if it was going to work out. Then, I realized, I was holding trump. Al Davis had hired me; no one in this room could overrule him. I said I would be working with both Tom and the coaches.

LoCasale looked at Grimes, calculating what that meant. He deduced that Davis must be thinking I would work on Doolittle Drive at the practice facility. I'd take the spot Ken Bishop had handled the first week of the season. "I know the coaches would like someone a little more stable than Bishop," LoCasale said, laughing, and Grimes agreed.

I let both of them know I was willing to do whatever with the coaches, but I still wanted to work with Grimes in the public relations department.

"We can make that work," he said. "I don't know what Al had in mind for you," he added, "but I know the coaches are in need of someone to field calls and type game plans. You could also work from a public relations standpoint by setting up the player speaking engagements."

I asked about *Pro! Magazine* and writing stories for the home game program. Grimes agreed I could do some stories for that too.

"Well, if you're on permanent staff, we've got some new forms for you to fill out," LoCasale said brightly. "Come down to my office."

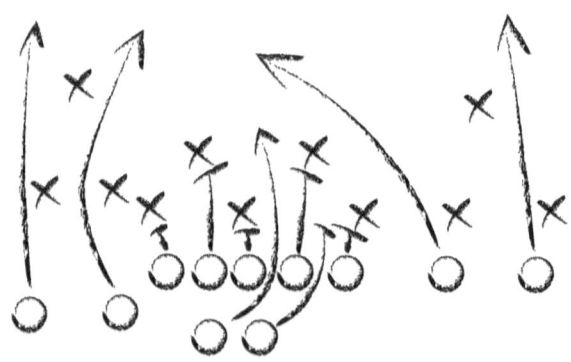

Chapter 8

Pay Phone

I MANNED A DESK IN AN OFFICE ADJACENT to the coaches' dressing room at the Raiders practice field on Doolittle Drive. The building was no better than trailer quality with gravel for landscaping. The inside of the training room smelled like a construction site, laid over the sweat of working athletes and the steam from the shower area. I had a metal desk with an IBM Selectric typewriter and a phone like the one at training camp. John Madden took one of the chairs in front of my desk to set me straight on my responsibilities as his field house secretary.

Nobody was in a good mood after losing our opening game to the Vikings, 24–16, and the prospect of losing our first two games of the season was very real. The defending world-champion Miami Dolphins were coming to town next.

"Can you type?" Madden asked while showing me an example of a Raiders game plan.

I assured him I could, and he explained that I would be typing the weekly game plans as well as fielding all incoming calls. Madden was lighting a cigarette when the metal door swung open, and Ken Bishop entered carrying a stack of newspapers. The PR assistant directed his first comments to the coach. "I know that on the body of this team, I am the armpit, but do you really think I deserve to have every desk of mine taken by the golden boy here?"

Bishop's comment could have been taken as either an arguing point or a joke. Madden chose the latter.

His blue eyes lit up, and he let loose a Santa Claus ho, ho, ho. "We just know you can do anything, and we need you free to be ready to go in for the team when we need it."

Bishop rolled his eyes and redirected his attention to me. "So, is this where you are going to be, or are you still at the desk on Oakport Street I used to have?"

I hadn't yet thought the matter through, but the truth was, my job in the Raiders organization was at the expense of Bishop. I had been assigned his desk when the internship program started in June, had taken over his work with the coaches and now totally usurped his spot at the practice field.

Madden engaged Bishop with good humor, giving him an opportunity to save face. Once his cheery banter prompted Bishop to break a smile, Madden stood up. As he disappeared into the coaches' locker area, he returned to his usual generalissimo mode. "None of us will be smiling next week," he warned us, "if we don't beat the Dolphins on Sunday."

The Miami Dolphins hadn't lost a game in two years. Don Shula's squad was coming off a perfect 17–0 campaign and had opened the 1973 season with a 21–13 win over the San Francisco 49ers. The Dolphins were looking to establish the all-time NFL winning streak record when they visited us.

The Raiders had played two preseason games on the University of California campus the previous month, while the Oakland A's baseball team used the Coliseum for their home games. Even though the A's would be in Chicago to meet the White Sox, LoCasale had convinced Al Davis to keep the Raiders meeting against Miami in Berkeley because of the anticipated interest in the game and additional revenue from increased ticket sales. The University of California stadium could accommodate nearly 80,000, while the capacity of the Oakland Coliseum was just over 50,000. For me, that represented a lot of extra work. While the Raiders would sell all those additional seats, the move created a massive logistical challenge. We had to accommodate all the media requests for the most anticipated early-season game in memory.

The move also shifted the hotel accommodations for the NBC television crew, including play-by-play anchor Curt Gowdy.

"You take Curt wherever he wants to go," Davis instructed me on Thursday at the Raiders practice facility. He handed me a note with Gowdy's flight number and scheduled arrival on Saturday at 11:40 a.m.

The Oakland Airport is smaller and less crowded than San Francisco International. All through the summer, the parking enforcement crew stationed curbside had been accommodating my request for special parking considerations. They did again this Saturday when I pulled Davis' black Cadillac past the baggage claim area and made a standard request to leave it in the loading zone while I retrieved my arriving parties.

"Who is it today?" asked George, whom I knew from past stops at the airport.

"Curt Gowdy," I said.

His eyes lit up with recognition. "The announcer?"

"Yeah, he will be calling tomorrow's game against the Dolphins."

"Are we going to beat those guys?" George asked me, as if I would know.

"We are," I said confidently.

"I'll keep an eye out for your car," George said. "Hope you're right about the game."

Curt Gowdy was wearing a light tan cowboy hat when he emerged through the tunnel at Gate 14. It was more elegant than any cowboy hat I had ever seen, somewhat smaller than what Roy Rogers would wear on television. I introduced myself, and he shifted his carry-on bag to his left hand before shaking mine.

"This is Phil Harris," Gowdy said while pointing to the gentleman on his left, whom I had already recognized without his introduction.

"Nice to meet you, Mr. Harris," I said respectfully, and then asked, "Do you have checked luggage to pick up?"

While acknowledging they did, Harris broke into a song about a cowboy traveling without luggage. Gowdy laughed and joined him for one chorus of the whimsical tune. It was the first of a series of inside jokes Gowdy and Harris shared throughout the day. The two men were on the tail end of a week together that had begun with five days of shooting an *American Sportsman* episode in Oregon.

Gowdy stopped at a newsstand and picked up an *Oakland Tribune*, *San Francisco Chronicle*, and *San Francisco Examiner* on the way to the baggage claim area. "Bet they've got a few stories in here on tomorrow's game," Gowdy told me.

"I think the fact that the Dolphins extended their winning streak against the 49ers last week is even causing more interest in this one."

"Moving this game to Berkeley so more fans can attend makes sense," Gowdy said, "but I tell you, no way would I have moved this game out of the *House of Miracles*." That was how he referred to the Oakland Coliseum, where he had called several incredible Oakland comeback victories snatched from the jaws of defeat in the final seconds.

After retrieving their bags and placing them in the trunk, I pulled a flip card and game program for tomorrow's game from the back seat and handed them over.

Gowdy studied the information while Harris asked me, "How long have you been with the Raiders? How do you like working for Al Davis?"

"It is the best experience of my life," I said succinctly.

"Davis knows how to find talent," Gowdy said, smiling my way. That was nice of him. He didn't have to say that, but that was the way he was.

When I asked if he'd like me to take them to lunch, he said, "Let's go to the stadium first. I'm not used to working at Cal, and I'd like to see the facility and my sightlines."

I drove them up through the sprawling university campus and to the large cement stadium. Afterward, Gowdy said he and Phil would just eat at the hotel. "Do you know where we are staying?"

"Yes, sir," I responded, "the Berkeley Marriott."

We were driving back down the hill to town when Harris asked from the back seat, "So, how is your team going to do tomorrow?"

"We're going to win," I said flatly.

"What do you think he is going to say?" Gowdy remarked. "He works for Al."

"Actually, there are more reasons than that why we are going to win," I said, like I had the inside scoop.

My information came from years of studying NFL games. I tried to measure point spreads, motivational factors, and team tendencies. When I was a kid, my dad and I would pick the games each Saturday during an NFL season. My interest in anticipating when a team would play above or below their talent level reached an early peak in 1965 when I was 15. That year, the NFL comprised seven teams each in the Eastern and Western Conferences; we didn't care about the AFL yet.

To start one Saturday selection process in November, my father picked the San Francisco 49ers to beat the Detroit Lions the next day. He put his initials next to the 49ers in the *San Francisco Chronicle* Sporting Green.

"Got to go with the Packers over the Rams," Dad said, and after I agreed, he moved to the third game on the schedule, the Baltimore Colts at Metropolitan Stadium, for a contest against the Minnesota Vikings.

"That's an easy one," Dad said. "The Colts don't have Unitas, so the Vikings should kill them." I quickly agreed. Baltimore's legendary quarterback Johnny Unitas was sidelined with a knee injury and was going to be replaced by someone we didn't recognize or know how to pronounce his name, Gary Cuozzo.

As it turned out, that year, Gary Cuozzo would throw seven touchdown passes in relief of Unitas; five of them were grouped in that one game against the Vikings. He triggered an unexpected offensive explosion for the injured Colts, and Baltimore blew out Norm Van Brocklin's Vikings, 41–21.

"How are they doing that?" Dad said as scores from Minnesota were announced with the Colts increasingly ahead. "Maybe this Cuozzo kid is something special."

I was not yet old enough to drive a car, but thinking about the Colts going into Metropolitan Stadium and ambushing the Vikings without their starting quarterback was a tantalizing question that intrigued me as much as physics captured the attention of Albert Einstein.

From that day forward, my handicapping with Dad took on a brand-new aspect for me. I calculated not only who had the better team or strength to attack an opponent's weakness, but which squad was more motivated.

Before we picked the games the following Saturday, I had developed a chart that showed how teams did when they were missing their starting quarterback. While they didn't always have the same success as the Colts in Minnesota, they did succeed more often than they failed.

With Curt Gowdy and Phil Harris, I went into a case study of how the Dolphins opening win off a perfect season plus a second-week road game ran smack into the Raiders road loss and opening home game, coupled with us being an underdog against the Super Bowl champions.

"That is why we are going to beat the Dolphins tomorrow," I concluded after identifying a list of motivational criteria that favored the Raiders. "And we are getting points on the spread, too," I added.

"Like I said," Gowdy commented to his partner, "Davis knows how to find talent."

Harris gave me a shrewd look. "You really think the Raiders are going to beat the Dolphins?"

"Absolutely."

"Pull over," he said. "I need to use a phone."

We were on University Avenue, and I spotted a phone booth at a dirty Shell gas station while at a red light. I couldn't imagine Harris using that phone booth.

"Do you really want to stop here?"

"There'll be a phone in the hotel lobby," Gowdy said.

"No," Harris said, "I want to do this now. Mind stopping?"

"Not at all, sir," I responded, and Gowdy laughed.

"The man trusts your information," Gowdy said as the two of us sat waiting in Davis' Cadillac while Harris used the pay phone in an outside booth that no doubt smelled of urine.

I knew what I was talking about. "You'll see, I'm right."

The next day, the largest home crowd to ever attend a Bay Area professional football game, 74,121, enthusiastically cheered each of four George Blanda field goals, which accounted for all the Raiders scoring. Coupled with a tenacious defensive performance, they proved to be enough to end the Dolphins winning streak by a 12–7 final score.

After the game, I was retrieving game stats when I spotted the press elevator with Gowdy and Harris inside. Just before they disappeared, Harris used his hand to stop the elevator door from closing. As it opened, he winked and said, "Good job."

— — — — — — —

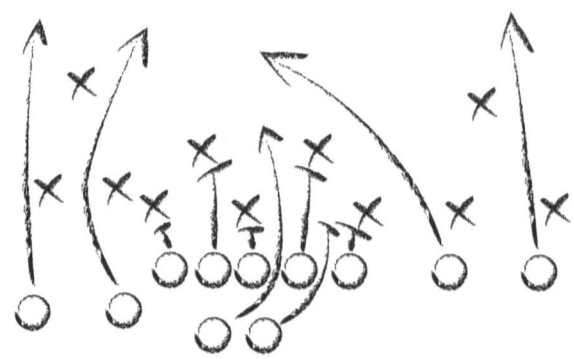

Chapter 9

Big Trouble

THE WIN SIGNIFICANTLY LIFTED THE SPIRITS around the Raiders camp. Davis greeted me enthusiastically the next Thursday in the hallway outside his corner office on Oakport Street. He was headed to his work-out and meeting with the coaches, and I had swung by to pick up mail.

"How ya doin', young man?" Davis said as he spotted me coming down the hallway. I responded with the standard "fine" reply.

Davis was probably expecting a similar automatic response to his next question, "And how's the team?" but was in for a surprise.

"We're in big trouble," I said flatly.

My answer hit him like an assassin's bullet. In an instant, his upbeat mood was gone. His cheery expression was replaced with reptilian green eyes that flashed danger. His dialect went from Southern gentleman to New Jersey thug. "What do ya mean?"

I didn't want to get on his bad side. I was only on my eleventh day as a full-time Raiders employee. Nor did I want to waste his time telling him how my father and I had spent hours each week handicapping games during my youth and how I had developed motivational charts while in college. Yet I had noticed the day before, when I ran my numbers, that the Raiders were in a monumental trap headed for Kansas City.

I didn't give Davis any of that information; I just cut to the chase. "We play the Chiefs in three days on their home field, and while they are preparing for us, our players are still talking about beating Csonka, Kiick, and Warfield."

The threat level melted. He had evaluated game factors of his own. He took a measured look at me and then said, "Listen, you just do your job. I'll take care of the team."

As he walked away, I felt better. I had told the genius of professional football that his beloved Raiders were in trouble, and I fed him the information in time for him to take corrective action. The Raiders now had a chance to win because Davis could fix the complacency I had noticed.

An hour later, back at the Doolittle Drive practice field, I got word from Ken LaRue that he was on his way over with the itinerary for Friday's flight to Kansas City. Tom Flores, slumped in front of his locker after a grueling workout, overheard my conversation and asked if I was traveling with the team.

"I'm not sure," I told him.

"If you don't go, I don't go," he announced. He turned to ask Paul Roach, who was sitting at his locker across from Flores, if he agreed. Before Roach responded, Raiders linebacker coach Don Shinnick burst in to check the thermostat that regulated the heat in the coach's area.

"What the rip?" Shinnick muttered while turning up the heat. "You think we're hanging meat back there?"

Flores got Shinnick's attention and said, "If Dennis isn't on the flight to Kansas City, we're not going. You with us?"

"I'm in," Shinnick responded. "He puts in the time with us all hours of the day and night, and he should get to go with us to the game." He gave Flores a conspiratorial smile. "I'm in. He's on the plane, or we stay home."

"I'm going to Kansas City with or without you guys," Roach deadpanned. "I think Denny deserves to go with us, but I'm going to beat the Chiefs in either case."

Flores smiled and said he hoped I was on the flight.

Flores was the only one in the clubhouse who owned a Super Bowl ring. Beginning his career as a Raider in 1960 as a quarterback out of the University of the Pacific in nearby Stockton, Flores had played nine seasons in the American Football League. His career in Oakland included all three years Al Davis coached the Raiders, 1963–65, and the first year John Rauch served as head coach in 1966. After two seasons in Buffalo, Flores joined the Kansas City Chiefs midway through the 1969 campaign.

Flores was a Kansas City backup but always a strong contributor to a team's success because of his intelligence and work ethic. Even as a young player, Flores was a steady influence and an attribute to the quarterback playing in front of him. His playing career spanned the life of the AFL, 1960–1969, and that last year was spent with the Super Bowl-winning Chiefs. His career passer rating is 67.6, but in 1970 with the Chiefs, he had only one pass attempt and completed it for a 33-yard touchdown to generate a 158.3 quarterback rating on the Super Bowl champions.

As the Raiders receiver coach, he was almost embarrassed to have a Super Bowl ring while being around a group of guys who had worked so hard, come so close, and still didn't have one. As much as anyone, he was dedicated to do whatever he could in order to ensure that the Raiders won their first Super Bowl.

I sure appreciated his standing up for me. A short time later LaRue confirmed that I was going, when he hand-delivered the weekend itinerary for Kansas City, including the list of passengers on the Raiders United Airlines charter flight.

The next evening, in the lobby of the Kansas City Hilton Hotel, LaRue warned me, "It is a working trip." My job was to make sure everyone had what they needed, and that the press didn't go where Madden didn't want them. LaRue wasn't talking about just the players. One of the perks for major advertisers was a seat on one of the Raiders charter flights and deluxe accommodations for an out-of-town game. The Kansas City trip and the game against the longtime rival Chiefs was one of the most attractive trips on the schedule.

"Where are we supposed to be?" Madden asked LaRue, in search of the Friday night team meal hosted in one of the hotel's banquet rooms. LaRue pointed to a stanchion that held a black message board with white letters pressed into place that read:

Olive Room

Raiders Team Meal

Friday * 10:00 p.m.

Being so close to the banquet room seemed to relax Madden, but only for a moment. Then he asked LaRue how many floors the players were on. LaRue pulled a room diagram from a black leather file he carried under his arm and asked the coach whether he had received his copy of the room assignments in the envelope with his room key.

"It's probably upstairs," Madden said vaguely as a number of his players filed by on the way to their late-night meal. "You just remember that curfew is at midnight," he ordered LaRue, "and tomorrow night at eleven, I want the halls policed. No girls."

LaRue raised his eyebrows, knowing both what the coach wanted and the difficulty in enforcing his request.

Madden didn't want his order taken lightly. "You," he said, looking at me, "I want you guarding that hall tonight and tomorrow night." Off he marched to the banquet room.

Bewildered, I asked LaRue what I was supposed to do.

"Stand in front of the elevator and just make sure no girls get off looking for players. Go up around eleven-thirty tonight and stay for about an hour. Tomorrow, get there about ten and watch the floor for a couple of hours."

I asked again, "So, what am I supposed to do?"

LaRue cracked a wide smile as he took a puff on his pipe. "Make the coach happy."

That Friday night Ken Bishop stood guard with me in front of the elevator on the sixth floor. He passed the time by telling me how he met his wife in Kansas City a few years earlier. As we chatted, the players emerged on the floor in groups, most returning from the team meal in the Olive Room. Around 12:15 a.m., LaRue came by and asked me how it went, and Bishop said, "Everything under control here."

I also informed him that a couple of times, girls came by. I had asked them what their room number was, and one threesome just giggled and stayed on the elevator. Another group of four girls blew off my request and sashayed down the hall.

"Did they go in a room?" LaRue questioned.

I told him I thought they were still in Warren Bankston's. Just as I spoke, the hallway filled with voices, mostly female, emerging from that very room.

We only heard Bankston's voice, bidding farewell from deep inside the room as two girls, dressed in revealing tight-fitting clothes, twirled at the door before saying goodbye.

The girls were moving our way but still looking back when Bankston appeared at the door they had left open. My attention was on the ladies, and I suspected Bishop's and LaRue's were, too, when all of us were drawn to the ding of the elevator and the imposing figure inside. I heard his voice before I saw his face.

"What's goin' on?" Al Davis said to LaRue.

The look on his face was in direct contrast to the high-pitched squeals of the girls.

"Hi, cutie," one of the girls said to Davis while pushing by him on her way into the elevator.

Bankston had either heard his voice or spotted Davis stepping off the elevator because the Raiders tight end slunk back into his room with the speed of a gopher disappearing into his hole.

The perfume of the girls lingered long past the time the elevator closed. LaRue was flabbergasted by the fact that Davis showed up just when the girls appeared in the hall.

His gaze then locked on me. It was our first exchange since I had alerted him to the potential for a Raiders letdown. Instantly, LaRue and Bishop were only observers while Davis aimed directly at me. "Ya gotta want to do everthin' for winning."

As if jolted by an electrical shock, I think I said hi. I might not have because whatever came out of my mouth was drowned out by the racket caused from another room opening. Two scantily dressed women emerged in the hallway. A voice came from deep inside the room, and it was obvious the player was oblivious to the fact Davis was within earshot.

"We'll talk tomorrow," the player yelled from out of sight. These two girls made more noise than the four had earlier as they approached the elevator.

Davis was truly pissed now. "I don't know what the fuck is going on here, and I've got to know who is with me in fucking doin' what we need to do in order to win."

The statement didn't need a response, but we all gave one.

Davis took them in with a wince of disapproval. "I just want us to know this is a business trip," he said as the elevator door closed on the second set of girls leaving a Raiders room.

"This is no fucking party," Davis said, turning his head our way for a brief moment. Davis then walked the length of the hallway before disappearing through a door under a green exit sign.

I confirmed with LaRue that Davis wasn't staying on this floor. I didn't know which room Davis was in because his room number was routinely left off the manifest of players, coaches, staff, media, and guest room assignments.

"He's got a suite upstairs," LaRue said while agreeing with me that his presence on the floor was totally unexpected.

"He got to see all the action," Bishop muttered while scanning the *Kansas City Star*'s late edition.

In another minute, he added, "Here's something the coach might want to see." He showed LaRue a column that compared Madden's relationship with Davis versus the Kansas City Chiefs head coach Hank Stram's relationship with Chiefs owner Lamar Hunt.

"What does it say?" LaRue asked, pushing the elevator call button. Bishop was still explaining when the two stepped on the elevator. LaRue looked back at me and said, "Better stay here for fifteen more minutes or so just in case he comes back."

He didn't.

At least not in the next thirty minutes.

— — — — — —

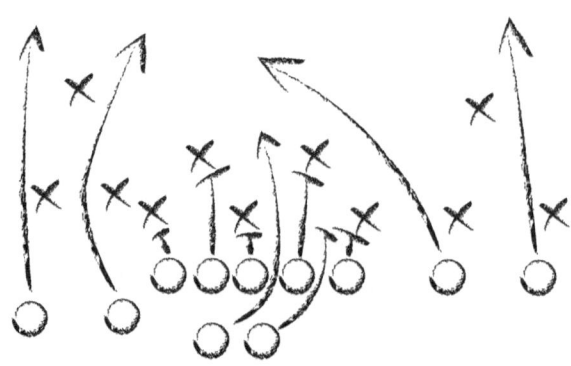

Chapter 10

Messenger

On Saturday night, I stood guard again in front of the sixth-floor elevator. I was joined by Ken Bishop, who staved off boredom by cutting stories out of the *Kansas City Star* for John Madden. In the final minutes leading up to the 11:00 p.m. curfew, a steady stream of players headed to their rooms. Shortly after eleven, the elevator door opened, and running backs coach Paul Roach greeted us with his engaging country banter.

"So they got you guarding the cattle." Roach pointed to the room-assigned manifest he was holding in his hand. "I'm here to make sure that everyone who's supposed to be in their rooms is, and any person not supposed to be in their rooms isn't."

The numbers written on the hotel wall indicated 602–632 were straight ahead, while rooms 601 to 631 were down the hall to the left.

Roach began his bed check with even-numbered rooms and greeted each room with his Wyoming twang.

Halfway down the hall, a door was not answered promptly, forcing Roach to knock a second time. The door still wasn't answered when the elevator ding announced its arrival and the doors opened. The back-lighting didn't offer any features until the elevator's occupant stepped forward, but his silhouette was unmistakable.

Madden towered over me. "No trouble up here tonight," he asked in a way that indicated I was responsible for last night's fiasco and should not let it happen again. He watched Roach knock on a few doors and then said to me, "You got to do the things leading up to the game right if you are going to win the game."

Madden pushed both the up and down buttons to call the elevator. Bishop called to him about his latest find in the newspapers, but Madden ignored him as the elevator arrived. He stepped on, and the doors closed on his imposing presence.

"And thank you for all your dedicated work," Bishop said in mock tribute.

Fifteen minutes had passed since Roach completed his room check when one of the rooms opened, and out came Raiders running back Pete Banaszak. He was not heading toward the elevator but toward one of the green exit signs at the end of the hall. He spotted Bishop and me in front of the elevator. I tilted my head as if to indicate I was hoping he was not leaving. He shuffled back up the hall sideways as if doing a football agility drill. "Hey guys, I've got to go see these relatives in town. This is just between us. You don't have to tell anyone."

He didn't wait for us to agree before jogging down the hall and out the door.

Bishop had left our lookout post by the time Ken LaRue arrived at midnight to relieve me of my watch. I asked him what I was supposed to do if I knew a player was sneaking out.

"Did someone?" LaRue responded.

I nodded while adding he wasn't with any girls and said he was just going to visit a relative.

LaRue almost dropped his pipe in laughter.

"Who was it?"

"Banaszak," I said.

"Oh, don't worry about that. Banaszak isn't anyone to worry about. He's no problem," LaRue assured me.

I didn't let the question go, though. I wanted to know what I was supposed to say to Madden if he asked. Did I have to give him names?

"It's usually a good idea to stay away from names," LaRue advised. "You don't want to get in the middle between the players and Madden or Davis."

I could tell I was going to hate hall monitor duty for the rest of the season.

Arrowhead Stadium in Kansas City is a near-perfect blend of understated elegance and magnificent facilities for players and fans alike. I was standing on the field with two Raiders, one of which lost here last year in Arrowhead's inaugural season. Rookie linebacker Monte Johnson was doing all the talking as he scanned the rows of bright red seats. By contrast, veteran Raiders middle linebacker Dan Connors was silent while studying the layout. Both players were still wearing their street clothes two hours before the scheduled kickoff.

Connors had his mouth open like he had just realized that there was a game to play today. During the week leading up to this game, his mind was still on the Dolphins game last week. He, along with most of his teammates, hadn't given much thought to this game. He knew it, I knew it, and we looked at each other in full communication without ever saying a word. Moments later, the three of us parted ways, Connors and Johnson to the locker room to suit up, me to the owner's box to sit with Al Davis.

Watching the game from the visiting owner's box in Kansas City is almost surrealistic because no live sound penetrates the thick glass window. Instead of hearing the crowd live, the cheers were pumped through a speaker located on the back wall. It meant the reaction from the fans was always a beat later than the action on the field.

Davis, dressed in a gray leisure suit with a white turtleneck, sat directly in front of me in the second of four short rows of seats. All during the game, the Raiders offense sputtered, and Davis scribbled notes on a white jot tablet that he kept with a black flow pen on the floor next to his foot. Half a dozen times during the first half, he folded one of his diagrams and handed it to me with instructions to deliver it to the upstairs coaches, working in a box three doors down.

Most of the game he watched with elbows on his knees while agonizing over another day of ineffective offensive play. As each Raiders drive ended with the Chiefs suffocating our efforts, Davis would contort in an anguished twist of his body.

Midway through the fourth quarter, Davis handed me another note to deliver to the coaches. "Get this to them," he commanded while folding the recommended formation sketch in half. I took the note gladly, knowing what an offensive genius he was. This might be the one the coaches really needed to expose a weakness in the Chiefs defense.

The door to the coaches' booth was locked, as it had been since early in the second quarter. I had simply been slipping Davis' plays and formations under the door ever since, but this time I knocked. The door opened to reveal Coach Bob Zeman slamming his headset on the table following a missed tackle on a third and short situation. Tom Flores was sitting to Zeman's right, Roach between them. I handed Flores the page from Davis while telling him this one seemed important. He took it without a nod. Meanwhile, Zeman screamed into the headphones he was now holding in his hands. I had the funny feeling that Davis' stroke of genius might not be put into play.

In the fourth quarter, Madden replaced Daryle Lamonica with Ken Stabler at quarterback. Even though he failed to get a first down in his first series and tossed an interception on the first play of his second attempt to move the Raiders offense, Oakland still had a chance to win after a Jan Stenerud field goal attempt was tipped at the line and recovered near the end zone by George Atkinson and returned 16 yards to the 18-yard-line. This was Stabler's first meaningful action since he scored the go-ahead touchdown in Pittsburgh before Franco Harris erased the Raiders advantage on the *Immaculate Reception* in the previous season's playoff game.

Yet hopes for similar heroics by the Raiders young quarterback were dashed moments later. A crossing-pattern pass from Stabler bounced off Pete Banaszak's right shoulder pad and into the hands of Chiefs linebacker Willie Lanier, who took it the short distance to the end zone to increase Kansas City's advantage to 16–3.

Both Davis and I were standing in frustration when the final seconds clicked off the game clock. The moment the contest ended, Davis spun around and grabbed my arm. He pointed an intimidating index finger at me. "And you knew, you knew." I stiffened, but he repeated the words more with a tone of appreciation than a threat, "You knew."

In the locker room, media gathered around Stabler. A reporter asked whether he thought he could pull off another comeback when he came into the game. Stabler retorted with a zinger, "We might not always need a last-minute comeback if I was in the game from the start." He was referring to the fact that this was the Raiders third straight game without an offensive touchdown.

He had broken a code by not supporting a teammate in front of the media. Stabler's insistence on being in the starting lineup rapidly spread through the locker room. Within minutes one reporter headed to Lamonica's stall and repeated Stabler's quote, waiting for his reaction. Lamonica, in true Raiders form, took the high road. "We are all here to win. No one is more responsible and more disappointed with our inability to get the ball in the end zone than me. I think I can still win for the Raiders, but they are going to do what they think is best."

I was standing in the group with Madden and Davis when Phil Finch, a reporter from the *San Francisco Examiner*, informed us of the quotes from the Raiders top two quarterbacks and asked for a comment.

Davis looked at Madden, offering him the first opportunity to answer. The coach began by addressing another concern: having to start the season playing six out of seven games on the road. "We've got four more games on the road in this ridiculous schedule that has us playing our first game in our home stadium in the eighth week of the season." Then he shifted to Finch's point. "We're here to win, and whatever man we pick to run our offense is capable of getting the job done. Lamonica has done it for years; Kenny has a big upside," Madden offered while remaining neutral on who would start the Raiders next game.

Davis added, "The greatness of the Raiders is in everyone doing their job. That includes on the field and in our preparation. We'll win as an organization."

Finch tried to explore the quarterback situation further. "Has a decision been made on who will start next week in St. Louis?"

"We've got a pretty good idea what way we'll go, but I'll make the final decision after looking at the game films and meeting with Al and my coaches." Madden stopped, realizing he needed to correct the impression he had just created. "I'll make the decision who starts at quarterback on my team!"

Everyone knew that a shift at starting quarterback would only happen if Davis wanted it, yet it was Madden's decision to make.

Madden was sensitive to reports that he was Davis' puppet and the real decisions on the team were dictated by the team owner. Madden had been willing to "co-coach" the team with Davis when he was first hired. He was smart enough to take advantage of what Davis had to offer in terms of offensive and defensive schemes, but five years into the job, Madden wanted to establish that he ran the Raiders on the field.

I wandered away to finish up my duties. Outside the Raiders locker room, I was putting extra sets of the play-by-play from the game in my briefcase when I heard a shout from a young voice, "It's Gene Upshaw!"

The kid didn't look more than 11 years old. He had apparently snuck by the security outside the corridor to the locker room and had positioned himself where he could see the Raiders leaving the dressing room door. He yelled their names to his friends standing where the Raiders bus was parked, trying to get autographs.

"It's Otis Sistrunk!" the kid yelled as the Raiders lineman ducked his head while walking past where I stood.

Here might have been the best advance man in the National Football League. This kid was able to recognize out-of-town players in their street clothes and give his friends an additional edge. Most often, particularly on the road, kids ask for autographs from men who look like athletes while not knowing who the player is. But when a player is referred to by name on the road, the chances of him taking the time to sign an autograph are greatly enhanced.

A 10-year-old with outstretched hands with a pad and paper is a lot more difficult for a player to pass by when he calls them by name.

"It's Ray Guy," the bright little advance man yelled while the Raiders punter made his way through the throng of waiting kids. Finally, after most of the players had left the locker room, I made my trek down the passageway. The barker knew who I was walking with and yelled to his cohorts, "It's Cliff Branch." Then he took a long look at me. He seemed to be running through his mind who I might be, and then shouted to his friends collecting autographs, "It's nobody!"

The mood boarding the plane in Kansas City after the loss was a total reversal from the levity experienced by the team flying in. Back then, I'd thought it was an honor to fly in the front-facing two seats with Madden, but LaRue had assigned me the position probably because no one else wanted to fly with the coach. He hated flying, perhaps because of the ill-fated C-46 charter that crashed on October 29, 1960, carrying the Cal Poly football team.

Madden had played at Cal Poly in 1957–58, and he knew a number of the athletes who lost their lives when the charter crashed on takeoff in heavy fog at Toledo Express Airport in Ohio. Sixteen members of the football team died, and he made a vigil on the Cal Poly campus to console the families of the lost players. At the time of the crash, Madden was an assistant coach at nearby Hancock Junior College.

Madden would later say that the Cal Poly crash was not the source of his fear of flying, but rather claustrophobia. Perhaps that was why the facing bench seats in the front, designed for four people, were occupied by only the two of us. Madden had his back to the cockpit, and I was facing forward.

"Just keep him calm, best you can," LaRue had requested.

I was already buckled up when Madden ducked his head to enter the plane shortly before takeoff. He looked at me with disdain. "And you knew," he muttered under his breath. "Fuck you knowing."

My assessment of the Raiders chances had obviously been shared with Madden, which did not score me any points.

"Fuck you knowing," he said, not loud enough for me to respond but loud enough to be heard. "Fuck you," he said a third time.

Moments later, his anger diminished as the United Airlines charter began its roll toward takeoff. The plane lifted into the air, and his red hands showed white-knuckled fear as a bump jostled our ascent.

I was not only a babysitter for the players at the hotel but also for the head coach in the friendly skies.

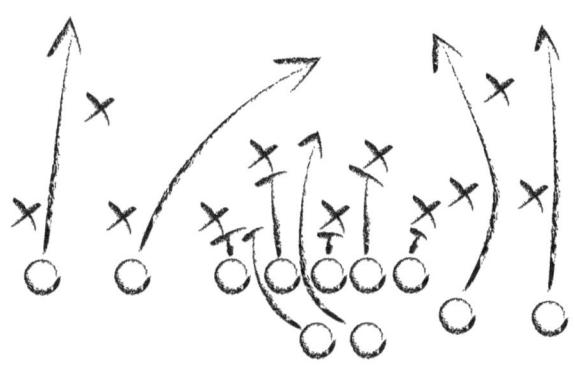

Chapter 11

Stabler In

KEN STABLER'S POSTGAME VENT brought the battle for starting quarterback into the limelight by the media and remained a major topic of discussion in private meetings between John Madden and Al Davis. Madden didn't want his team to be distracted by a quarterback controversy, while Davis appeared to respect Stabler for putting the hammer down. In the end, the decision was made to start Stabler the following Sunday against the St. Louis Cardinals.

The night before Stabler's first start, the hallway guarding duty was now accepted as my ongoing job. For a second week in a row, I realized that Davis was sure to appear at some time during my guard duties, and he had an uncanny knack of showing up not when the hall was quiet but when the players were most active.

He was again talking in his New Jersey thug accent. It almost rolled from the back of his throat and dropped off his lower lip in a tone that silenced any other voice. It has been a particularly stressful week, and the fact that we had opened the season with two losses in our first three games added to the concern around the quarterback switch. I stood as if getting inspected by a sergeant in the army. After a brief exchange, Davis headed down the hallway of the St. Louis hotel.

He was maybe ten yards down the corridor when a burst of smoke that billowed out of the room the defensive back was exiting forced him to stop. The sudden explosion of smoke in the hallway was as jolting as the burst from a steam engine leaving a train station.

George Atkinson teamed with Jack Tatum on the field to make one of the NFL's best, and certainly hardest-hitting, pair of safeties. As a player, he was aggressive but appeared to be having fun, which is exactly how he was off the field.

Atkinson ventured into the hallway, closing the room door behind him. Upon seeing his boss, he made a futile grab to turn the knob, only to find it locked. Atkinson cocked his right hand to knock on the door but then appeared to have second thoughts. He headed directly toward Davis while running his knuckles on the wall to steady his walk.

It was a brave act for a man, facing those reptilian eyes. The showdown in the sixth-floor hallway ended without a word after Atkinson fished a room key out of his pocket and zipped through a door two rooms closer to the elevator than the one he had exited. Now the hallway was filled with the smell of cheap perfume and clouds of marijuana smoke. In the middle of this haze stood Davis, fuming at what he had discovered.

"This is no fucking party," Davis said, turning his head my way for a brief moment. Davis then walked the length of the hallway before disappearing through a door under a green exit sign.

Busch Stadium is a near carbon copy of five other stadiums built in the same period, including Three Rivers Stadium in Pittsburgh, Jack Murphy Stadium in San Diego, Fulton County Stadium in Atlanta, Riverfront Stadium in Cincinnati, and the Raiders own Oakland/ Alameda County Coliseum. I viewed a circular sea of concrete with plastic seats as I sat in the owner's box. Davis was sitting two seats away to my left.

Again this week, Davis had a white jot tablet and a black felt pen by his foot. My understanding was that he and Madden had agreed no notes would be passed to coaches in St. Louis for Stabler's first game, but Davis kept a chronological log of the plays he would have called with the time of the play noted on each scribble.

Even with the new quarterback, the Raiders failed to score a touchdown in the first half. Once again, the defense kept Oakland in the game. A first-quarter Cardinals touchdown was countered by a short George Blanda field goal in the second period that limited the halftime deficit to 7–3.

Davis stayed frozen in his seat as the first-half clock ran out, and his beloved Raiders trotted off the field toward the locker room. With elbows on his knees, he stayed long after nearly everyone else around him had begun moving. I didn't budge from my position either. After what seemed an appropriate time to mourn another half without a Raiders touchdown, I asked him if I could get him anything.

"Touchdowns," he said softly. "Can you get us some fucking touchdowns?"

He didn't remain mournful for long, however. "You watch this fucking team in the second half. We are about to come together. This is going to get good." His mood lifted with each word as if giving himself a halftime pep talk.

Even though the Raiders offense had still not pierced the end zone, the offensive play in the first half did seem significantly upgraded from the first three weeks. The failures were not a result of missed long passes but rather drives that didn't finish. They were orchestrated with a better combination of short and long passes, with runs up the middle adding consistent yardage.

When Lamonica was at quarterback, everyone always had their eyes peeled for the next long pass. This was a player who had earned the nickname *Mad Bomber*. The Raiders had become accustomed to his style, but it was not the formula to resurrect them from a 1–2 start to championship caliber. The future of the Raiders success was now pegged to the left-handed, free-spirited 1968 second-round draft selection from Alabama.

Stabler had all the promise of greatness, but the longer a game progresses before a team scores their first touchdown, the more pressure builds. The Raiders attack finally climaxed into the team's first offensive touchdown of the season when Stabler handed the ball to Charlie Smith in the third quarter, and the veteran back carried it two yards for a touchdown. From his perspective in the box at Busch Stadium, Davis stood in a salute with a clenched right fist and a tightened jaw.

While celebrating the Raiders go-ahead touchdown, I bent forward to get a look at the score from Atlanta, located somewhat out of my view on the bottom right corner of the Busch Stadium scoreboard. The team I had rooted for all my life, the San Francisco 49ers, was playing the Falcons that day. Davis might have noticed my checking the out-of-town scores, but he said nothing.

When Raiders running back Marv Hubbard tallied our second offensive touchdown early in the fourth quarter to counter a game-tying

Cardinals Jim Bakken field goal, I took another peek to check on the 49ers progress. This time Davis didn't let it go unnoticed.

"Dennis," he said in a dire tone, "the only team you need to be concerned about is right down there wearing white."

I did not in any way want Mr. Davis to think I thought the 49ers result was as important as the Raiders, and he must have recognized my sincere contrition because he added, "The Niners are ahead, 13–9."

The more important result that day was 17–10, Raiders.

— — — — — —

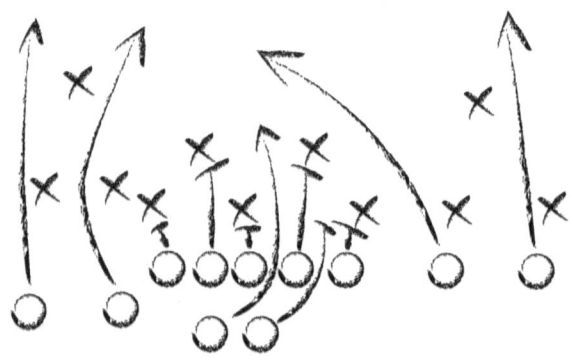

Chapter 12

Night and Day

Monday Night Football in 1973 was the center of the sports world. It played to astronomical ratings, spiked by announcers Howard Cosell, Don Meredith, and Frank Gifford. Meredith and Gifford were former star players, the former a quarterback for the Dallas Cowboys and the latter a New York sensation both on and off the field. Cosell's demeanor and voice were the same in person as on-air—louder than anyone else. He also assumed that his analyses were more insightful than others.

I was thrilled to sit near them. A year earlier, I'd been drinking beer with my buddies in college, watching Cosell, Meredith, and Gifford on TV. Now I was sitting next to Al Davis while watching them at Mile High Stadium.

Minutes before the *Monday Night Football* telecast aired, Cosell came out of the ABC booth and yelled to Davis, who was sitting on my left at a press table in the front row of the press box.

"You go on with us at halftime," Cosell shouted over all other pregame noise.

Davis shook off Cosell's request with a negative wave of his hand and a scowl.

"Mr. Davis," Cosell persisted, "the sports world wants to hear from you. They want to hear about your rookie kicker and the exciting new quarterback." He was referring to Stabler and the Raiders top draft choice that year, punter Ray Guy. Much of the pregame hype coming into this Monday night contest in Denver focused on just how high and far Guy's kicks would go in the thin mile-high air. The week before, Ken Stabler had, in his second start, guided Oakland to a pair of fourth-quarter touchdowns to earn a 27–17 win over the Chargers in San Diego.

Davis muttered under his breath, which only I could hear. First, Davis made a tick, tick, tick sound with his lips and then growled, "I'm fucking working here. You can do your entertaining without me."

Davis then crumpled a piece of paper and threw it on the table. "Do you understand what is important here?" he asked me.

I nodded, and Davis then threw a second wad of paper. "Let's just fucking win."

Someone from the ABC booth called Cosell. He took a puff from his cigar before assuming a standing position behind Meredith and Gifford, seated in front of their microphones. On the monitors, we could see the opening of the telecast the channel had taped earlier, and then the lights illuminated the ABC booth as the transmission switched to live commentary.

Ray Guy started the action on the field with a kickoff that sailed over the Broncos end zone. Denver moved to midfield on their first drive before being stalled by the Raiders defense. Our first drive lost yards as Stabler was sacked on third and seven for minus eight yards. After forcing Broncos into a punt following a three-and-out defensive stand, Stabler directed Oakland deep into Denver territory. However, Clarence Davis fumbled, and the ball was picked up by Broncos cornerback Bill Thompson, who returned 80 yards for a Denver touchdown.

Mile High Stadium was mostly aluminum, and the noise of the fans banging their feet in the stands was deafening. The press box would literally rock whenever the fans celebrated Broncos successes. Davis sat seething as Thompson crossed the goal line.

The Raiders went to work again, moving the ball efficiently into Broncos territory. On a third-and-four from the 18-yard line, Davis reacted instantly to the formation. "No, no, call time-out."

He saw the defense, knew the offensive formation, and considered it a bad matchup on a key play . . . but Stabler called for the snap. He was quickly buried for a 10-yard loss by a trio of Denver defenders.

"Fuck, fuck," Davis said to me. "Did you see that? I bet you did. Why the fuck can't the fucking coaches who are hired to see it, see it?"

In truth, I didn't see anything, but Davis quickly scribbled a formation and double-underlined a play on his tablet. He had been tearing pages off the entire first half. The "no messages" to the coaches rule was over, and I was handed the page with the instructions: "Get that to the fucking coaches."

Dutifully I found where Tom Flores, Paul Roach, and Bob Zeman were stationed upstairs, and handed Roach the note just after Blanda had connected on a field goal to cut Denver's lead to 7–3. On the ensuing kickoff, which I watched while walking back, the Broncos fumbled Guy's kick out of bounds and were forced to begin their offensive series from the 2-yard line.

Still, Denver ran 16 plays to advance the ball across midfield and set Jim Turner up for a 52-yard field goal midway through the second quarter. The ball hit the crossbar and was no good. The Raiders very next play from the 20-yard line was an 80-yard connection to wide receiver Mike Siani for a touchdown.

Davis didn't celebrate, instead pleading with his team from the press box to stay focused. They did.

Gerald Irons intercepted Charley Johnson's pass on Denver's next possession, and that led to a Blanda field goal to close out the first half with the Raiders leading, 13–7.

"It isn't over," Davis warned as the two teams headed to their halftime locker rooms.

He was right. The Raiders didn't move the ball on the opening possession of the second half, and Denver capped a 59-yard drive with Floyd Little taking it one yard up the middle for a go-ahead touchdown. The Raiders turned it over on their next possession when Marv Hubbard fumbled, and the Broncos converted that into a field goal to give themselves a four-point lead.

"Tell them to run this fucking play," Davis said to me while scribbling a formation and numbers on another piece of paper.

None of the coaches looked up when I came from behind, so I tapped Flores on the shoulder and whispered, "Davis says to run this play."

"Get the fuck out of here," Zeman yelled. "Tell him we are doing our fucking work, and let us do it."

I didn't report that to Davis when I returned.

Moments later, Stabler connected with Cliff Branch for a 16-yard touchdown. Oakland regained the lead, 20–17, as time ticked off in the third quarter.

Early in the fourth, Turner connected on his second field goal of the night, tying the game at 20. The aluminum-accented fan celebration again vibrated through the press box. They weren't making much noise six minutes of game clock later, though, when Blanda drilled a 49-yard field goal. The Raiders took a three-point lead with 41 seconds left in the contest.

"Stay focused," Davis said while Oakland lined up for Guy's kickoff attempt.

"Fuck," he said as the ball dribbled out of bounds short of the end zone, resulting in a five-yard penalty and re-kick. It was taken by Joe Dawkins at the 13 and returned 25 yards to the 38. Two runs and a pass garnered the Broncos 34 yards and set Turner up with a 35-yard field goal attempt with three seconds left on the clock.

The battering of the stadium was as loud as it had been all night. The press box swayed in the Denver evening when Turner connected on the kick to end the game in a tie, 23–23.

The Broncos celebrated like they'd won; the Raiders responded like they'd lost.

Davis wadded a piece of paper in the press box, threw it aimlessly in front, and said under his breath, "I knew this was going to be fucking tough."

Madden was wearing the same striped, brown dress shirt he had on during the game when he boarded the plane and slumped in the chair across from me.

"A tie feels the same as a loss," Madden said while buckling his seat belt.

The two-and-one-half-hour flight from Denver to Oakland departed Colorado just after midnight, and with the hour we'd pick up flying west, the Raiders United Airlines charter would be in Oakland before 2:00 a.m. local time.

"I hope you don't have any plans with Pammy tonight," Grimes said shortly following takeoff. "We've got a short week, and we need to work when we get back."

"I need you at the practice field before 10," Madden added.

"Okay, I will," I said to both requests.

As we soared through the night, I tried to figure out going to San Jose—I was still living in the same rented house from my senior college days—and returning to Oakland in the available time. The commute was nearly an hour each way, and if I had eight hours between the time we landed and when my duties would start at the Raiders practice field, my five-hour sleep time was going to be reduced in direct relation to how long I worked with Grimes at the office.

It was nearly 4:30 a.m. when Grimes typed the final notes I had helped him research for the Raiders weekly press release. On the plane ride home, he had updated the Raiders stats for the six regular-season games, and once we arrived at the office, Grimes began inserting them into the press release. The notes were the final piece of the mailer sent to media outlets throughout the country, 318 in all.

The envelopes were already printed with addresses and ready to be stuffed when Grimes placed the original of the four-page press release on Sandra Gardner's desk—the PR secretary. Every Tuesday during the season, she would make Xerox copies of the press release and stuff them in the envelopes to get them mailed by 4:00 p.m.

It was almost 5:00 a.m. when Grimes said, "Good job . . . see you a little later this morning." He then put some papers in his briefcase and said, "Don't forget to lock the door when you leave."

I checked my watch again, contemplating whether to attempt my two-hour commute or sleep in the office. I had my luggage from our trip to Denver and decided the extra hours of sleep would be better. I instead opted for the 10-minute drive to the Raiders practice field facility on Doolittle Drive.

Once there, I called Pam, who lived with me and five college students in the San Jose house.

"You were on TV," Pam said after I explained I was still in Oakland and would spend the night.

"I was?"

"Yes," she said, "they were showing Al Davis all night, and you were there right next to him."

As it turned out, I spent the time required to drive home on the phone instead of sleeping. At 6:00 a.m., Pam ended the conversation because she needed to get ready for her nursing school classes.

It was one of those nights I am not sure if I ever really fell asleep. I awoke to the cowbells' ringing sound, hooked to the practice field's front doors, that announced someone was entering the building. George Anderson, the Raiders trainer, poked his head in, and when I asked what time it was, he replied, "You spent the night here? It's 8:15."

"Oh man," I said, "I need to get some sleep before the coaches get here."

He laughed before heading to his training room to set up for the day. That Tuesday was a day off for the players, but those with bumps and bruises were required to come in for treatment.

I still had not caught up on sleep the following Friday when the team, staff, media, and guests were boarding the United Airlines charter to Baltimore. Luckily, given our short week, the Colts were in a down year, and we eased to a 13–0 halftime advantage before trading points in the second half en route to a 34–21 victory.

We had been airborne for less than an hour when Ken Bishop approached the front compartment to announce to Madden the final score from Kansas City. "Chiefs 14, Bills . . . 23," Bishop said, pausing for dramatic effect. Any score of a division opponent mattered, but this one assured that seven weeks into the season, the Raiders were alone atop the AFC West race.

"Four-two-and-one," Madden said proudly. "The league schedules us on the road six times in the first seven weeks in four different time zones, and still, we lead our division."

It was an uncharacteristic claim to dominance for the Raiders coach, who, like Davis, more often considered the challenges ahead. He, too, always thought in terms of keeping the edge necessary to succeed.

His confidence faded the following Sunday during warm-ups at the Oakland Coliseum. I was assisting a photographer who needed an extra pass when I encountered Madden less than an hour before kickoff.

The players were going through warm-up drills. Fred Biletnikoff had caught a pass from Ken Stabler that took him close to where Madden and I were standing.

"It's a beautiful day for a big win," Biletnikoff said to his coach with a big smile.

The breezy enthusiasm of the Raiders star receiver, often the most intense player in the pregame ritual, caught Madden off guard. After Biletnikoff was out of range, he groused, "It just doesn't feel right to me." He looked at me for a reaction. "This one just doesn't seem intense enough. I just don't know if we are ready to play our best."

His candor took me by surprise, just as Biletnikoff's confidence was out of character. Madden sharing a concern with me was totally a new experience.

"I think Fred is right," I said enthusiastically. "I think we kill the Giants today."

Alex Webster, the Giants head coach, came up to us and offered Madden a handshake greeting. New York had been in a dive, having lost their last five games since earning a tie against the Philadelphia Eagles in second-week action.

"You've got another strong team," Webster said to Madden.

Since it was our first regular-season game at the Coliseum, a number of local media people, who didn't travel with the team, were seeing the Raiders live for the first time. Grimes had recommended to bring a few extra sets of the league media guides, the annual books each franchise puts out with the history, stats, and particulars of their teams. Media people were always offered a complete set of 13 plastic holders that held each team's guide.

When I pulled an AFC binder out of the box to give it to Mac Hyman, the books drained out and spread across the concrete press box floor behind his chair. Hyman, who wrote for Post Newspapers, didn't move out of his chair; rather, he just looked over his shoulder and made a disparaging comment about my competence.

I dropped to my knees and began collecting the scattered guides when another person came to offer assistance. I saw his hand first, a tan one with perfectly manicured fingernails, a lavish diamond ring on his little finger, and a Rolex watch on his wrist. As I scooped up the Bengals and Browns books, I thanked him for his assistance.

"No problem, happy to help," he said with a distinguished accent while I began to reassemble the binder with the books collected from the floor. He was wearing a blue blazer with a gray turtleneck sweater. His slacks were perfectly tailored, and his black shoes shined to military standards.

"I'm Dennis Ranahan," I said while extending my right hand in both thanks and greeting.

"Domenico," he said.

I wasn't sure if that was his first or last name, so I just said, "Thank you, sir."

"You do good work," Domenico said while I handed the reassembled media guide binder to Hyman. Just then, a roar went up from the Oakland Coliseum crowd in response to Bob Moore catching a 21-yard touchdown pass from Stabler to advance the Raiders first-quarter lead to 14–0.

"Not so good when I'm taking media guide binders out upside down," I laughed.

"That aside," Domenico nodded, "you do good work."

I really didn't know what he was referring to. I had never seen him before nor did I think he was from media. But he was wearing a Raiders game day credential on the button of his blazer.

"Who is the gentleman in the blazer?" I asked Grimes a short time later.

Grimes hesitated before answering. "They call him Mr. Dom," he deadpanned. "Why?" Grimes added.

"Because he was really helpful when I dumped a set of media guides. Does he work for a paper?"

"He is a friend of Art Snyder," Grimes said. Art Snyder worked on the Raiders stat crew.

That day, the stats were all in favor of the Raiders as they white-washed the Giants 42–0. In retrospect, I wondered if John Madden had been trying my odds on the game. Naw, I told myself, he had a lot more important things to think about.

– – – – – –

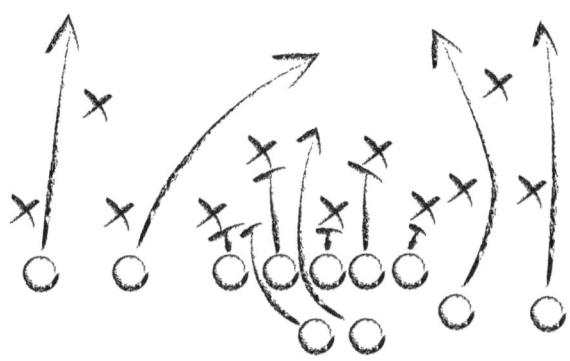

Chapter 13

Immaculate Revenge

Narrow home losses to the Pittsburgh Steelers and Cleveland Browns followed, but a victory over the San Diego Chargers sent us to Houston still holding first place in the AFC West with one more win than both the Denver Broncos and Kansas City Chiefs.

Whether the Raiders chartered their team flight for a Friday or Saturday departure depended mostly on geographic considerations. If we were playing east of Colorado, our travel plans called for a Friday afternoon departure. If we were playing a game closer to Oakland, such as San Diego or Los Angeles, the team charter would leave on Saturday.

Texas pretty much split the difference, and yet the decision was made to arrive for the Oilers game on Friday night. I think Davis wanted time to visit Houston. He requested I drive his rented Cadillac for a city tour after the Saturday morning walk-through.

After parking the car, he pointed at a building in downtown Houston. "This is where we ran the American Football League from while I was the commissioner." I was walking with Davis and had never seen him so reflective. His normal demeanor was edgy and challenging, but today he was visibly sentimental, reminiscing about his AFL stewardship that brought about the merger with the NFL.

He wandered off the main drag and into a fashionable clothing store. He took a shirt off the rack and held it up for me. "Is this black?"

I knew why he had asked that; he was color blind. Some mornings Davis would slip out of his house with Mrs. Davis discovering later that the clothes she had marked with numbers that went together were not used. A call to the office would have Rosemary inform Mrs. Davis of what he was wearing. Occasionally his garments clashed, and the two ladies would share a laugh about his wardrobe if he was still in the office or get concerned about his impression if he was in public. A closet in Davis' office included color-coordinated items he could change in case of any mishap. No wonder he liked silver and black.

"That's dark blue," I said to Davis.

"Don't want any fucking blue," he chuckled under his breath. "How about this one?" he queried again, holding a silk shirt.

"Black," I nodded.

After a leisurely stroll around the heart of Houston, we got back in the Cadillac to return to the Marriott Hotel. He was reading stats from a legal-size mimeographed report when I made a left turn, off a four-lane road that had a left-turn lane, and soon noticed the island of the four-lane road was on my right side. Somehow, I ended up driving into oncoming traffic. A couple of cars were coming my way; one passed on my left while honking. The second car shared the lane I was driving in, and we were heading for a collision. Luckily, I could see a break in the divider not too far ahead.

The car jerked into the passing gear at the same moment I accelerated to make it to the opening in the same lane. Alerted by the sudden acceleration and kick down, Davis looked up from his paper.

He didn't say anything, only watched my dash for that opening in the divider. I darted through it and onto the proper side of the highway. The car coming right at us sped by on the left.

"Everything okay?" Davis said while looking my way.

"Yes, sir," I snapped while feeling sweat accumulate on my forehead.

"Good," he said with a smile as he returned to his reading.

The Houston Astrodome was dubbed the eighth wonder of the world when it opened in 1964. I was excited to see it but was surprised to find it more of a dump than most NFL venues. The place had the feeling of a large cargo area instead of an NFL stadium. It appeared uncared for and old even though it had opened less than ten years ago.

The seats were hard and uncomfortable. George Blanda was using three of them while smoking a cigarette, sitting alone in his street clothes more than two hours prior to the Raiders December 2, 1973, game against the Oilers. Blanda was Houston's first quarterback when they became a charter member of the AFL in 1960.

He had led the Oilers to the first two AFL championships, both times beating the Chargers, the team where Davis served as an assistant coach on Sid Gilman's staff. Davis traded for Blanda before the 1967 season, who joined the Silver and Black as their kicker and backup quarterback. He saw limited duty as a quarterback in his first three years with the Raiders but was a reliable field goal kicker.

Then, in 1970, everything changed for Blanda. It began on November 1, in a game against the defending Super Bowl champion Kansas City Chiefs at Municipal Stadium. The Raiders trailed 17–14 with time running out on the clock when Ben Davidson was called for an illegal hit on Chiefs quarterback Len Dawson. Even though the penalty was against Oakland, the play stopped the clock and gave the Raiders just enough time to regain possession and set Blanda up for a field goal attempt that appeared longer than his range.

Still, the master competitor booted the ball, which cleared both the crossbar and leaping attempt by a Kansas City defender to prevent it from going through and ended the Raiders/Chiefs game in a tie. The following Sunday, back in Oakland against the Cleveland Browns, Blanda was part of another improbable comeback that ended when he connected on an even longer field goal in a 23–20 win.

The following Sunday in Denver, Blanda pulled the Raiders from the brink of defeat for a third straight week, this time both as a kicker and quarterback, in defeating the Broncos 24–19. Against the San Diego Chargers seven days later, he again provided the winning margin with a late kick that downed the Chargers, 20–17. His heroics prompted Raiders announcer Bill King to acknowledge his feats with a clear declaration for Oakland fans: *"George Blanda has just been named king of the world."*

I didn't want to interrupt his pregame preparation when I spotted him alone in the stands at the Astrodome, but I did pause to look at him and he noticed me. Instead of turning away, Blanda motioned for me to join him. As I took the seat that left one unoccupied between us, he appeared as melancholy as Davis had the day before.

"I sure love this game," Blanda said while puffing on his cigarette, "but I wish I could just play it, do my job, and not have all the distractions around it." At 46, Blanda was two years older than Davis, the oldest active player in football.

At first, I thought he was referring to the requests I often made of him for an interview with a writer or electronic media person, but I soon realized that he was taking a more global perspective.

"That damn 1970," Blanda said while crushing out a cigarette on the concrete with his right hand. "Had a good thing going here, nobody paid much attention, and then all the hype around that month. Everyone wants to talk about that season when they interview me, when all I care about is the next game." He then paused after lighting another cigarette, and said to me, "Never lose yourself in the hype, Dennis, it is a fickle friend."

He uncoiled himself from the posture that covered three seats and nodded to me as he headed to the locker room for another battle.

An hour later, I heard Davis' distinctive voice: "You have them get that fucking sign down now."

He was talking to Al LoCasale, and was referring to a sign hanging from the second deck that read, "Madden is a FAT SLOB."

LoCasale didn't respond at first, thinking whom to assign the sign removal task. Davis took umbrage at his delay. "Listen, Al, I don't care if you have to go over there and pull that goddamn sign down yourself; just get it outta here before John brings his team on the field."

Jim McLemore, the Oilers public relations director, overheard Davis and spotted the sign. He offered to get the job done. Minutes later, a security guard was booed by Houston fans as he pulled up the hanging sheet and rolled it under his arm.

We won that day in Houston and clinched another AFC Western title the next Sunday against Kansas City at the Oakland Coliseum. All that remained on the regular season schedule was a rematch of the overtime tie in Denver against the Broncos. Most of the preparation time in the week leading to the meaningless contest against Denver was dedicated to preparation for possible postseason opponents.

"We aren't going to spend time on dogs that don't hunt," Raiders offensive line coach Ollie Spenser said while I was typing the game plan. "Pittsburgh, Cincinnati, and Miami are the only teams we care about now. They are the only ones between us and the Super Bowl," he added. "Our film studies are dedicated to those teams."

I mentioned I had grown up a 49ers fan and how big it was for me on the final day of the 1970 regular season when San Francisco beat the Raiders to earn a postseason slot. He laughed, "We didn't prepare for them either. I think it was the only time I ever saw Al not intent on winning. He almost conceded that a 49ers victory would be good for football in the Bay Area."

"Mr. Davis not care about winning?" I questioned with a shake of my head. "I can't even imagine that."

"Well," Spencer said, "he cared a lot more about our next opponent, and we spent two weeks getting ready for the Dolphins. Beat them that year."

In 1970, the 49ers beat an unfocused Raiders squad 38–7, but even an uninspired Oakland team outscored the Broncos to close out the 1973 season, 21–17.

The Pittsburgh Steelers were, for the second year in a row, our opening-round opponent. But this time, under Chuck Noll, they were no longer new kids in the playoff arena. Pittsburgh was now better than the one that beat us the prior season and six weeks earlier as well. Pittsburgh was 22–8 over the prior two seasons, Oakland, 19–8–2. In head-to-head matchups, the Steelers were 3–0 against the Raiders since an opening-day Steelers win at Pittsburgh in 1972.

In the midst of preparing for the December 22 playoff game, I got a call at the Raiders offices from my dad, asking me about Christmas.

"I'm making reservations for the Wharf," Dad said, referring to Christmas Eve. "Will you and Pam be able to join us?"

My family had celebrated Christmas Eve at Grotto #9 in San Francisco every year since they moved to California from Nebraska in 1943. My mother was pregnant with my brother Mike when they first went, taking my oldest brother, Jack, with them. The annual trip to dinner at the Wharf served as an opportunity for my grandparents to play Santa Claus while we had dinner. The family celebration always included them, along with opening presents on Christmas Eve night.

In other words, missing a family dinner at the Wharf was paramount to missing Christmas.

"I don't know if I will be able to come this year," I said honestly. I had not made any plans since summer camp that were not trumped by my work with the Raiders. "If we win Saturday, I might have to work."

"On Christmas Eve?" Dad asked with concern.

"I don't know," I said again.

"Well, first, I hope you win, and second, I hope you can have dinner with us on Christmas Eve."

The Coliseum was sparkling in silver and black for our Saturday showdown against Terry Bradshaw, Franco Harris, Joe Greene, and the rest of the Pittsburgh squad. The prior losses, and revenge for the dramatic defeat in last year's playoffs, made our easy-romp win over the Steelers that much more satisfying. We scored the first 10 points of the game on a Marv Hubbard run and a George Blanda field goal. After the Steelers got on the board with a TD pass from Terry Bradshaw to Barry Pearson, we added 16 more points before they scored again.

Hubbard book-ended his opening-period touchdown with another scoring run late in the fourth quarter to provide the final margin of victory, 33–14.

While most of the Raiders staff attended the postgame party at the Oakland Hilton, Grimes and I returned to the office following the game to prepare our press release for next week's AFC Championship Game against the winner of the Miami Dolphins versus Cincinnati Bengals game on Sunday.

Del Courtney had been celebrating at the post-game party and was in a particularly good mood when he stopped by Oakport Street to retrieve something from his office.

"Why aren't you guys at the party?" he said with a grin on his face.

"Some of us have work to do," Grimes murmured, not looking up from his IBM Selectric typewriter.

"It's a good party," Courtney said while leaving the office.

Grimes and I were still working an hour later when we got a call from Del's recently divorced second wife, Connie Haines, who reported that he was involved in a traffic accident. It was fortunately not as serious as it could have been. On his way home, he had somehow entered the wrong bore of the Caldecott Tunnel and sideswiped an oncoming car before putting his car up against the wall.

"Is he all right?" Grimes asked Connie. She must have said he was because when Grimes hung up the phone, he looked at me and said sarcastically, "Seems Mr. Courtney's party didn't end when he left here."

After explaining what Connie had reported to him, he said, more to himself than to me, "How does someone get in the wrong tunnel?"

I was more familiar with the Caldecott Tunnel than Grimes because it was the route I used to visit Pam in Orinda. I explained that there were three bores and that the center one was opened for traffic in both directions at different times to accommodate weekday traffic flows. Westbound for the morning commute and eastbound for the afternoon. Still, the tunnels were clearly marked, and the only way someone could get in the wrong bore toward oncoming traffic was if they ran through the orange markers that rose from the roadway to direct them into the right bore.

"Well," Grimes said again with good humor, "the old bandleader found his way through those barriers and into the westbound bore in an easterly direction."

"He's all right?" I said to confirm his condition.

"Better than his car, as I understand," Grimes said again before returning his attention to the paper in his typewriter.

On Sunday, the Dolphins easily handled the Bengals in their playoff game, setting up the second meeting of the year between the Raiders and defending world champions. The coaches worked on Sunday, pulling film of the Dolphins win, and began preparing to stop Bob Griese's attack and pierce the No-Name Defense.

Monday night routinely had been an early evening for me. In most weeks, we worked all day after playing a game on Sunday, half of the time requiring travel. Once I got the coaches their dinner, which was their choice between Mexican food, hamburgers, steak sandwiches, or something from one of the players' restaurants, I was free to go. Gene Upshaw owned Uppy's, which was located on the upper side of Oakland and featured chitlins and other Black ethnic selections. Fred Biletnikoff had his name on the Flanker Steak House, which was located just across Hegenberger Road from the Edgewater Hyatt. On Christmas Eve, the coaches opted for a steak dinner while I was still hoping for fish at Fisherman's Wharf.

I thought that Christmas Eve was a great reason for me to get off early, but preparing for the AFC Championship Game was all that mattered to Madden.

"What is more important to you?" he said in an intimidating voice when I asked at about 4:00 o'clock how long I would be working that evening.

"I'm here to do whatever you want me to do. I was just thinking because it was Christmas Eve, I might get off early," I responded as politely as I could.

"We can find someone else that would love your job," Madden bellowed. "Do you want me to do that?"

"No, sir, sorry I mentioned it," I meekly replied.

"What time do I get off?" Madden muttered under his breath as he disappeared into the coaches' locker room.

Once he was out of sight, I placed a call to my home in San Bruno to let Dad and Mom know I would not be able to join them for Christmas Eve dinner. It was the first time in my life I hadn't spent that night at Fisherman's Wharf.

My father was not only understanding, he praised me for my commitment to work.

"Don't worry about the dinner," he said, "you should be glad that they need you."

"Okay, thanks."

Around 7:30, Madden poked his head into my office. I was manning a phone that wasn't ringing and reading *Sports Illustrated*.

"You can take off. Just get the reports to the Oakport office before you go home," he said in a tone that was markedly friendlier than the one before.

"Thanks," I said eagerly, almost like a little kid. In a flash, I picked up the updated list of players, coaches, staff, and media invited to Miami. I was to deliver the envelope to Rosemary Butt, so she could forward it to Mr. Davis for final approval. When I handed them to Rosemary, I spotted Mr. Davis sitting in his corner office. The fluorescent lights in the ceiling were turned off, and he was reading under the illumination of a desk lamp. I poked my head inside his office and said, "Merry Christmas, Mr. Davis."

He looked up from the notes he was reading. "Christmas? Christmas? When's Christmas?"

"Tonight, sir, tomorrow. I mean, this is Christmas Eve, and tomorrow is Christmas."

"Tomorrow is Christmas already?" he asked. "No, no. Can't be already."

I thought he was kidding, but I didn't want to say the wrong thing. "See you tomorrow."

"You're going to be here tomorrow? On Christmas?" he said, almost playful.

"Yes, sir," I said flatly.

"Working on Christmas," Davis said, not as a question but as an acknowledgment of my commitment to our objective. "You must really want to win."

"I do, sir."

"You have a good night; see ya tomorrow."

— — — — — —

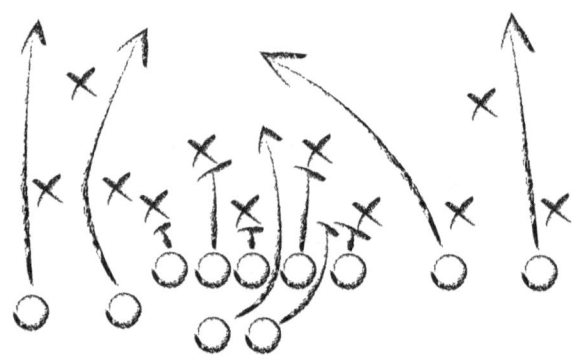

Chapter 14

Kentucky Christmas

THE RAIDERS ENDED the Dolphins 19-game winning streak with their victory in September. Miami would go on to lose only one more time the rest of the season, leading up to this showdown with Oakland to determine which team would represent the AFC in Super Bowl VIII.

The only other game Miami had lost in 1973 was a week-13 defeat at Baltimore against a lowly Colts team that won only three other games the entire season. Baltimore did not present any real threat to the Dolphins. They had defeated Baltimore 44–0 four weeks earlier when they still had something to play for. Before that game, the Dolphins had won 10 straight games, including a week-12 conquest of Pittsburgh, 30–26, to clinch their division title. The Dolphins were playing out the regular season with nothing at stake, and the Colts improved on their 2–10 record with meaningless wins in the final two weeks of the season.

Still, Madden was looking for more information to get his team ready for a battle. On Christmas Day, he asked me to get Howard Schnellenberger, head coach of the Baltimore Colts, on the phone. He thought that if the Colts beat the Dolphins, maybe they had discovered something that the Raiders could use in the AFC Championship Game.

I knew it was faulty logic, but if Madden wanted to talk to the Baltimore coach on Christmas Day, my job was to find him. I didn't expect he would be working. Why would anyone from an organization eliminated from the playoffs weeks earlier be working on Christmas Day? But I called the Colts offices anyway as a starting point and was greeted with a Christmas recording that assured me my call would be returned after the holiday if I left a message. I didn't leave one and went to my Public Relations Guide that gave inside and home phone numbers for staff members from all 26 NFL teams.

The inside line at the Colts office scored a live voice, a female with an accent I didn't recognize who first explained she had stopped in the office only for a moment when she saw the phone light blinking. After telling me how lucky I was to reach her, she answered my inquiry on Coach Schnellenberger by telling me he was spending the Christmas holidays with relatives in Kentucky.

"Is their last name Schnellenberger?" I asked, confident that if they were listed in the phone book, there wouldn't be too many Schnellenbergers in Kentucky to choose between.

"No," the voice on the phone explained. "He is with his wife's family, and Beverlee's maiden name is Donnelly."

"Donaldly, like the boy's name Donald?" I asked.

"D—O—N—N—E—L—L—Y," she clarified before adding, "they live in Lexington."

"I have listings for six Donnellys in Lexington," the phone operator said when I continued on my quest to get the Colts coach on the phone for Madden. I took them all, and the first one I dialed produced a friendly male voice wishing me a Merry Christmas before knowing who I was.

"I'm looking for Coach Howard Schnellenberger and wondered if he was there," I responded to his holiday greeting.

"He sure is."

"I work for the Oakland Raiders. I'm looking for Coach Schnellenberger for John Madden."

"Oh," the voice said, "just a minute."

Schnellenberger's voice was lower than I had ever remembered hearing a person, and his greeting had me on quick alert to again explain my mission. "My name is Dennis, sir. I'm calling on behalf of John Madden. Can you wait just a moment while I go get him for you?"

"Sure," Schnellenberger replied. I put the receiver on the desk and headed through the coaches' locker area to find Madden sitting next to a projector, studying films of the Dolphins defense.

"I've got Coach Schnellenberger on the line."

Madden snapped off the projector and unfolded himself from a chair more suited to a high school kid than a man of his bulk. Moments after greeting Schnellenberger, he used both hands to light a cigarette while holding the phone to his ear with his shoulder. After taking his first drag on the cigarette, he said through a cloud of smoke, "Howard, tell me how you beat those guys and what I need to know to do the same."

From that glib comment, the conversation turned more serious. Madden continually prodded Schnellenberger on keys he had found in unlocking the secret of how to exploit the Dolphins. I could only hear my end, but his responses to Schnellenberger indicated that the coach in Kentucky didn't have any special knowledge.

When Madden hung up the phone, he said, "No magic bullet." He lifted himself out of the chair, then lit another cigarette. "Where did you find him?"

"He was spending the holidays with his in-laws in Kentucky."

Madden nodded in approval.

"I wish it could have helped," I said, "but you know the only reason the Dolphins lost to Baltimore was because they had clinched their division title the week before."

Madden appeared irritated by my assessment. "I think they'll be a little better prepared for us than they were for the Colts. No magic bullets," he said again before heading back to his projector for film study.

— — — — — —

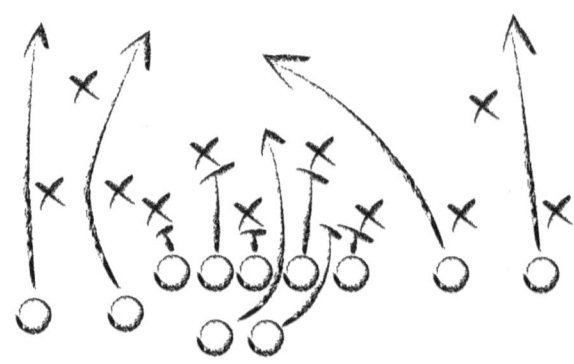

Chapter 15

Guard Dogs

We arrived in Miami for the 1973 AFC Championship Game on Thursday, a full day earlier than we normally would for an away game. Madden wanted to hold a couple of practices on the Orange Bowl artificial turf, which was spongy and like none other in the league. He also thought to get his team acclimated to the time shift. He scheduled a pair of practices at the Orange Bowl, both for 1:00 p.m. local time.

On Friday, the late December weather in Miami was warm, nearly 80 degrees, and muggy. Yet when I showed up, I found that Al Davis was not hot about the weather, but by the possibility that the Dolphins had spies watching our practice.

"Dennis," he said, pointing to a section of empty stands, "any fucking guy could be up there right now watching us, learning our plays, and stealing away our chances for a win. I want security up there to make sure nobody is watching."

"What would you like me to do?" I asked, not mentioning the impossibility of his request.

"Find the guy in charge of security. Tell him I want guards up there to sweep this stadium for onlookers."

So, off I went on a mission to find the Orange Bowl security chief and have him secure the stadium.

Less than 15 minutes later, I located the security office and found the man in charge sitting in a swivel chair behind a metal desk cluttered with paper and manila envelopes. The shabby office smelled like a janitor's closet.

"I'm with the Raiders," I announced while walking in on him. He didn't seem impressed.

"Mr. Davis wants the stadium secured from any onlookers while we practice," I said, hoping he would jump to attention and know just how to enforce that request.

"What exactly do you want me to do?" he responded without budging one inch.

"How can we make sure no one is spying on our practice?" I asked.

"Nothing I can do," he said.

"Really?" I responded. "Aren't you in charge of security?"

He took a deep breath. "Listen, kid, I don't know exactly what you want me to do, but I can't guarantee you privacy for your practices."

"Okay," I said, shaking my head, "but my boss is Al Davis, and he usually figures there is a way to get things done whatever he wants to get done. So," I said, crooking my finger for him to follow, "why don't you come with me and tell Mr. Davis in person you can't do anything."

He seemed astounded. "You want me to go tell him we can't do anything?"

"That's right," I said, "because I think we can. I believe if you have a conversation with him, he might just bring up some new possibilities on how to handle this."

"Seems like a waste of time to me," he mumbled. Yet he picked up a collection of keys on a silver ring and finally rose to his feet. He was shorter than me but weighed at least a hundred pounds more. He clipped the key ring on his thick brown belt and checked to make sure his office door was locked before we started our walk through the bowels of the Orange Bowl and onto the synthetic playing surface.

Davis was standing near the end zone when I introduced him to Frank, the security chief.

"Listen," Davis said to Frank without diverting his gaze from the players on the field, "how are you going to make sure no one is up there watching our workout?"

"Like I told your boy here, there is no way to secure this stadium for absolute security."

"Maybe you didn't understand me," Davis said, peering at Frank in a menacing manner. "We are guests in your stadium, we are the Raiders, and I'm requesting security for our practices. How are you going to fucking provide it?"

"I don't know that we can," Frank said stubbornly.

"You misunderstand," Davis said in a voice less threatening and more engaging. "I'm not asking if. I'm asking how you are going to provide security. Are you with me?"

I was enjoying the exchange. Obviously, Frank did not often have a conversation with someone not satisfied with excuses or reasons but only focused on the objective.

Frank was beginning to understand that and shifted gears for the first time. I could see it happening. Frank was now becoming a partner with Davis in solving a security issue that only a moment before he thought was impossible.

"Well," Frank finally offered, "short of guard dogs roaming the stands, I can't think of any other way to assure security."

For Saturday's practice, in addition to Oakland personnel on the field, three dog handlers showed up to control five German shepherds secured in harnesses with heavy brown leather collars.

Commands were barked out to the dogs in a foreign language, I think German, and their handlers looked like the three toughest cops I wouldn't have wanted to break up a dorm party on campus.

Gene Upshaw, the Raiders great offensive guard, unthinkingly reached out to greet one of the dogs as if it was a family pet. The dog snapped at him with a growl that might have removed a mere mortal's hand. Fortunately, one of Upshaw's strengths was his quickness, and he used it to snap his hand out of harm's way. One of the gloved handlers yanked the dog back and yelled something I didn't understand.

If a Black man could turn pale, Upshaw did.

"Wow," Gene said in his thunderous voice, "I feel safe now."

"You shouldn't reach out to them," the handler said in English.

"You are absolutely right."

Davis was not happy about the encounter. "You're here to roam the stands and make sure we don't have anyone spying on our practice," he said. "Not fucking eating our players."

George Anderson, the Raiders trainer, was standing next to me and gave a mock injury report. "Upshaw, doubtful, lost limb."

When the Raiders beat Miami early in the season, Daryle Lamonica was our starting quarterback, and we were underdogs at home. This time the Dolphins were at home, again favored, and we had Ken Stabler running our offense. The Dolphins were beyond swagger. They carried themselves like champions who expected to repeat. They had followed up their perfect season with another campaign that proved them to be the class of the league. We would have to play a special game, indeed, if we were to earn a spot in Super Bowl VIII.

The Orange Bowl filled up with Miami fans basking in South Florida weather. Raider support was pretty much limited to the stack of good luck telegrams Grimes had handed me on Saturday after practice to post in the locker room.

On Sunday, I was the only one sitting next to Al Davis during the game. The Dolphins, by request from Ken LaRue, had given Davis a private viewing area that was the size of a school classroom. We sat next to each other in plastic chairs that abutted an 18-inch counter and had a view of the field from the 25-yard line. The Dolphins were on the far side of the field from where we sat, but Davis often spoke in a conversational manner as if his team could hear him. He stood for most of the first half, often gripping the back of his plastic chair with both hands.

The first half was a defensive struggle. He was saying, "Stop 'em here, stop 'em here," when Larry Csonka scored his second touchdown on a third down play in the final minute of the first half. The score advanced the Dolphins lead to 14–0 and capped a 16-play drive that consumed nearly eight minutes, and all but the final 17 seconds of the second quarter.

When Csonka scored the touchdown, Davis said, "Return the kick."

Dolphins kicker Garo Yepremian booted it six yards deep into the end zone and Clarence Davis took a knee after fielding it.

While the teams headed to their halftime locker rooms, Davis wadded a piece of paper, tossed it aimlessly on the table in front of him, and looked at me. "We can get them in the second half."

Yet his voice was not very convincing. Playing on the Dolphins home field with a Super Bowl berth awaiting the winner was not an ideal time for his Raiders to overcome a 14–0 halftime deficit. Maybe Davis wanted me to agree with him. Since I had informed him before our week-3 game at Kansas City that we were in trouble, Davis had often asked me how the team looked for upcoming games.

I had been right every time he asked, and fortunately, I could consistently tell him his team looked ready to win. He seemed to ask me straight out, though, what I thought about this game.

I don't think he wanted my answer.

Instead, he answered it himself. "No matter what you think," he drawled, "these guys can win."

Hope ended for every Raider except Davis less than two hours later when Csonka scored his third touchdown of the game on the first play after the two-minute warning. The score advanced Miami's lead to 26–10, and while the two teams were lining up for the extra point, Davis, who had been slumped in his plastic chair for most of the second half, now leaped to his feet and pleaded with his team from his perch at the Orange Bowl, "Just block the fucking extra point." He then looked at me and said, "If we can just block this kick, we still have a chance, you know that?" The man simply refused to surrender to the obvious.

His remark could have been viewed as a futile cry in the fading afternoon sun, but I realized by now that it meant something more. This unflagging belief in his team had guided Davis through his life. His strength of character, refusing to surrender to defeat, had carried his beloved Raiders more times than any other NFL team to revive games that appeared lost.

The Raiders successful last-minute comebacks was a character trait that had burst on the national scene five years earlier when NBC shifted from action in Oakland and missed the Raiders two late touchdowns to beat the Jets in the Heidi Game. There were 65 seconds left in the contest when Jim Turner of the Jets converted a field goal that put Joe Namath's team up by three points. Seven o'clock was approaching in New York, and NBC had contracted with Timex to show a made-for-television version of the classic movie *Heidi*. Most NFL games were played in less than three hours in the '60s, but this battle between the Raiders and Jets, considered the best two teams in the 10-squad American Football League, had run long because of numerous fights on the field.

In a move that had forever changed how networks handle covering games to their conclusion, NBC shifted off the Raiders/Jets game and began the *Heidi* movie on schedule at the top of the hour.

What everyone missed seeing, except those fans in attendance at the Oakland/Alameda County Coliseum, was the Raiders amazing comeback. They scored a pair of touchdowns in the final minute of play to post a 43–32 win. When NBC ran a scroll at the bottom of the movie 20 minutes into their broadcast, they were besieged by angry phone callers demanding to know what had happened. How they could be so stupid to shift from the game in the final minute?

Two years later, in 1970, the Raiders had gone on a four-game winning streak sparked by the magic engineered by George Blanda. Behind all those wins was Al Davis' faith that the game wasn't over. Now, on this Sunday in Miami, he was once again the lone person standing in the Orange Bowl holding out hope that this one wasn't over.

"Just block the fucking extra point, and we still have a chance," Davis said again through clenched teeth.

If the NFL had the two-point conversion rule in 1973, then maybe Davis' plea would have had some basis for logic. But the NFL limited conversion attempts after touchdowns in 1973 to a single point, meaning whether the Dolphins converted this extra point or not, the Raiders would still have to score three times in the final two minutes to catch the defending champions.

Yepremian's kick was as routine as the perfect snap and sure hold that preceded it; and when the 27th point of the day was added to the Dolphins total, Davis slumped back in his chair, wrinkled another sheet of paper in his hand, and tossed it a couple of inches in the air in surrender.

He didn't say another word as the Raiders turned the ball over on their last desperate attempt to score, and the clock ticked to zero.

Then, as if inspired by the defeat, Davis' bottom jaw jutted forward. With an intense look that would have melted any opponent, he said, "Never again. We will never lose to this fucking team again. Never again."

— — — — — —

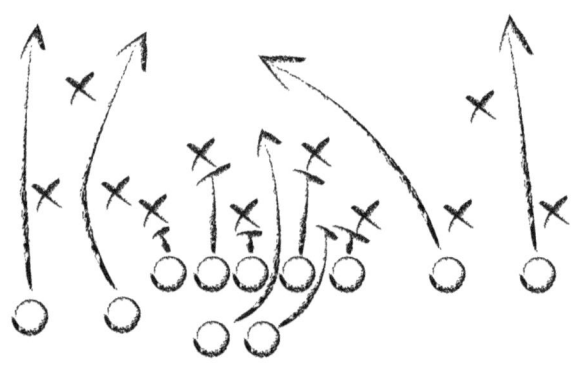

Chapter 16

Donuts

L<small>ESS THAN A MONTH</small> after the Miami Dolphins dominated the Minnesota Vikings in Super Bowl VIII, the NFL conducted their annual college draft.

"This is my Super Bowl," Ron Wolf said on the Friday before while thumbing through a set of reports on offensive linemen in a blue binder.

Ken LaRue was cleaning his pipe and watching me do work for Ron. "You might be in a position to make all the difference in this year's draft," he said to me. He turned solemnly to Ron. "Do you think he is up for donut detail?"

"That's a pretty hefty position," Ron responded slowly. "Can't mess it up, got to work. I don't know." He gave me a level stare. "He might be, but he'd have to get some real good direction."

They had my attention. I wasn't sure what "donut" stood for, but I was up to the challenge.

"I can do it. What is it?"

"Most important thing in setting up the day to work. Sets the tone for the whole draft," Ken said, puffing on his pipe.

"If you take it on, I'm counting on you," Ron put in.

"What is it?"

"Come with me," Ken said.

I marked where I had progressed in the work I was doing for Ron in player research, and then I was off to my next assignment.

"My office," LaRue directed when I reached the bottom of the stairs, and I went out in front. He closed the door behind him and went behind his desk. "I've got to have your full agreement that you will not fail on this responsibility," he said while emptying the contents of his pipe with three firm taps in an ashtray. He looked up at me significantly.

"You have to order, have to pay for, pick up, and deliver on time. One day, one opportunity to succeed," LaRue said while leaning forward on the elbows he rested on his desk.

"What is it?" I said, now more intrigued than ever.

"You've got to know that this task may seem trivial, but in fact it sets the day for everyone in this building. Mess up, and everyone will know. Do it right, and everyone will have a better day because you set it up to work," LaRue said in a way that would have prepared me to storm the beaches of Normandy.

"Let me show you something," LaRue advised. He led me out into the lobby. "This is where the table would probably be best set up."

LoCasale appeared in the lobby, and he seemed to know instantly what responsibility I was being offered.

"Can he handle it?" LoCasale said ominously to LaRue. "Got to be on time. Can he get up here all the way from San Jose?"

LaRue directed a question at me: "Can you be here by 5:00 a.m. on Tuesday?"

"Draft day?" I verified.

"Right," LaRue said.

"Sure; what do you need me to do?"

"Donuts," LaRue said while LoCasale added, "Nothing more important to set up the day to work."

For a moment, I was deflated. So, "donuts" really meant donuts, but then I took to heart the importance of how the task was presented to me. It was another opportunity to help out the team, even if it was as mundane as picking up donuts.

LaRue drove me to the donut shop on Park Avenue in Alameda to place the order, confirm what time they would be ready, and rethink how many dozen to order.

"I'd rather have a few go stale than Madden coming down to grab one and be out," LaRue said. "You know the press," he added. "That group lines up for free food like cows at feeding time."

"Five dozen?" I asked.

"Make it eight," LaRue suggested, "and make sure they are good donuts. A lot of jelly, maple and chocolate bars, and twists. Madden likes bear claws."

The morning of the draft, offensive line coach Ollie Spencer was the first to arrive. "Good job," he said, taking a bite of one. He put two more on a napkin that he balanced on top of the notebook he carried. He moved along the table I had arranged with the first two dozen donuts neatly aligned on trays atop a black tablecloth with white napkins and a large silver coffee carafe. As I saw three donuts disappear up the stairs with just the first person in the building, I was hoping eight dozen was enough.

Actually, I thought Spencer was the first to arrive, but when I went upstairs, I noticed Ron Wolf was already here. He must have arrived before I got to the office, just after 4:30.

"Can I get you anything?" I asked. He told me he'd be down in a moment to get himself some donuts and coffee. He stubbed out a cigarette in the ashtray. He patted the stack of material on his desk. "This is a year's work focused on today's and tomorrow's picks."

Later that morning, the draft started, and all the Oakland coaches and football staff huddled around a speakerphone in the conference room. Madden sat at the head of the table with Wolf on his left and Al Davis to his right. The rest of the Raider coaches manned the chairs around the table, and Grimes was standing in the open doorway behind Madden. On the other end of the speakerphone were the Raiders representatives stationed at the NFL Draft headquarters in New York. They were led by East Coast scout Roy Schleicher, who informed us that Pete Rozelle was headed to the podium to announce the Dallas Cowboys first pick.

Dallas had advanced to the National Football Conference Championship Game the year before, where they lost to the Vikings. Still, Dallas had the top pick in the draft by virtue of a trade with the Houston Oilers. We could hear Rozelle's announcement from New York over the speakerphone: "With the first pick in the 1974 NFL Draft, the Dallas Cowboys select Ed Jones, defensive lineman, Tennessee State. The San Diego Chargers are on the clock."

The Raiders staff had decided that the early rounds of our draft would be dedicated to offense, which had struggled most of the year, even with Stabler at quarterback. The loss of Raymond Chester in the trade with Baltimore that brought Bubba Smith to Oakland the previous July had robbed the Raiders of one of their most explosive weapons.

"Roger Carr if you want a receiver," Wolf said to Davis in response to who the best athlete on the board was. Position-by-position had been written on the chalkboard. Wolf spun his chair around to look at the board as Tom Flores erased Randy Gradishar's name off the top of the best athlete available list after the Denver Broncos made their first-round selection.

"If we go for an offensive lineman," Wolf said, "Henry Lawrence is the best. In fact, I'd say right now Lawrence is the best player still available."

"Receiver, running back or lineman?" Davis said to Madden. The head coach checked notes he'd made while studying films.

"Depends on what we can expect from Bob Brown," Madden said, referring to the talented but often injured veteran offensive lineman.

"Let's say he is out of the picture," Davis suggested.

"I say we go for the tight end out of Notre Dame," Madden declared.

Wolf didn't say anything, seeing by the way Davis was framing the conversation with Madden, he was leaning toward the player Wolf thought was best to take with our first pick . . . Henry Lawrence.

"The Bills might grab him," Wolf speculated with some apprehension. Buffalo was the final team before the Raiders made their first selection. "Yes!" Wolf celebrated, slapping his hand on the black table, when Rozelle announced the Bills pick: "With the 18th selection in the 1974 draft, the Buffalo Bills select Reuben Gant, tight end, Oklahoma State. The Oakland Raiders are on the clock."

The Raiders had 15 minutes to submit their first-round selection, and when the countdown began, Davis pushed his chair back from the table and walked out of the room to the projector he had set up in his office.

"Oh no," Wolf said softly.

"He's gonna find someone none of us have been thinking about," Special Teams Coach Joe Scannella speculated while the room sat silent.

"Is he that good?" Madden asked Wolf in reference to Lawrence, and Ron nodded in the affirmative.

"Nine minutes," Schleicher said into the phone while eyeing the clock in the draft room.

"Have you seen this kid out of Minnesota?" Davis said as he reentered the conference room.

"Matt Herkenhoff," Wolf stated while turning pages in his binder to review reports. "He can play," he added without looking up, "but he's no Henry Lawrence."

"What do you think?" Davis said to Madden.

"I can go with either of them."

"What are we missing here?" Davis said, seemingly not hearing Madden's response.

"Okay," Wolf said, "Benny Malone and Delvin Williams are two good running prospects still available. Roger Carr and Lynn Swann are the best two receivers on the board. If you want to look at tight end, with Gant now gone, I'd lean toward either Paul Seal from Michigan or, of course, Casper."

"We are missing something," Davis said.

"Danny White," Wolf responded. "If we are missing anyone, if you don't want Lawrence, and you want another first-rate quarterback prospect, Danny White from Arizona State is a possibility." Then he added, "But if we take him here, we are taking him too high . . . he could still be available when we pick in the second round."

Wolf's appraisal of other available talent was thorough but said in a tone that pleaded with Davis not to miss on Lawrence. Wolf then offered the factor Davis seemed most interested in, he said, "If we take Lawrence here, Casper could still be available in the second round. But if we take Casper here, Lawrence will not be on the board when we next pick."

"Two minutes," Schleicher announced over the speakerphone while all eyes in the Oakland draft headquarters focused on Davis.

"You think he is the guy, huh?" Davis confirmed.

"I think he is," Wolf said.

"Okay," Davis said, "let's make Henry Lawrence a Raider."

"Put it in," Wolf quickly relayed to Schleicher. Moments later, we could hear Rozelle's announcement: "With the 19th pick in the first round of the 1974 NFL Draft, the Oakland Raiders select . . ."

Madden went downstairs and grabbed a bear claw off the donut table. Then he addressed the media on what the Raiders saw in the team's first pick in the draft.

He would have an even greater level of excitement a few hours later when he announced the Raiders second-round selection. Four tight ends were listed as primary draft candidates on the Raiders board, and it was a priority to get one of them. Raymond Chester's replacement in the Raiders lineup, Bob Moore, was a solid blocker and high-character guy but had pedestrian speed and average hands.

Madden craved a playmaker in the tight end spot, and after Gant went to Buffalo in the first round, the New Orleans Saints took the tight end the Raiders had listed as the fourth best in the draft with a pick nine positions ahead of Oakland in the second round. His name was Paul Seal, leaving only Notre Dame's Dave Casper and Texas Tech's Andre Tillman from the Raiders list of top tight ends.

Wolf quickly reviewed the eight teams picking ahead of Oakland to gauge whether the Raiders might need to make a trade-up in order to ensure getting one of the two remaining tight ends the organization coveted.

"Not Baltimore, maybe Miami, not Detroit or Cleveland, maybe Kansas City, not Denver or San Diego or Atlanta," Wolf informed the Raiders draft room with his knowledge of what team needs were and what organizations might pick a tight end. After the Baltimore Colts took Ed Shuttlesworth with the first pick after Seal was taken by the Saints, Wolf said, "We could lose one of them right here, although I don't think they are taking Casper."

That was good news to Madden.

In his film studies, Casper was at the top of the coach's list. Wolf knew that his counterpart in Miami, Dolphins player personnel director Bobby Beathard, was higher on Texas Tech's Andre Tillman than he was on Casper. His information proved correct as Miami took Tillman with their second-round pick.

Detroit and Cleveland both went for linemen before the Chiefs were on the clock. Davis leaned over the speakerphone in front of him and asked Schleicher, "How close are you to the Chiefs table?"

"They are a couple away," Schleicher said. "Why?"

"Should we have made a fucking trade to get in front of them?" Davis said, looking straight at Wolf.

Wolf didn't look up from the binder he was paging through. He knew enough to allow Davis to vent.

"Did you want me to do something?" Schleicher's voice came over the speakerphone before he quickly added, "the Chiefs pick is in. It is about to be announced."

Don Weiss, Executive Director of the NFL, had taken over for Rozelle. Everyone in the Oakland conference room took a collective deep breath as Weiss said, "With the 41st pick in the 1974 draft, the

Kansas City Chiefs select Charlie Getty, tackle from Penn State. The Denver Broncos are now on the clock."

One more hurdle had been cleared in our attempt to get Casper. Now only three teams were left to pick ahead of us. Madden wished out loud that Casper would still be there for the Raiders. As he did, Davis looked at Wolf and said, "Who else should we be looking at? Let's be ready if Casper is gone."

"Benny Malone and Delvin Williams are the best two runners left," Wolf said while checking both the binder on the table in front of him and the names written on the chalkboard behind him. "If we go for a receiver, Gerald Tinker is the best still on the board."

"Do we still gain anything trading up?" Davis asked again.

"Broncos pick is in," Schleicher said, and our draft headquarters in Oakland went silent. Don Weiss announced Broncos had taken defensive end Carl Wafer from Tennessee State. Wolf's assistant, Ken Herock, muttered, "Mistake."

"Why?" Davis snapped at Herock.

"He looked better than he is because Ed Jones was getting all the double teams. They are going to be disappointed."

"I hope you're fucking right," Davis said. Above all, he was focused on beating opponents in the AFC West.

"What are we missing here?" Davis asked Wolf again in an attempt to assure himself we weren't.

"White could be special," Wolf said in regard to the Arizona State quarterback who was still undrafted. "I'd say he is the best offensive player still on the board, while I like Matt Blair, the linebacker from Iowa State, if we go for a defensive player."

"You promised offense this year," offensive line coach Ollie Spencer blurted out.

Davis pressed the mute button on the speakerphone, so Schleicher couldn't hear what we were saying in Oakland. "We will take the best fucking player . . . that's what we're fucking looking for here," Davis snapped at Spencer in a tone that stopped all talk in the room dead in its tracks.

Spencer cocked his head, suddenly on the wrong side of Davis' lightning. Then he pushed his chair back from the table while mumbling something inaudible.

"What the fuck was that?" Davis pursued in a voice louder than any used earlier in the morning.

Softly, Spencer said, "It just seems to me that if we spend three weeks going over a plan, and decide we are going to focus on offense, we shouldn't now be talking about maybe picking a defensive player." He made his statement as humbly as possible, but defiance still rang in his voice.

At this moment, he was all alone. No one was backing him up.

Davis ended the confrontation by defusing the situation. "We are here to fucking win, to not back ourselves into a corner without seeing all the fucking possibilities. No one said we were now looking for a defensive player over our commitment to bolster the offense," he added, shifting from condescending to constructive. "But if the next Dick Butkus is out there, I fucking want him. Do you understand that?"

It appeared Spencer was going to agree, but before he spoke, Schleicher announced over the speakerphone, "The Chargers pick is in."

San Diego chose Penn State center Mark Markovich with their second-round pick. Only the Atlanta Falcons were left to choose before Oakland.

A few minutes later, when the Falcons tabbed Gerald Tinker with the 44th pick in the draft, Weiss completed that announcement with the words, "The Oakland Raiders are now on the clock."

"What quarterbacks are still available that can help us for ten years?" Davis posed to Wolf.

"Did you get that? We're up," Schleicher said on the speakerphone.

"We got it," Davis said into the box in front of him.

"Are you there?" Schleicher said again.

For a moment, Davis looked confused. Noticing what was happening, I pointed out, "The mute button is pushed. He can't hear you."

"You're fucking right," Davis said with a chuckle. "How the fuck would that go over if we were making picks over a muted phone?" He pushed the button that reconnected us with Schleicher. "We're here," Davis assured him.

"We've got a shot here at the best quarterback in the draft," Davis said while looking at the position list on the board and noting that no QB had yet been chosen.

"Danny White is the best QB in this draft," Wolf said knowingly.

"I've got a quarterback," Madden reiterated. "What I need is a big target for him from the tight end slot."

"Seven minutes," Schleicher said.

Davis knew both Wolf and Madden were in agreement on what Oakland should do with their second-round pick, and while he had leaned on Wolf's expertise during the first round, with less than three minutes left to submit a pick, he looked to his head coach.

"What's your call?" Davis said to Madden.

"I want the big guy. Get me Casper," Madden said.

"The coach wants to see Mr. Casper in silver and black," Davis said, looking across the table to Wolf. "Can you live with that?"

"Absolutely," Wolf said, which completed the process. Davis motioned Madden to submit the pick to Schleicher.

"You want me to call it in?" Madden confirmed with Davis before proceeding.

"It's your guy," Davis said in his Southern gentleman dialect. "Tell Roy we're bringing Mr. Casper to the Raiders."

"Roy," Madden said, "send in Dave Casper, tight end, Notre Dame."

"It's in," Schleicher reported less than a minute later, and soon thereafter, we heard Weiss' announcement in New York.

"The Steelers are on the clock," he said in closing, but only moments later, Weiss was back at the podium to announce who Pittsburgh picked.

"They knew who they wanted," Madden said.

"Probably more defense," Wolf judged.

"With the 46th pick in the 1974 draft, the Pittsburgh Steelers take Jack Lambert, linebacker from Kent State. The Miami Dolphins are on the clock."

"Lambert is a wild man?" Linebacker Coach Don Shinnick said, directing his assessment to no one in particular. Wolf was paging through his reports in search of the best players available, and Davis reacted to Shinnick's comment.

"I don't give a fuck about Jack Lambert anymore," Davis said. "He's off the fucking board. Focus on something that makes a difference. Who are we going to get next?"

Before the Raiders made their first pick on Wednesday, the second day of the draft, Davis came bounding into the conference room beaming with approval. "Did you see his fuckin' legs?" he gushed, holding his hands far enough apart to allow a basketball to pass through. "Oh yeah," Davis continued, "he's a first-round choice."

Henry Lawrence had arrived early that morning and was sitting in Davis' office. "You got another good one," Davis said to offensive line coach Ollie Spencer.

Uncharacteristically giddy, Davis spun around on his tiptoes. Then he headed back down the hall to complete his conversation with Lawrence. I followed him out to deliver donuts to both his secretary, Rosemary, and Wolf's secretary, Beverly Swanson. On the way, I could see Henry Lawrence uncomfortably parked on the black couch in front of a glass chrome-rimmed table. Davis strolled back into his office and took a seat across from Lawrence. "What you've got here is an opportunity."

Lawrence nodded.

"Being a Raider is special," Davis said. "You'll line up with greats like Jim Otto, Gene Upshaw, Art Shell . . . just being with them can make you a better player."

I was watching the exchange from outside the corner office, mesmerized by Davis' challenge, when Rosemary said, "Don't let that drop."

I was holding a jelly donut at her desk and it was about to drip on her work area. I quickly handed Rosemary the donut and a napkin. But I would never forget Davis' art of negotiation. I would soon have an opportunity to apply that lesson with another offensive lineman.

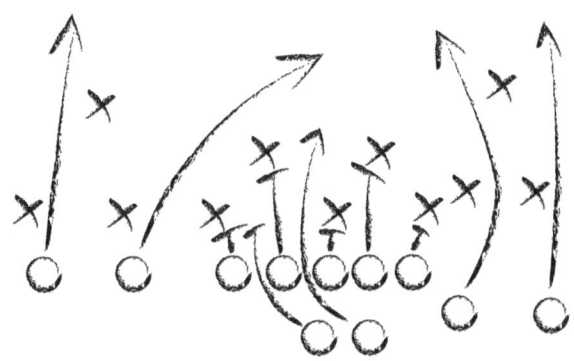

Chapter 17

Stabler to Birmingham

W HO HENRY LAWRENCE WOULD BE BLOCKING for came into serious question before he ever played his first down. Quarterback Ken Stabler had entrenched himself as the Raiders field general during the 1973 season, but before he arrived for training camp, he jolted the organization with a teletype message on April 2, 1974.

I was making Xerox copies when the TWX machine kicked into motion and printed out a pair of messages from Stabler and Henry Pitts, his agent in Alabama. The first TWX was addressed to Al Davis or Rosemary Butt and arrived at the Oakport Street offices at 8:29 a.m.

"MR DAVIS, TRIED TO CONTACT YOU THIS A.M. KENNY
WILL SIGN WITH BIRMINGHAM. NO NEED TO ASK YOU
TO MEET OFFER AS HE SIMPLY WANTS TO PLAY IN
ALABAMA. HE WANTS YOU TO KNOW IT HAS NOTHING
TO DO WITH YOU OR YOUR ORGANIZATION. BOTH OF
US HAVE THE UTMOST RESPECT FOR YOU. FURTHER
WANTS YOU TO UNDERSTAND HE WILL HONOR ALL
CONTRACT OBLIGATIONS WITH RAIDERS. HE WILL
REPORT TO CAMP WHEN INFORMED AS OF DATE. HE
WILL CALL YOU ON APRIL 3, 10PST. RESPECTFULLY
PHILIP HENRY PITTS"

I didn't touch the communication, not wanting to make a mistake
in tearing it out of the machine. Instead, I went to tell Al LoCasale,
since neither Tom Grimes nor Ken LaRue had yet arrived. As I left the
TWX machine, I heard it kick into gear again with another message
from Alabama.

"You've got to see this," I told LoCasale.

"What is it?" he said in a mood too buoyant for this early in the
morning.

"I think you better see it," I responded, not wanting to be the one
that announced our quarterback was jumping ship.

He peered at me more carefully. "Who died?" He hurried into the
hallway to retrieve the TWX messages. LoCasale was also silent as he
read the first, and I looked over his shoulder to see what the second
message had to say. It was addressed to John Madden.

"FELT OBLIGATION TO YOU AS MY COACH TO
INFORM YOU PERSONALLY I WILL SIGN TO PLAY IN

BIRMINGHAM IN 76. WANTED TO CONTACT YOU
EARLIER BUT CIRCUMSTANCES WOULD NOT PERMIT.
I APOLOGIZE FOR THIS. WANT YOU TO KNOW I HAVE
THE UTMOST RESPECT FOR YOU AS A COACH AND
THE ENTIRE RAIDER ORGANIZATION. IT IS NOT A
MATTER OF ASKING RAIDERS TO MEET MY OFFER. I
HAVE ALWAYS WANTED TO PLAY IN ALABAMA AND
NOW HAVE THIS OPPORTUNITY. I WILL HONOR MY
CONTRACT WITH RAIDERS FOR 74 AND 75. LOOK
FORWARD TO REPORTING TO CAMP AND WORKING
WITH YOU FOR THE NEXT TWO YEARS. RESPECTFULLY
KEN STABLER"

"He's not playing with us anymore," LoCasale said with disdain. "He can't be a Raider if he is already committed somewhere else."

Tom Grimes arrived while we were still hovering over the messages on the TWX. His contribution was a calming influence on the situation.

"No telling if the World Football League will be around in two years, let alone Kenny will play for them," he pointed out.

"I'll be the one to tell Al," LoCasale said while ripping the messages off the TWX and heading down the hall.

The World Football League was scheduled for its inaugural season in 1974, and they had adopted the Davis method of gaining credit-ability by signing high-profile players. In March, they signed contracts with three key players from the roster of the World Champion Miami Dolphins. Larry Csonka, Paul Warfield, and Jim Kiick were inked for a staggering $3.5 million to begin play with the Toronto Northman in 1975. That March announcement had given the new league instant significance with a number of players, and salary negotiations in the NFL had taken a new turn.

Csonka was now guaranteed $1.4 million for three years, a far cry from his first NFL contract with Dolphins in 1968, which paid him $75,000 for three years plus a $34,000 signing bonus and a new car.

In Oakland, the signing of the three Dolphins had given us a welcome relief. Miami would be greatly weakened without the trio of its primary offensive weapons. But now we were the ones taking the hit. The idea that Stabler had spent his entire professional career working to earn the starting quarterback job in Oakland and, now that he had it, was talking of leaving the organization struck me as ironic. LoCasale viewed it as desertion.

At least, that seemed to be his state of mind when he headed to his office to alert Davis of the news from Foley, Alabama. Davis must have had a different take on the situation because when he returned, and plopped into the chair between Grimes' and my desks, he announced: "We go on as if nothing has happened. We'll see how it plays out."

Henry Pitts, Stabler's attorney and agent, was a friendly Southern gentleman. He had a quick wit and engaging manner. A couple of weeks after negotiating the contract with Birmingham, Pitts was scheduled to meet for the first time with Davis face-to-face. He flew into San Francisco with Stabler and Kenny's wife, Debbie, on a Tuesday afternoon, a day before the meeting with Davis. I was sent to the terminal to pick them up.

"Denny," Pitts said while extending his hand in a welcoming shake. His upbeat mood was in stark contrast to the surly demeanor that both Kenny and his wife displayed. I did not have to be a talented detective to know that the two were in the midst of a serious disagreement.

"It's not a cold war," Pitts confided to me out of earshot of the Stablers. "Been on each other's case since Alabama."

Some girls are cute, some beautiful, and a few combine those two with a measure of hot. Debbie scored high on all three of those attributes. After collecting everyone's luggage, we walked to the car. Henry introduced me to her. When they first arrived, the battle between her and Kenny was too involved to interrupt, but now the tension seemed to be easing a bit and Debbie said good-naturedly, "I must have made a great first impression on you. Sorry, I just was in the middle of it with my man."

"I hope you were at the end of it," Kenny contributed.

"That could be arranged," Debbie snapped at him, which sent the Raiders quarterback into a silent, grim walk to the car.

Henry sat in the front with me, the Stablers in the back, for the ride from San Francisco to the Oakland Hilton. After checking in, Henry recommended we have drinks. I went ahead to get us a table in the almost empty bar, and Henry was the first to join me.

"Whew," he said with his thick Southern accent, "when those two go at it, they really dig in." We each ordered a drink when Stabler, without Debbie, joined us and ordered a Southern Comfort.

"She is just freshening up," Kenny said. "That lady can be tougher than facing Willie Lanier," he quipped while shaking his head. "But I love her. When we met, she knew nothing about football, didn't know who I was or what I did. I was attracted to the fact that here was a lady who liked me, and not because I was a professional football player."

The war of the Stablers seemed settled when Debbie joined our table.

"Let's drink to happiness," Pitts said while ordering Debbie a drink, "and what do you want to do for dinner? What's that restaurant you took me to last time we were here?" Henry asked his client.

"Which one?" Kenny said.

"The one right down the street. The Italian place."

"Vince's," Stabler said.

"Let's go there. You joining us, Denny?" Henry said to me.

"I'm having dinner with my girlfriend, Pam, tonight. I just got an apartment in Alameda, and she is over there now."

"Bring her along," Henry said grandly. "Let's make it a fivesome."

Vince's restaurant is located on Hegenberger Road between the Oakland Hilton and the Raiders offices on Oakport Street. It is Davis' favorite, and he has a space with a phone attached under the table that is always reserved for him.

Debbie and Pam took seats next to each other at the round table we were escorted to in the middle of the dining room. As Stabler was handed his menu, he spotted Davis in his corner booth.

"Oh geez," the quarterback said. The upbeat mood that we had brought into the restaurant was suddenly replaced by a quiet reserve because of Davis' presence. Oh no, I think, knowing Davis frowned upon fraternizing with the players, and here I am with his quarterback and agent shortly after Stabler had signed with a competing league.

Only Pam and Debbie seemed unaffected, as they were enjoying each other's company. Henry remarked, "Well, isn't this cozy."

We were working on our main course when Davis came over to our table on his way out of the restaurant.

"Everything good over here?" he asked no one in particular.

I stiffly nodded and began to rise when he put his hand on my shoulder and coaxed me back into my seat. "You all have a good evening. I look forward to meeting you tomorrow," Davis said, directing his comment to Pitts, not even looking at Stabler.

He marched off, leaving the three men at the table powerfully affected by his brief encounter.

"He is the only person I know," Stabler said, "that can change the taste of food from across the room."

— — — — — —

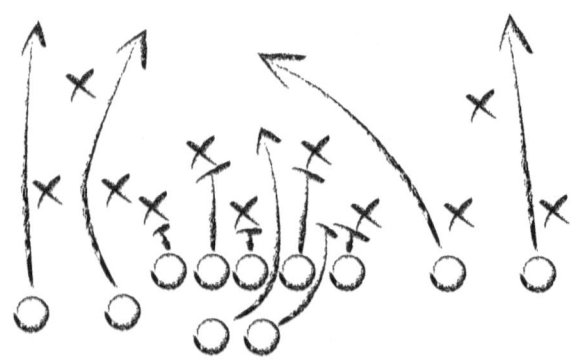

Chapter 18

Sightseeing

O<small>NE DAY THAT</small> <small>SPRING,</small> I was assigned to chauffeur three of the top draft choices from Santa Rosa to Oakland. Ken Bishop had left an hour before me, driving third-round draft selection Mark van Eeghen to his airplane connection in Oakland. In my car, Dave Casper was sitting in the front passenger seat, Morris Bradshaw, a wide receiver selected in the fourth round, was seated directly behind Casper, and I had to move my seat up as much as possible to allow maximum room for the man sitting behind me, top pick Henry Lawrence.

The final session at the Raiders four-day rookie camp had finished before 10:00 a.m., and most of the players had stopped by the cafeteria to make sandwiches or pick up fruit on their way out of Santa Rosa. Lawrence had picked up two bananas and two apples; they were bulging out of his leather jacket pockets.

Light Sunday morning traffic made our trip down 101 easy, and we quickly reached the junction that split toward the San Rafael Bridge to the left and Golden Gate Bridge straight ahead.

"We've got time before your Oakland departures if you'd like to see San Francisco," I offered to my passengers. All three flights were scheduled close to 4:00 p.m. "You guys want a little tour of San Francisco?" I asked again when no one answered the first time.

"Let's do it," Casper said, motioning to the right as we approached the freeway split.

"Can we see the bridge?" Henry Lawrence piped up.

"We might be able to do that."

While a sense of direction has never been a personal strength of mine, I learned about the streets of San Francisco during my three years serving as a janitor with multiple work locations in the city. Lawrence's request to see the Golden Gate Bridge was easy, though, because staying on 101 led us right onto the historic span.

On this day, the Chamber of Commerce might have done well shooting pictures of the span along with the glistening San Francisco skyline beyond. I could see in my rearview mirror Lawrence's eyes open wide in appreciation. I said, "Pretty cool, huh?"

"Amazing," Bradshaw said while Lawrence continued his wide-eyed gaze.

Once in the city, I took a route that included Fisherman's Wharf, the recently completed Transamerica Pyramid, Chinatown, Nob Hill with the Fairmont and Mark Hopkins hotels, and a look at cable cars climbing San Francisco hills. I turned off California Street onto Van Ness Avenue before driving the three new Raiders down Broadway and onto the ramp that put us back on 101 and past Candlestick Park on our way to San Francisco International.

"That's where the 49ers play," Lawrence said as much a question as a statement.

"Moved there three years ago," I said. "Played at Kezar Stadium prior to that. If we had gone straight off the bridge, I could have shown you Golden Gate Park and Kezar," I said while thinking that may have been a better route to have taken on my tour of the city.

I pulled up in front of the curbside entrance to the United Airlines departure gates in San Francisco to drop off Bradshaw before proceeding to Oakland for the first- and second-round draft pick flights. "Thanks for everything," Bradshaw said, extending his hand. "See you in a few weeks when camp opens," he continued as I made sure he had his ticket.

"Perfect," he said, slapping Casper's hand and telling Lawrence he looked forward to working with him.

"What a good guy," I said once the three of us were on our way to their gates across the Bay.

"Hope he makes it," Lawrence said in regards to Bradshaw's chances of joining the Raiders, who already had outstanding receivers.

"No hope to it," Casper said. "If he runs and catches, he makes it; same for us. If I run, catch and block, I make it. If I don't, I don't. Same for you, Henry," Casper continued. "Being picked one or two won't mean anything if we don't take advantage of the opportunity."

Casper's intensity changed the sunshiny mood. Neither of the rookies said another word before we arrived at the Oakland Airport, and after I unloaded their bags from the trunk, both shook my hand and thanked me for, as Casper said, "the extraordinary private tour."

Al Davis was not in the office on Monday, but early Tuesday afternoon, I was summoned to come upstairs by Beverly Swanson, who had recently become his secretary.

"What did you do?" Grimes said softly after hearing the request to visit Davis.

"Nothing that I can think of," I said. "Maybe he's just got something for me to do."

I quickly made my way up the stairs to Davis' office.

"Close the door," Davis said in a tone that indicated something different than good wishes.

"Yes, sir," I said instinctively.

He began talking to me before I had turned from latching the knob. "Did you take our fucking players on a sightseeing tour?"

I was shocked for several reasons. How did he find out? What did it matter? What was the problem here?

"On Sunday, Casper, Lawrence, and Bradshaw," I said, thinking I had nothing to hide.

"And where the fuck did you guide this little impromptu tour of yours?"

"Sir?"

"Where the fuck did you take the Oakland Raiders on Sunday!" he thundered.

"Sir?" I said again, still not grasping the reason for his anger.

"Did you show them Oakland?"

Suddenly I realized what the problem was. "No, sir," I said softly.

"What the fuck did you show them?" he demanded.

"The Golden Gate Bridge, Fisherman's Wharf, Nob Hill."

"Is the Golden Gate Bridge in Oakland?" he asked.

"No, sir."

"Is Fisherman's Wharf in Oakland?"

"No, sir."

"Is Nob Hill in Oakland?" he barked.

"No, sir," I said, wishing I'd never had my brilliant spur-of-the-moment idea.

"Listen," Davis said sternly, "you work for the Oakland Raiders. If you take Oakland Raiders for a tour of anything, you show them the sites in our city. Do you understand?"

I nodded my head.

"You fucking show them Lake Merritt or the Oakland Tribune Tower, features in Oakland, if you want to conduct sightseeing tours again," Davis said before adding, "do you understand?"

"Yes, sir," I snapped.

"Get the fuck out of here," Davis said, turning away.

Beverly didn't look up while I sheepishly inched by her desk and slunk back down the stairs to my lowly station across from Grimes.

- - - - - -

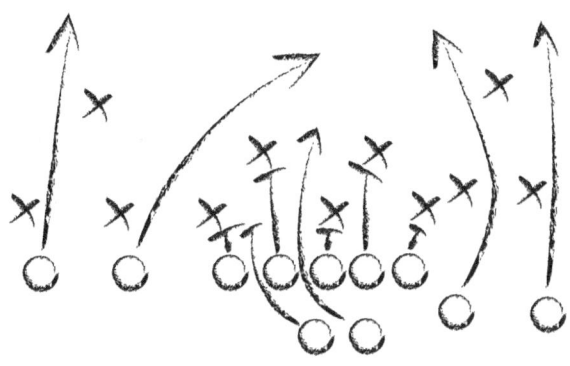

Chapter 19

Chicago

"I'm in Chicago," I told Dad by phone from a hotel room.

"Where are you staying?" he asked. "Are you going to have time to see any sights in the city?"

My father had grown up in Chicago; his dad was a night watchman at the University of Notre Dame and later a bartender for one of Al Capone's establishments during Prohibition. Dad had taken me for a tour of Chicago in 1968 on a family vacation, showing me the lion sculptures he had climbed on as a kid and the street where John Dillinger had been shot, not far from where Dad had sold papers.

After telling him the hotel I was staying in, which was right next to the facility used by the College All-Star team, I added that I didn't think I would have any time to see the city. Before he had time to ask me another question, I said, "I was in the elevator with Ed Garvey."

"The head of the union?" Dad said about the executive director of the NFL Players Association. "Did you say anything to him?"

I hadn't, but I had met Jim Finks, who had been named NFL Executive of the Year for his work with the Minnesota Vikings but had recently left the team and was now representing the NFL Management Council. He was heading up the NFL talks in Chicago opposite Garvey. I was scheduled to meet with Finks in a meeting at 7:00 p.m. with a number of representatives from other teams.

Al Davis had sent me to Chicago to monitor the trio of Raiders draft picks that had been selected to play in the 41st Annual All-Star Football Game sponsored by the *Chicago Tribune*. Two of the athletes had taken my little San Francisco tour a few Sundays earlier: Henry Lawrence and Dave Casper.

Prior to the meeting with Finks, I put on the new pair of white pants and black patent leather shoes I had purchased for the trip. I felt somewhat out of place when Stan West, a scout for the St. Louis Cardinals, strolled in wearing jeans and cowboy boots. He gave me the once-over. "What did you think this is, kid, a goddamn fashion show?"

Despite my attire, by the next night, I had collected enough information from the players to gain insight into the way they were leaning in their private negotiations with Garvey. The first attempt by NFL players to form a union had occurred in 1956, headed by five NFL players: Don Shula of the Baltimore Colts, John Gordy of the Detroit Lions, Norm Van Brocklin of the Los Angeles Rams, and a pair of New York Giants, Frank Gifford and Sam Huff. Their initial demands of the owners called for minimum league salaries, per diem pay, and costs to maintain equipment and pay while players were sidelined with injuries. Those requests did not grab the attention of NFL owners until the following year when Creighton Miller, a former Notre

Dame football player and current attorney, threatened an antitrust suit. That action gained momentum when the United States Supreme Court ruled in 1957 in *Radovich v. National Football League* that the NFL did not enjoy the same antitrust immunity afforded to Major League Baseball.

The owners wanted to avoid further legal battles and agreed to most of the demands made by the players before the 1958 season. From that meek beginning, the players' organization had gained little strength until Ed Garvey became executive director in 1971, implementing negotiating methods that rivaled those Al Davis had used in his short term as commissioner of the American Football League. Garvey had threatened the league with a strike, a tactic that had failed in previous attempts by player representatives in 1968 and 1970 but had more momentum in 1974.

The first action Garvey decided to implement was to interrupt the College All-Star Game. He had gained an audience with the All-Star team, which was gathered in Chicago to begin practice under Southern California head coach John McKay on Monday. I didn't say a word at the Saturday night meeting Jim Finks held for team representatives to discuss strategy, overawed by the more experienced team representatives.

Yet on Sunday, I did all the legwork, following the advice I had gotten from my Saturday night call with Davis. "Listen," he said, "you just make fucking sure the players are thinking about football instead of labor negotiations. Let them know the Raiders are going to be playing football, and it would be nice to have them along. Keep in contact with all of them, hear everything there is to hear . . . I'll talk to you tomorrow."

On Sunday, I felt like a spy, spending most of my time in the players' hotel lobby and coffee shop. Henry Lawrence had little to say after the

Sunday night meeting with Garvey, but Dave Casper clearly articulated the position Garvey had outlined for the incoming rookies.

"We're in a tough spot here," Casper told me, cognizant that I was on management's side but with an open ear to what had transpired in the union's meeting. "The Dolphins are not going to play if the league is having a strike, which means our first game after being drafted by the NFL would be against a second-tier team that may or may not be NFL players."

"The Dolphins aren't going to strike," I quickly replied.

Casper looked at me like I didn't know a thing. "We've got nothing to gain," he said, "by playing without assurance the Dolphins are going to be the opponent."

His argument resonated with sound logic, and I headed back to my hotel in search of Finks to let him know what I had gained about the players' meeting with Garvey. He was in a restaurant, sitting with four other team representatives, and I knelt on one knee before asking him if he would like the information I had just gotten on the results of Garvey's meeting.

He put out his cigarette and asked me what I had learned.

"Garvey told the players that if they played in the All-Star game, they would be viewed as scabs by the NFL veterans because the Dolphins have already agreed not to play."

He said to the other four people at the table, "That is his best tactic, getting the rookies afraid that they will be blackballed by their teammates if they agree to play."

"It really puts the players here in a tough spot. I don't see how they can stand up against the threat of alienating their future teammates," I said.

Finks reached out and gave me two pats on my cheek. "You're such a bright kid. How does Davis find you guys?"

Buoyed by the compliment from a man I had admired for years, I caught the eyes of West, who was sitting at Finks' table. More than a fashion show, I thought as I headed for my room to make my nightly call to Davis.

I related the information, thinking he might be pleased that I saw the strength in the case Garvey was making to the players. "Listen," Davis said, "your fucking job is not to only locate their fucking strengths. I sent you there to make fucking sure our guys get their minds on football. Fuck Garvey. You need to have them excited about playing, not fucking walking."

The next morning, the players were locked in a long Monday session with Ed Garvey and Jim Finks. Then they held a closed session among themselves while the media gathered outside the lobby-level conference room. Their hours of speculation among themselves, milling around the lobby and eating donuts came to a halt as the door opened and the players filed out of the meeting. One player moved to the front of the group and was surrounded by microphones held by reporters kneeling in front of him with outstretched arms. The area outside the conference room was suddenly brightly illuminated by television camera lights.

"No, no, no," I said under my breath. The player drawing all the attention was none other than Dave Casper. He had been chosen as the spokesperson for the All-Star players.

Before speaking, he paused for a moment, seemingly collecting his thoughts and straightening the paper he held in his hands.

"We are issuing one statement," Casper said while scanning the assembled crowd. "We, the All-Stars, in light of a difficult situation, will honor the picket lines. We have signed an agreement to that effect."

Casper looked up in response to a few reporters already shouting follow-up questions. He quieted them with a glare and returned to his prepared statement. "We feel that an All-Star game with practices under pressure from the NFLPA and management, and a game against a team of seconds, is not in the best interest of ourselves as players in the NFL and not in the interest of fans and football in general."

After refusing to answer questions from the media, he left. I headed for my room to face what I was sure to be consequences from Davis.

I could hear the phone in my room ringing as I searched for the large room key, shoved in the right front pocket of my white pants. I was relieved to pick up the phone before it stopped ringing.

"I got him," Beverly Swanson said in response to my breathless, "Hello?"

"Dennis," Davis said in his most businesslike voice, "seems like you need some help in Chicago."

The wrath I anticipated was entirely absent. Instead, he understood that the circumstances dictated the results by the All-Star players, and the fact that a Raider was their spokesperson wasn't all bad.

"I'm sending Kenny in to handle this situation," Davis said.

"LaRue?" I questioned.

"No," Davis said flatly, "Mr. Herock. You pick him up at the airport. Beverly will give you his flight information."

When I hung up the phone, I experienced a feeling of defeat. My efforts not only didn't get done what Davis wanted, but my failure also didn't even warrant his anger. I stood in the room, looking at myself in the mirror, and noticed the white pants I had worn for three days now had dirt stains leading into both front pockets. I leaned forward and took a closer look at the tears welling up in my eyes. "Fuck," I said softly to myself. "You are a piece of shit. Loser."

The first thing Herock noticed when I met his flight at the United Airlines gate at O'Hare International was the dirt leading into my pockets. "What the fuck are you wearing?" he said, laughing at my appearance.

"I only have—" I began to explain, but he launched straight into the matter at hand.

"Have you talked to Casper since he became the spokesperson?"

I hadn't, and he remarked, "You must have been real pleased to see him step in front of the cameras."

The light comment began to reduce my stress level. He put his arm around me while we headed for my rent-a-car. "It isn't your fault. This is a mess with Garvey and the players' union; you just were in the path."

Reassured, I proceeded to explain all that I had witnessed with the negotiations while I was in Chicago.

When I got back to my room, the message light was blinking, and the hotel operator informed me I had a message from Al Davis and that I should call him at his home number.

"Dennis," he said after I dialed his home on Mountain Avenue, "I have another assignment for you."

It was music to my ears. I wanted to do right by Mr. Davis, and I welcomed a new assignment so quickly.

"I want you to go to the World Football League opener at Soldier Field and scout the teams. Give me a report on Thursday when you get back," Davis ordered.

The World Football League was attempting to duplicate the success the American Football League had accomplished more than a decade earlier. This time around, though, Davis was on the other side, protecting the success of the established NFL.

I followed up that call with a request of Ron Wolf to guide me in my scouting.

I reached him in his Oakland office on Tuesday morning, and Wolf asked, "What does he want?"

"He wants me to 'scout' the teams," I said with little more detail to add.

"I don't know," Wolf said at first. "He probably wants to know what formations they are running. Maybe he wants some designs so if he sees someone excelling in a system that might help us, he could skim a few players off the top of their talent pool," Wolf surmised.

"I think Doug is going to the game too," Wolf said, referring to his friend Doug Hafner, who had worked on his staff in Oakland for several years beginning in 1966 and was now assistant director of player personnel for the Cincinnati Bengals. "Let me give him a call and see if he can meet you at the game and help you create some stuff Davis would probably appreciate."

I met Hafner in the press box before the game, and while shaking his hand, he said, "Do you want to sit up here? I don't like it. I prefer the stands when there is enough room."

I liked the press box but quickly acceded to Hafner's wish and followed him into the press box elevator and to a location in the north end zone at Soldier Field. Hafner was interested in seeing how a player he had drafted and developed in Cincinnati, Virgil Carter, would fare in the new league. Carter was the starting quarterback for the Chicago Fire, and in their inaugural game of the new football league, he was leading his squad against the Houston Texans.

Carter threw more interceptions than touchdowns, 3 to 2, but his two scoring tosses and a Chicago field goal were enough to dominate the Texans. Houston was held scoreless with a totally ineffective offense that was a combination of incomplete passes, sweeps that were still looking for a hole when the runner was run out of bounds, and an inside running game that went nowhere.

"I think what Davis wants is formations and stuff," I said to Hafner in an attempt to get insights that I could not generate on my own.

He quickly obliged. "Tell him this and show him these," Hafner said while scribbling formations and patterns on a jot tablet and explaining what defensive and offensive alignments each team was running.

If I didn't understand something, I asked him to explain it again. While I knew I was still short of a full grasp of what he was offering, I thanked him for his work and sat there studying his pages of formations and alignments.

The next afternoon, I appeared in Davis' office more prepared with football information than I had ever been after a night of cramming for a college exam. Before Davis even made the request, I was showing the formations Hafner had written out for me and explaining what patterns the Fire and Texans were running.

"No, Dennis," Davis said with a laugh, "I don't care about any of that. I just want to know if you found the game entertaining. Was it exciting?"

"What?" I said, looking for clarification.

"Was the fucking game exciting?" Davis asked again, showing no interest in my detailed scouting report.

"Oh, no," I said. "They got Jim Nance trying to run sweeps, and he couldn't get out of his own backfield."

"That's all I care about," Davis said. "You'd say the action was a dog?"

"A dead one," I contributed with a smile.

"Dennis," Davis said, studying me, "what business do you think we're in?"

"To win."

Davis laughed. "No, young man, that's what we're here to do. I'm asking you what business we're in."

"Football?" I replied.

"Entertainment," Davis said emphatically. "If we just played the game, like you said they did in Chicago, it doesn't mean anything. People don't pay for tickets, buy souvenirs, or talk about the game with their friends because we run, block, and throw. They do it because we entertain them. Do you understand that, Dennis?"

I nodded slowly.

"We fucking entertain with the Raiders," Davis said, adding triumphantly, "and you're telling me that new league isn't getting that done."

"I know that's true," I said confidently.

"Good," Davis responded, rising from his chair. "I guess your trip to Chicago wasn't a total waste."

— — — — — —

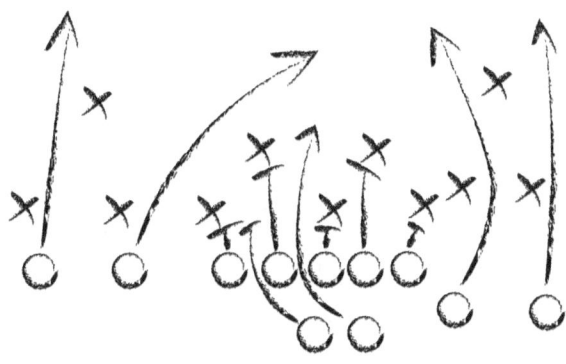

Chapter 20

Car Phone

THE ONLY CAR PHONES I HAD EVER SEEN were in the movies or on television in *Burke's Law* and *Banachek*. Still, I knew how much time Mr. Davis spent with me driving, so I suggested he get one in his black Cadillac.

I proposed the idea while driving him from the airport to his home. When I mentioned that the only people I had seen with car phones were James Bond and Banachek, his head jerked up from the papers he was holding on his lap. "They have those?"

"I checked on it this morning," I said, responding to his enthusiasm. "There is a company in Oakland that installs car phones in just a few hours. Do you want me to make an appointment?"

Two days later, I drove the car to his house after the phone was installed. I showed him how to use it, which required contacting the mobile operator first, giving the mobile phone number, which for Davis was JR60476 Oakland, and have that operator connect him with a desired number. It was an expensive service, but he immediately sat down in his car, right in front of his house, to test his new phone.

"He looks like a kid on Christmas morning playing with a new toy," Carole Davis said, observing from the front door. "Do you want something cold to drink?" she asked me while heading for the kitchen. I requested a Coke, but she returned with a glass of Tab on ice while saying, "Is this OK?"

I hated Tab but gladly accepted it from Mrs. Davis with a thank-you. She was one of my favorite people in the world. She was always nice and thoughtful, with a willingness to engage in conversation with constant good cheer.

Most of our conversations took place while I was waiting for Mr. Davis at their Piedmont home. I had never had such a long one with her as on this day, and I had turned down a second Tab when she said, "Do you think he is going to do all his phone calling from out front now?"

Mrs. Davis had walked back to the front door to watch him. "How long has he been at it? Is he calling everyone he knows to tell them he's on his car phone?" She smiled at me. "I think you gave him his gift of the year. I'm so glad he has you, Dennis; you're a gem."

At long last, the door opened and Davis entered in high spirits. "'Where do you think I'm calling you from?' I asked everyone I called, and none of them guessed my goddamn car. Bob didn't believe it . . . bet you he is next to get one." Then Davis turned his attention to me. "He might be calling you. He wants to know who you had install this one."

"Dr. Albo?" I asked to assure I knew what "Bob" he was referring to.

Davis nodded while adding, "I'm going to be able to get a lot of work done with a phone in the car. What will they think of next?"

"Whatever it is," Mrs. Davis said in a friendly tone, "I bet you'll get it."

— — — — — —

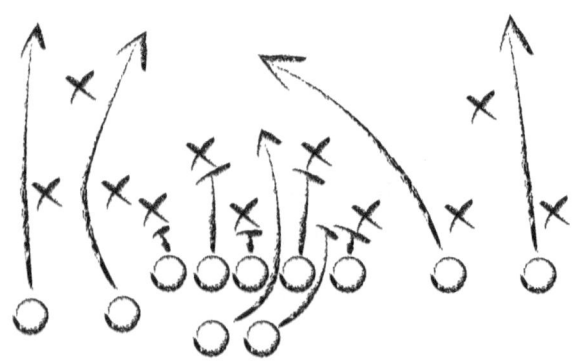

Chapter 21

Trash Talk

I HAD JUST DROPPED DAVIS OFF at the Oakland Airport and was headed back to training camp in Santa Rosa when his car phone rang.

"Are you still at the airport?" Ron Wolf asked.

"Close," I said. "I'm on 17, headed back to camp."

"I need you to go back. Ron Sellers is arriving, and I need you to bring him up here."

"On my way," I said, immediately moving to the slow lane and preparing to take the Broadway exit in Oakland.

When I pulled up to the curb in front of the commuter helicopter service, I was met by George, the parking enforcement officer.

"All right if I leave Davis' car here?"

"Sure, I'll keep an eye on it," George said. "Who you picking up this time?"

"Ron Sellers, a receiver we just brought in for a look at camp."

I noticed that Gary was unimpressed. He was probably hoping for someone more prominent like Ken Stabler or Jim Otto.

After putting Sellers' bag in the trunk of Davis' black Cadillac, I pulled myself into the driver's seat and struck up a conversation with Sellers. "You know, you broke my heart a couple of years ago when you beat the 49ers with that catch in the playoff game."

"You were with the 49ers then?" Sellers asked.

"I was a fan," I stated. "It was the year before I joined the Raiders."

"You know who really lost that game for the 49ers?" Sellers asked as if he knew the answer.

"Yeah," I said, "Preston Riley," in reference to the 49er that was vilified by his loss of a late onside kick.

"Nope," Sellers said, "Dave Wilcox."

That didn't make sense to me. Wilcox had been a stud linebacker for the 49ers the last ten years, and I hadn't seen him make any mistakes on the field.

"We might have quit that day. The 49ers were handing us our butt," Sellers recalled. "But that fucking Wilcox just couldn't let it go. For most of the second half, beginning late in the third quarter, he would run by our bench every opportunity he got to rub it in," he said, getting more animated.

"'How's it feel to lose, you fuckheads?' he'd yell while pointing at our sidelines. 'Eat shit, you motherfuckers,' he said another time. Even if we wanted to quit, we couldn't allow that asshole to rub it in like that without a fight. He kept us in the game with that crap," Sellers said.

"Don't tug on Superman's cape," I said.

"Exactly," Sellers said. "He was stupid."

－ － － － － －

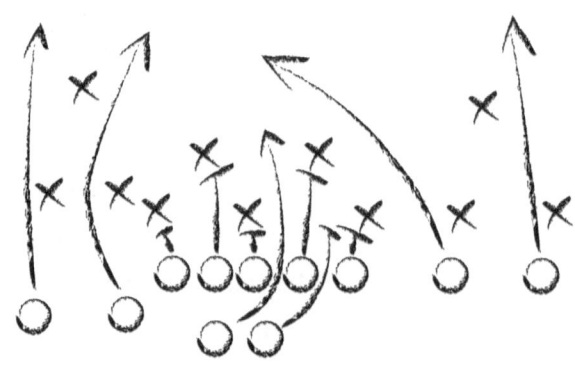

Chapter 22

At Your Service

At the height of his popularity, Don Meredith decided to end his career on *Monday Night Football* voluntarily after the 1973 season. Who would replace him caused quite a controversy, and some suggested Cosell would be better working only with Frank Gifford.

Fred Williamson, a one-time Oakland Raider who played defensive back for the Kansas City Chiefs in Super Bowl I, was the first hire, but he got terrible reviews during his preseason work in 1974.

The importance of *Monday Night Football* to ABC and the NFL made executives unwilling to gamble that Williamson could turn around his low ratings. Just prior to the start of the regular season, *Monday Night Football* creator Roone Arledge brought in Alex Karras. He was scheduled to make his debut in the Monday night booth when the Buffalo Bills hosted the Raiders to open the 1974 prime-time schedule.

It was a controversial hire. Karras, a former Detroit Lions defensive lineman, had been banned from playing in 1963, along with Green Bay Packers running back Paul Hornung, by NFL Commissioner Pete Rozelle for gambling on NFL games. ABC was not deterred. Instead they were drawn to his dry sense of humor, demonstrated shortly after his return from his one-year suspension. A referee asked Karras to call heads or tails while preparing to flip a coin to determine who would get the ball first.

"I'm sorry, sir," Karras responded, "I'm not permitted to gamble."

The day before Karras made his *Monday Night Football* debut, I was invited to a hotel suite in New York with Cosell, his wife Emmy, and Mr. and Mrs. Davis. He had me serve drinks and police the room while the four of them spent the day together.

"There are men far more qualified, that have paid their dues, that deserve those spots, and here the job is given to a jock with no command over the talents necessary to carry a broadcast, but hired simply on the fact that he once played the game," Cosell said while taking a fresh drink from my hand. Davis was standing in front of a 36-inch color television tuned to the New England Patriots home opener against the Super Bowl champion Miami Dolphins. John Brodie, one of the quarterbacks Davis had signed to an AFL contract eight years earlier, had ended his playing career the previous season and was now serving as color analyst for the NBC telecast.

"The supposition that simply on the basis of playing the game, one can now serve as a broadcaster is akin to assuming that after an operation, the patient is now suddenly capable of performing surgery," Cosell continued.

Davis interrupted with a mocking laugh. "You benefit from athletes in your Monday night booth."

Before Davis could finish his thought, Cosell jumped back into the conversation. "The Gif is an icon and worked his way up, and Dandy, well, I knew Don was something special in our very first telecast when Bob Matheson made a tackle for the Browns and Meredith said, 'That is our old friend Paul Crane making another key stop for the Browns.'"

Davis cackled out a laugh while Cosell clued in the two ladies, who failed to see why Meredith's statement was so funny: "Bob Matheson and Paul Crane both wore number 56. Dandy had simply looked at the wrong roster in identifying the tackler and then added to the error by calling the misidentified player an 'old friend.'" Davis laughed again. Cosell had gotten another dose of Meredith's natural humor when he corrected him off-camera, and Meredith simply shrugged off the mistake with the words, "I like him too."

"We are going to miss his persiflage in the press box for sure," Cosell said, grabbing a handful of nuts off the bar.

"Freddie didn't work out?" Davis asked in regards to Fred Williamson.

"Alex seems a good fit," Cosell responded in a matter-of-fact voice. "He, too, has a great wit and should leave me plenty of room to express my sagacious observations."

The New England Patriots upset the two-time defending Super Bowl champion Dolphins. Davis watched the kickoff of one of the day's later games, the Denver Broncos hosting the Cincinnati Bengals. Finally, he said, "We better get ready to get out to the stadium."

The Raiders were having an evening practice at Orchard Park, and Davis asked Cosell if he would be joining him for his limo ride to the stadium.

Once Cosell announced he would, Davis turned his attention to the wives in the room. "Will you young ladies be all right while your husbands go out and earn a living?"

At the stadium, Madden was directing the Raiders light workout and game walk-through. The practice was almost over when Cosell began a rant. "Leave him," Cosell advised at a volume as loud as a megaphone would produce. "He is only holding you back, Coach Madden. The great Al Davis will always cast a shadow that will only stifle your true potential."

Madden smiled sheepishly as Cosell attracted an audience. Standing right next to Cosell, Davis appeared amused at the exchange.

"Only when you free yourself from his dominating presence will you be able to rise to your full potential and gain the recognition you so richly deserve. Go now, Mr. John Madden, to show the world the person you can be on your own! You don't need Al Davis as much as he needs you." They began following the team off the field and into the tunnel toward the visiting locker room. Cosell's diatribe generated appreciation and laughter from his growing number of listeners when he said, "Go now, Coach, while you still have youth on your side, and free yourself of Mr. Davis' rather untenable grip."

"I think you're right, Howard," Davis said, seemingly not offended. "John is perfectly capable of being great anywhere. But," Davis said, "why would he want to give up the best job in the world, head coach of the Oakland Raiders?"

Cosell smiled broadly, then went back on the attack. "Mr. Davis is once again attempting to blur your vision from the world of possibilities that await a man with your immense talent. He would have you think your success is only available here while working for his beloved Raiders. But, Mr. Madden, your time of destiny is right before you. Call it quits now, leave this man, and announce it tomorrow night just before kickoff on our *Monday Night Football* telecast."

"So that's it, Howard," Davis said, realizing what Cosell really wanted. "You are fishing for stories, manufacturing them in fact, to pump up your telecast ratings now that you have lost the man that carried your show. The irreplaceable Don Meredith."

"Ratings are not a problem when we have the fiery redheaded coach of the Raiders on one side and the splendid skills of the Juice on the other," Cosell said. "I'm here for you, Coach, to free you from the harness that is truly preventing you from getting the credit you truly deserve."

The next night, Alex Karras made his debut in the ABC booth, located just to my right in the press box at Orchard Park. The game between the home underdog Buffalo Bills and Raiders was mostly controlled by the defenses into the fourth quarter. With Oakland nursing a 13–7 lead midway through the fourth quarter, Marv Hubbard fumbled and set the Bills offense up at the Raiders 33-yard line.

Joe Ferguson, the Bills quarterback, completed only 10 of 20 passes in the *Monday Night Football* opener, but one of them was caught for a touchdown by Ahmad Rashad on the first play after the two-minute warning. The ensuing extra-point kick by John Leypoldt gave the Bills a 14–13 lead with only 1:51 left on the game clock.

Rooting for a team with boisterous outbursts is forbidden in the press box by NFL policy, but when Stabler missed on pass attempts first to Cliff Branch, then Fred Biletnikoff, and another to Branch, the Bills media corps was outwardly rooting for their home team. With only a minute and a half left in the game, and trailing by six points, Madden opted to punt on fourth down and Ray Guy booted it 41 yards to Donnie Walker, who brought it back 7 yards to the Bills 31-yard line.

O.J. Simpson was limited to 78 yards on 12 carries, while his blocking back, James Braxton, carried the ball 19 times. His last carry was on first down after the Guy punt, and the ball was jarred loose and picked up by Oakland defensive tackle Art Thoms, who broke out of the scrum and toward the Raiders end zone.

I found myself matching the unprofessionalism of the Buffalo media by jumping out of my chair and exploding with one loud word, "YEAH!" Then, even before sitting down, I said under my breath, "Lay down at the one."

I thought that with just over a minute remaining on the game clock and the Raiders trailing by a point, if Thoms lay down at the one-yard line, we could either use the rest of the time before Blanda kicked the winning field goal or force Buffalo to exhaust all their time-outs while we worked the ball from the one while waiting to push it across the goal line.

As Thoms crossed the goal line, I looked at the clock, which showed 1:08 left in the game.

It was enough time for Ferguson to run off eight plays without ever requiring a third-down call. Rashad caught his second TD of the night, and Leypoldt's extra point gave the advantage back to Buffalo, 21–20.

Still, this is the Raiders. It's not over till it's over.

A short kickoff to Pete Banaszak was returned to the 41-yard line, and two Stabler pass plays later, the Raiders had moved the ball to the Bills 33 when they called their final time-out with six seconds left on the clock. In any other year, this would have been a 40-yard field goal for Blanda, but for the first time in NFL history, the goal posts had been moved from the front of the end zone to the back. That made a Blanda kick for the win 50 yards—which came up short as time on the clock expired.

The bus ride from the stadium to the airport was entirely silent. Yet after we found our seats on the United Charter flight for our trip back to Oakland, I mentioned to Madden my thought that Thoms could have stopped short and not given the Bills an opportunity to come back. I tried to word it in a way that was not accusatory but more in a partnership on how to win the game.

Madden didn't see it that way.

His disgust at my suggestion was obvious on his face, and he dismissed it with a growl. "You can't tell a player not to score."

"But if he had, we could have won," I said.

"No one can think that in the heat of the game," Madden said.

"I did," I said and quickly wished I hadn't.

"It's pretty fucking easy from an air-conditioned press box," he snapped.

Before he uttered another word, the plane began its takeoff down the runway. His fear of flying took precedence over every other possible feeling. I was spared by aviophobia.

— — — — — —

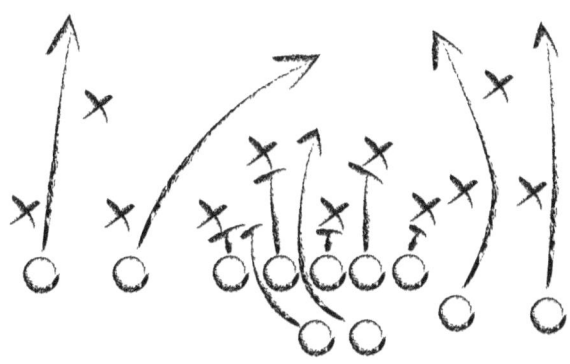

Chapter 23

Good Guys

Six straight wins since the opening night loss in Buffalo added bounce to the Raiders front office. The team was steamrolling most opponents, and four of the six wins were won on the road. Last week, in San Francisco, the Raiders beat the 49ers by eleven points, and after Sunday's contest in Denver, Oakland would host six of their final seven regular-season games at the Oakland Coliseum.

The upbeat mood even pervaded Al Davis' demeanor, and with a skip in his step, he bounded into the public relations office on the Wednesday before we played in Denver.

Baron Wolman, who made a name for himself as a photographer in the world of rock 'n' roll, had signed on to take behind-the-scenes photos of the Raiders in 1974. His friend, and partner on the project, Fred Kaplan, would take game-action shots of the Raiders while

Wolman photographed the coaches, staff, players, and football life off the field.

Wolman was a cool guy, easy to talk with, and the first person in charge of photography at a successful publication started a few years earlier, *Rolling Stone Magazine.* A year earlier, the Raiders had granted locker room access to eccentric writer Hunter Thompson, and that provided a spike in the Raiders brand-name recognition to many readers who would not otherwise have been exposed to a sports story.

Al LoCasale had identified the benefits of expanding the Raiders recognition to a new group of fans, expanding still on a market that had swelled success to include a waiting list to buy season tickets of more than 14,000. The access afforded Wolman was first suggested by LoCasale, but Davis was clearly in favor of the project too. He nodded Baron's way while walking between us and the press releases hanging on clipboards.

Dressed in all white, Davis had his back to Baron and me while paging through a *Pro Football Weekly* that was on the credenza next to Tom Grimes' desk.

"Have you named that book of yours yet?" Davis asked of Wolman without turning his head.

Wolman offered a few titles that had been discussed without any real conviction, and Davis said the name would come. "Something will happen, you'll notice it when it occurs, and you'll have your name," Davis assured.

Wolman smiled while glancing at me, Davis still with his back to us.

My brother was on a bowling team that we named over a family dinner. It was Jack's team, he was the best bowler in the family, and the name was The Good Guys.

I was thinking about that while Davis paged through *Pro Football Weekly,* and Baron smiled my way, seemingly asking me if he should say something since Davis still hadn't made eye contact. To take the pressure off Wolman, I decided to speak next, and I took a flyer.

"How about calling the book, The Good Guys," I offered, not sure how the suggestion would be taken by Davis or Wolman.

Davis spun around and made eye contact for the first time since his brief glance when he entered the room four or five minutes earlier.

"The Good Guys," Davis repeated with eyes wide open. "That's what we fuckin' are, and we should say it. The fuckin' Raiders are the fuckin' good guys," Davis said while laughter burst through his speech.

"Do you like The Good Guys?" Davis said to Baron.

"I like it if you like it," Wolman said with a smile.

"Fuckin' a, we are the good guys," Davis said again, amused at the thought. A moment later, he headed for the door, saying over his shoulder, "It's a name; it's a possibility; give it some thought."

We could hear Davis ask Kris how she was doing in his Southern gentleman dialect before he headed up the back stairs to his corner office. Wolman asked me if I really thought Davis liked the idea of calling a book on the Raiders The Good Guys, and I offered that he seemed authentically enthused.

Davis was not enthused a few hours later when his secretary, Beverly Swanson, asked if Gene Upshaw had been taken off the waiver wire. It was four minutes to the deadline, and she hadn't yet seen a TWX to confirm the Raiders maneuvers that would have taken the Raiders All-Pro offensive lineman off the waiver wire. If his availability was not rescinded in the allotted time, he would be available to any team that chose him, starting with the team with the worst record.

Gene Upshaw could have woken up on Thursday morning and found himself a member of the Houston Oilers.

Why was Upshaw on the waiver wire in the first place?

Often when the Raiders were trying to slip a player through the waiver process, they would put Upshaw, Jim Otto, George Blanda, Ken Stabler, Fred Biletnikoff, or some other established star on the list with him. This was an attempt to sway attention from a would-be prospect the Raiders were trying to keep without needing to have him count against our roster number.

On this day, Upshaw was included on the list and the order to call him back had not yet been submitted. Neither Ron Wolf nor Ken Herock were in the office, both on the road scouting college games, and the Davis directive to include Upshaw on that day's waiver wire was faithfully submitted, but his obvious call to take Upshaw off was never made.

Beverly noticed it at a time when the transmission on the TWX, which was required, would be in a close race with the time left on the clock.

"Jesus Christ, we didn't pull Gene yet," Davis said in response to Beverly's announcement at his door. At the same time Davis said to do it, Beverly pounded on the TWX keys while Davis dialed the league office to assure Upshaw was not lost.

"I just want you to know the Raiders are not offering Gene Upshaw on the waiver wire," I could hear Davis say while watching Beverly efficiently work to beat the deadline.

"On fucking time or not," Davis said in a louder voice, "we are not offering Mr. Upshaw."

He stopped as Beverly informed that the request was complete and ahead of the deadline.

Davis nodded but continued his conversation on the phone with the league representative.

"Listen," he said, biting his bottom lip, "I just want to know what your policy is for someone like myself calling in and telling you something in no uncertain terms versus a transmission received in the office?"

The person in New York must have had an answer to that because Davis listened for an extended time. Finally, he said, "I'm telling you, Upshaw is off the waiver wire whether you receive transmission of that now or in five minutes from now."

I suspect the league official talking to Davis got confirmation that the Raiders had gotten Upshaw off in time to meet policy. The expression on Davis' face changed, and he made his final point. "I'm just confirming with you that we had a conversation that could have accomplished what that TWX did."

After a brief interruption on his side of the call, Davis said, "We can't fucking lose who we are in these matters. If we can't talk, we can't do business."

When Davis hung up, he noticed I was peering in from his door; I had seen the whole drama unfold. "What do you want?" Davis snapped at me in an uninviting tone.

"Nothing, sir," I said, backing away from his door.

"That was amazing; good job," I whispered to Beverly while she just shrugged her shoulders.

Four days later, we opened November play with a win over the Broncos at Mile High Stadium and returned home with only one road date left on our regular season schedule, a December game in Kansas City.

— — — — — —

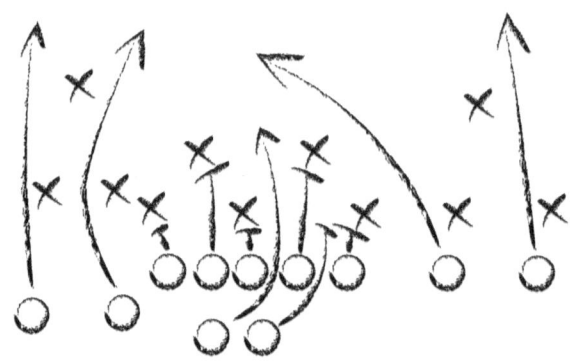

Chapter 24

Wing
and Prayer

"WHAT'S THAT?" JOHN MADDEN WOULD SAY, his eyes widening in fear, when our craft was encountering turbulence. From his face, you'd think that at any moment, the wings would be ripped off the jet.

"It's okay," I would croon, as though comforting a child.

He would fasten his gaze on me, hoping I was right, and then glance down the aisle to see if his terror was shared by anyone else. It almost never was.

It was painful to see the fearsome head coach sit erect, fear in his eyes, clutching the seat armrests with white knuckles.

Al Davis would sit three rows back in an aisle seat. The seating arrangement allowed Davis to face Madden, so the owner had a front-row view of raw terror. While I believe Davis considered Madden's fear of flying irrational, he accepted it. The coach did fly with the team in order to do his job.

While Madden feared every flight we took, on one trip in 1974, his terror was warranted—and shared by everyone onboard.

Despite the loss in Buffalo to start that season, quarterback Ken Stabler led the Raiders to the postseason in 1974 and was completing a campaign that would earn him Most Valuable Player. The Raiders playoff position was locked in after a home blowout win over Jim Plunkett and the New England Patriots, 41–26, on December 1. The next week in Kansas City, the decision was made to keep Stabler out of action and allow untested backup Larry Lawrence a chance to start. The move avoided subjecting the second quarterback on the Raiders depth chart, Daryle Lamonica, to possible injury.

In a game that meant nothing, played in a freezing cross breeze at Arrowhead Stadium, the Chiefs and Raiders banged each other around for 60 minutes. In the end, the Raiders won, 7–6. Heavier snow than we encountered during the game was in the afternoon forecast, and the need to get out of town before the severe weather arrived was receiving more attention than the game itself. The buses from the stadium to the airport were able to negotiate through the weather, but by late afternoon the skies were dark, not from the setting of the sun but rather from the gathering storm clouds.

The players had left the bus and were already milling about the airport when we learned the bad news. "They're going to close the airport," Stan Glazier reported. He was a silver-haired gentleman with chrome-rimmed glasses who managed the Raiders charter flights for United Airlines.

"That can't happen," Al Davis exclaimed with an anguished look. "What do we need to do in order to get out of here tonight?"

"They'll give you no more than 12 minutes," Glazier related while conversing with an airport manager on the phone. "If you can get the team onboard and the doors closed in less than 15 minutes, we can probably get out before the airport is completely shut down."

The players were scattered all over Terminal A. They had been told we wouldn't be leaving for another hour. I looked out the large terminal windows and saw the snow blowing sideways, falling at a rate significantly harder than when we rode the buses just minutes before.

"We can fucking do that," Davis said in his New Jersey thug dialect.

"We can fucking do this," he then said to me and three others standing around the registration podium in front of Gate A16. Al LoCasale was first to snap to attention and fired off to no one in particular, "Everyone here now goes. Those that aren't here get left behind."

"We don't want to leave any players," Ken LaRue said, asking Tom Grimes and me to form a search party. LoCasale asked Glazier if he could make an overhead announcement that the Raiders charter was leaving in ten minutes.

"Check that way," LaRue told me while pointing in one direction and sending Tom Grimes in another to round up players from bars, restaurants, and newsstands.

I heard the overhead announcement: "Final call for United Charter 193, now boarding at Gate A16 . . . Final call for United Charter 193 now boarding at Gate A16 . . . All passengers for United Charter 193 should now be at Gate A16."

The announcement was playing a second time when I spotted a group of Raiders—Bob Moore, Phil Villapiano, and Warren Bankston—eating sandwiches and chucking down cold drinks in a restaurant just off the airport concourse.

"You've got to get on board now," I told them. At the same time, I spotted over my shoulder additional players huddled around a newspaper stand about ten yards away.

"We've got almost an hour," Bankston said while reaching for his sandwich.

"No," I said, "the bad weather might close the airport and we need to leave now to beat the storm."

They were hurriedly gulping down the rest of their drinks and laying more money on the table than their tab warranted as I headed for the newsstand.

Ten minutes later, I returned to the podium in front of the departure gate and found Davis in a heated argument with an airport representative who had been summoned to the Raiders gate.

"No other flights are leaving," the man in a blue blazer and red tie said firmly.

"I don't give a fuck about any other flights," Davis said. The airport rep seemed stunned by his language and demeanor. "I only care about the Raiders flight. And we are getting out of here now."

I had seen Davis bent on getting his way in the past and knew that the chances were very strong that we were going to lift off. But this was one time I thought it might be better for Davis to lose his battle. The snow was falling even harder, and I wished the airport representative could withstand my boss' heat.

Captain Hank Silliman, the Raiders charter pilot, was already in the cockpit and preparing for departure. All players were accounted for except defensive lineman Horace Jones, according to the manifest LoCasale was holding.

"We can't fly if it isn't safe," Stan Glazier said in an attempt to prepare Davis for the possibility of not leaving tonight.

"Listen," Davis said, "if we go now, right fucking now, can we get the fuck out of here?"

It seemed more like a directive than a question, and the airport representative agreed that if the plane left right now, we could get clearance to depart.

"We go without Horace," LoCasale said as Davis disappeared through the entrance to the jetway, followed closely by Grimes. Just then, Horace appeared, startled that the plane was already set to leave.

"I didn't hear any announcement," Jones said.

"See?" LoCasale told Glazier. "Saying 'Flight 193' didn't mean anything to them. We should have said on the overhead announcement, 'The Raiders charter is leaving.'" This must have been an argument I missed while I was rounding up players. Still, LoCasale wasn't letting Jones off the hook. "You've got to know what flight number you're on, sir," he said sternly.

Madden was sitting in his seat with his safety belt already buckled as I hustled into mine moments before Glazier slammed the jet passenger door shut and firmly pulled the latch closed. He had never done that before; that task was always done by the head stewardess. Yet protocol on this flight had been abandoned in favor of doing whatever necessary to get us out of Kansas City pronto.

"Let's go," Glazier said, taking a seat in a fold-down metal chair commonly used by the stewardesses.

"Is this all right?" Madden asked me, wanting assurance Davis hadn't bullied us into a flight we shouldn't be making.

"We wouldn't fly—the airport wouldn't allow it—if it wasn't safe," I said, trying to convince myself as much as the nervous coach.

The flight crew rushed through the emergency announcements and took their seats while the plane was pulling away from the gate.

I rubbed the window on my right to get a better view. The driving snowstorm barely allowed me to see the blinking lights on our wings and the headlights of the airport vehicles moving bags. I glanced at the wing behind where I sat and could see snow accumulating at a rapid pace. In front of me, Madden closed his eyes to impending doom.

The engines sounded different from anything I had ever heard before as the jet labored down the runway. They emitted not a consistent, powerful roar but rather the whining of an old air conditioner unable to combat stifling heat. It took forever to lift off. I felt the aircraft struggling to get off the ground and wanted to bury my face in my hands. But I didn't. I knew my job was to offer Madden some semblance of security even if my own was whirling down the sink.

Finally, the craft became airborne, but it didn't ascend with the serene strength enjoyed on the usual flight. Noises never experienced before rattled the Boeing 727. One of the overhead compartments a few rows back was jarred open. That prompted Cheryl, one of the flight crew, to quickly unclasp her belt and close it with a slam.

She had just returned to her seat when the aircraft suddenly lost altitude. The drop was drastic, shoving our hearts in our throats. Madden was wretched in anguish, and we all froze in our seats, anticipating the worst. He said nothing, but the irises of his eyes were full circles, and his pupils grew to a larger size than I had ever witnessed. His look pleaded with me to say something that would relieve his fear.

With an outward calmness that belied my true feelings, I said, "Hank told me that we would encounter a few of those and not to worry. Everything is okay."

Madden seemed to accept my lie, looking anywhere he could for relief from the terror that had spread throughout the cabin. His knuckles remained white, but he nodded in approval and closed his eyes while resting his head on the seat back.

I looked over my left shoulder at Davis, not with the security I had offered Madden, but with a question: What the hell are we doing up here? Is it really worth risking all of our lives to get out of town on this ill-advised flight?

Davis seemed to acknowledge my question, and for one of the only times I had ever seen him, he looked unsure of himself. He had strong-armed his way into a dangerous situation.

The aircraft experienced more sudden drops and jarring trembles in the inclement weather for nearly an hour. Even after the flight gained a more steady keel, I sat rigidly in my chair, deathly afraid, until we landed safely on the ground in Oakland.

"I'm glad to be off that one," Madden said with a laugh and a huge sigh of relief as he headed through the Oakland terminal, two steps in front of me on the way to the luggage carousel. I didn't respond. Davis, who was just off my right shoulder, seemed to sense my anger that my life had been put at risk.

"Drive me home tonight," he ordered.

I turned to him in surprise, wondering why he needed me to drive him.

"Your car is here, right?" Davis asked.

I nodded yes.

"Well, you can pick it up tomorrow. Take me home in my car."

I know the standard odds, and I was aware that the drive from the airport to home is statistically more life-threatening than the flight itself. But tonight, I thought Davis had twisted those odds, and turned what could have been a routine flight into an unsafe adventure. For the first time, I had a different reaction to the man's drive to get whatever he wanted because his desires had crossed the line into simple belligerence. He always had to get his own way. The last thing I wanted to do was drive with a man whose fanatical behavior had put my life in danger. During the long flight, I had considered for the first time that working in this organization might not be my best option in the future.

We were driving down Broadway in Davis' black Cadillac when he asked, "You like pastrami sandwiches?"

After I said I did, Davis said, "They have some of the best ones right up here at Doggie Diner. Let's stop and get one."

At midnight on a Sunday night, I was able to find three parking places available on the street where the Doggie Diner was located.

"Do you want me to get you food to go?" I asked Davis.

"No," he said while unhooking his seat belt, "let's go in and eat."

Only two other customers were in the brightly lit restaurant, two young Black men who didn't seem to notice Davis or me as we made our way to the ordering counter.

"Do you want one?" Davis asked while ordering his pastrami sandwich with extra mustard, and I said yes while adding a Coke to my order. Davis was silent while we waited for our food. Then we found the cleanest table and sat in chairs across from each other.

"Well, we got our team home on time, goddamn ahead of schedule," Davis said with a hint of accomplishment in his voice.

Instinctively, my lips tightened and I shook my head.

Davis caught that, and asked me why I was so quiet.

I couldn't tell him what I really felt, not if I wanted to keep my job.

"You think we should have stayed in Kansas City?" Davis said with venom in his voice.

"I'm just not sure it was safe to fly," I finally replied.

"See," Davis said while wiping a glob of mustard from the corner of his mouth, "that is the difference between you and me."

"Sir?" I asked, trying to understand what he meant.

"You do what you think is right. I do what is best."

I was still trying to wrap my mind around that notion when Davis added, "You'll never seize the moments when the greatest gains can be made if you're always hooked on doing what is right. Right is not as good as best. Best requires being alert, doing what you have to do to get an edge when opportunities arise."

He warmed to his subject: "When the storm was coming in Kansas City, would you have waited to be overcome by its effects and be spending tonight in Kansas City just because our departure time was 7:12?"

The two guys in the corner were now looking over at our table as Davis became more passionate.

"We did what was best. We took action, we overcame circumstances, and tonight we are in Oakland and on schedule as an organization. Greatness occurs when you do all the things necessary to achieve it. That always requires doing what is best."

For more than two football seasons, everything Davis had taught me had been taken as gospel, but the logic of this lesson was wobbly for me.

He saw that.

"You fucking think it would have been right to stay in Kansas City? To wait for the fucking storm to beat us?" Davis leaned across the table and motioned with his hand within inches of my face, "Listen, Dennis, when you take on what is best, you pay the prices, and when you win, you should celebrate the rewards. We're fucking in Oakland tonight, and trust me, that is a huge reward over the fucking alternative. You should be celebrating that."

- - - - - -

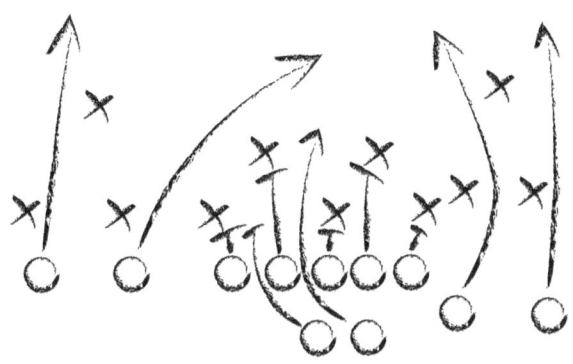

Chapter 25

Walkie-Talkie
Squawking

DAVIS' FIRST CHANCE TO LIVE UP to his previous declaration in the Orange Bowl, that he would never lose again to the Dolphins, occurred that December in Oakland. The Raiders had won the West in 1974 in Stabler's first full season at quarterback, and the Alabama alum won the NFL's Most Valuable Player Award. The Raiders offense was a juggernaut because of an offensive line of Jim Otto flanked by Gene Upshaw and George Buehler at the guards, while the outside rush was protected by Art Shell and John Vella from the tackle positions.

Snake, a nickname Stabler gained returning punts in college and darting back and forth across the field to avoid would-be tacklers, was to football in 1974 what Sandy Koufax was to baseball in 1965: nearly perfect.

Behind excellent protection by the best offensive line west of Miami, Stabler dissected opponent defenses with precision on crossing patterns to Fred Biletnikoff, Mike Siani, and Bob Moore. When a quick score was available, Cliff Branch was the most likely target to break a long one against an overmatched cornerback. Stabler carved up defenses at venues across the country with the grace of a conductor leading a full orchestra in Carnegie Hall.

Between his accurate passes, Stabler handed the ball to Marv Hubbard and Pete Banaszak for the tough yards, or Charlie Smith and Clarence Davis for outside bursts.

The season had delighted fans, but neither Lamonica nor Stabler had ever gotten Davis the one prize he put ahead of all others—a Super Bowl win.

In 1974, the team standing between Oakland and the Vince Lombardi Trophy was once again the Miami Dolphins.

Don Shula's team had won back-to-back championships, matching the Green Bay Packers two-game streak in Super Bowls I and II. The Dolphins were looking for their fourth straight Super Bowl appearance.

"Dennis," Davis said on the phone I answered in my Alameda apartment about 20 minutes after I got home on Thursday night, "Did ya pick up Mr. Gowdy at the airport?"

"He comes in tomorrow," I said, suddenly alarmed. Had I blown the assignment of picking up Curt Gowdy?

"And you'll take care of that when it's time?" Davis responded.

"Yes, sir," I dutifully recited while relaxing. I had not made a mistake, after all.

"And how does the team look?" Davis said in what might really have been the reason for his call.

While I had studied point spreads and team motivation before joining the Raiders, I got the message that gambling was not an option for an employee of the league. It was a rule I took seriously, and while I had not been tempted to gamble since going to work for the Raiders, I did continue to chart team tendencies, motivational stats, and my own database. In fact, my firsthand knowledge of a football organization has now given me even more insights into what drives a team's performance.

"We look good, don't we?" I said.

"You take care of Curt," Davis said, ending the conversation where he started it.

I took care of Gowdy on Friday, and on Saturday, he was behind the mic for the NBC telecast of the Raiders-Dolphins game from the Oakland/Alameda County Coliseum.

"We're back in the House of Miracles," Gowdy said to his broadcast partner, Al DeRogatis, as I watched from the doorway.

"Is there anything else I can get you?" I asked.

"Dennis," Gowdy said, "you've been great. Tell your boss to give you a raise."

"I could use a drink, some kind of soda or juice," DeRogatis responded.

I nodded to him and checked with Gowdy one more time if he wanted me to get him anything too. He waved me off with a friendly gesture, and I headed for the elevator located on the third floor, right over the 50-yard line. The elevator had three stops: The top floor was the press box, the bottom one led to the locker room at field level, and the second-floor elevator door opened right in front of the stadium lunch area. The smell of Kentucky Fried Chicken blew in first when the elevator doors opened.

To the left of the elevator was the entrance to the space underneath the stands that the stat crew used. It was a hollow, cold cement area the size of a high school gymnasium with windows that offered a view of the playing field. The stat crew used this area so they could do their work without distraction, and for all the regular season games, they were alone in this cave-like setting. But today, because of the high interest in the game and increased media attention, 63 additional seats were set up here on the risers to accommodate the extra press credentials requested for this playoff game.

I grabbed both an orange juice from a cooler and poured a Coke from the machine for DeRogatis, and headed back to the elevator to deliver the drinks. Davis was sitting at a round table nearest the door, and he nodded to me as I walked by. On most game days, I would sit with him, but LoCasale had requested my assistance today to help him handle the extra demands.

Before some of the people had taken their seats, the game opened with George Jakowenko kicking to the 11-yard line and Dolphins return man Nat Moore returning it the distance for an 89-yard touchdown. After Garo Yepremian added the extra point, the Dolphins led 7–0.

The Raiders tied it midway through the second quarter when Stabler connected with Charlie Smith from 31 yards out, and the Dolphins countered with a field goal to take a 10–7 lead to the halftime locker room.

Before the Amador High School Marching Band completed their halftime show on the field, the stat crew had produced the totals from the first 30 minutes of play and copied them on a Xerox machine located in a small room next to the lunch area. I distributed copies to the media first in the makeshift press area below the stands, leaving most on empty chairs, as the reporters were congregating in the lunch area.

Upstairs in the press box, I made the rounds of television and radio booths and followed that duty by putting a copy at each seat in the press box. The two rows of media seats both had windows and a work counter that ran the length of the press box. On the far left were two seats set off from the rest of the press area, and that was where Al LoCasale and Tom Grimes were working, armed with phones and LoCasale's walkie-talkie.

On the opposite side of the elevator, another press area had been set up in the cement stadium structure where four rows of seats, six stadium seats to one side of an aisle and four to the other. This area was used as private boxes for baseball games, but the Raiders needed it for the media and executives from visiting teams. Because it had no worktables, the area was mostly dedicated to electronic media. On this December afternoon, the press area was cold, made worse by the cement. The electronic media press area smelled like a gas station garage on a rainy day. Among other inconveniences, a 19-inch Sony television fastened to the cement wall near the ceiling could be seen easily from where I was standing, behind the seating area, but required those in seats to crane their necks to watch the direct game feed.

Included in their numbers was Monty Stickles of KGO-Radio. Stickles was a former tight end and punishing blocker with the San Francisco 49ers, their first-round draft selection out of Notre Dame in 1960. After his playing career, he was involved in a number of business projects, including a beer distributorship, and he was working with KGO-Radio in the early days of sports talk radio.

I was standing behind him in the third quarter of the Raiders-Dolphins game when Stabler completed a 40-yard pass to Fred Biletnikoff that he caught with a spinning move. The 53,515 fans at the Coliseum first roared with approval, thinking their beloved Silver and Black had taken their first lead of the game, but then booed in opposition to the stripe-shirted official waving off the score, ruling Biletnikoff was out of bounds.

Instant replay was limited in 1974 to seeing if a call was right or wrong, but was not subject to any review and possible reversal by game officials. Still, everyone in the press box wanted a look at the replay.

Stickles had played his last NFL season in 1968 with the New Orleans Saints, a team that had a kicker in 1970 that was born without any toes on his right foot, Tom Dempsey. While New Orleans won only two games in 1970, one of them was provided by a record 63-yard kick from Dempsey, who wore a kicking boot with a blunt, flat surface on his right foot that looked more like a sledgehammer than a typical shoe.

I took a step forward to see the television replay of Biletnikoff's catch, and the camera confirmed the official got it right. His foot came down with the tip of his shoe on the white chalk that outlined the end zone. Stickles was at waist level in front of me, leaning back and looking up to see the replay.

At the moment Fred's shoe was shown hitting the chalk, Stickles softly said, without knowing anyone was in listening range, "Dempsey would have been in."

I was laughing at Stickles' comment when I noticed Domenico was standing at my side, again dressed and manicured impeccably, in stark contrast to most media people. I had seen him around the Raiders for more than a year now. I still wasn't sure if Domenico was his first or last name, but addressed him the way I had heard other people greet him in Davis' box, "Mr. Dom."

"Perfect day for football," Domenico said while watching the Raiders drive continue on the field.

"Yes, sir," I agreed.

"Are you confident in the Raiders chances today?" he asked in a way that put me on the defensive.

"Confidence against the defending world champions is tough," I said succinctly. "But if you're asking me if I think we are going to win . . . I do."

He smiled while disappearing through the metal door toward Davis' box.

Seven plays after Biletnikoff was ruled out of bounds, the Raiders enhanced their prospects when Stabler completed a 13-yard touchdown pass to him to give Oakland their first lead of the game midway through the third quarter.

That advantage only lasted until Dolphins quarterback Bob Griese found Paul Warfield for a score from 16 yards out on Miami's next possession. In one of his few heroic efforts for the Raiders in his final NFL campaign, Bubba Smith blocked the ensuing extra-point attempt by Yepremian. The defending Super Bowl champions lead was a precarious two points, 16–14.

Less than four minutes into the final quarter, Yepremian booted a 46-yard field goal, and the Dolphins lead expanded to five points. The Raiders failed to pick up a first down on their next possession, and Ray Guy punted to the Dolphins with ten minutes left on the game clock. Larry Csonka ran the ball five times on the first seven plays of the ensuing drive, but with third-and-seven from midfield, Griese handed the ball to rookie runner Benny Malone, and he swept around the right end before being knocked out of bounds by Otis Sistrunk right at the first down marker but short.

The fourth-and-inches call from the 46-yard line was an automatic punt for the defensively strong Dolphins, and Larry Seiple booted it 29 yards and out-of-bounds at the Raiders 17-yard line. Less than five minutes remained on the game clock, the Raiders trailed by five points, and Gowdy was talking of the House of Miracles when Stabler lined up behind Jim Otto.

On first down, Snake found Biletnikoff for 11 yards up the right side, and on second down, magic.

Branch had been setting up defensive backs all game, looking for his opportunity to exploit the Dolphins sturdy secondary. On first down, his chance for glory presented itself as he gained one-on-one coverage from nickelback Henry Stuckey, who, as it turned out, was playing his last game in a Dolphins uniform.

The defender honored Branch's speed and turned his back on Stabler to try to keep up with number 21 in silver and black, which left only Branch to see the pass up the left sideline that Stabler had lofted short of the sprinting receiver. With Stuckey still turned the wrong way, Branch came back for the ball and caught it with a dive in front of the defender at the 27-yard line. Then, before Stuckey could even come back to down the receiver, Branch leaped to his feet, skirted around Stuckey, and scored on a 72-yard pass, dive, catch, get up, and run-in touchdown.

The Coliseum went wild.

No one in the stands was more excited about the turn of events that put the Raiders up 21–19 than Al LoCasale.

I was standing next to him when the Raiders took the lead, and he couldn't shove his papers and notes into his briefcase fast enough to get down on the field and celebrate this magnificent Oakland victory.

"You take this," LoCasale said while handing me one of his walkie-talkies. "I'll keep in touch with you over it. You man this station." He shoved his way through the metal doors and toward the elevator.

A few minutes later, Tom Grimes approached and said, "Glenn and a few other reporters want to know officially how long of a pass play it was, what yard line Branch caught it on, and how far he ran after he jumped back up." Glenn Dickey, who was requesting the details, was a columnist for the *San Francisco Chronicle*. "I can't reach the stat crew because Lokee took their walkie-talkies for his own use today," Grimes continued.

"He left me in charge of this one right here," I said, pointing at it on the table where LoCasale had left it. "He told me to stay here and man it while he went down on the field."

"I'll watch it. You go get the information from the stat crew and have them include the distance both for the pass play and where Branch caught it and got back up on the play-by-play, too," Grimes instructed.

By the time I reached the stat crew, the Dolphins were driving. Larry Csonka had just run around the right end for seven yards, and Miami was already in Oakland territory at the 38-yard line. The stat crew was working feverishly to track the on-field moves, and my request for a play that had happened on the previous series was not an interruption they welcomed. Still, Art Snyder, while calling out that Csonka had gained 15 yards on the previous play, moving the ball to the Oakland 23, also provided me the information that the Branch to Stabler touchdown was 72 yards and that the ball was caught at the 27-yard line.

"Grimes wanted that included in the play-by-play," I said.

"It is," Snyder said over his shoulder, giving me the strong impression that my intrusion had better have reached its end.

I left the downstairs area and, before hitting the elevator call button, took a peek into the lunch area, where on a 32-inch color television mounted on the wall, I saw Miami running back Benny Malone dash around the Raiders defense and score a touchdown for the Dolphins from 23 yards out.

It had taken the Dolphins slightly more than two minutes of the game clock to answer the Stabler to Branch touchdown with one of their own. The extra point put Miami back on top, 26–21, with just over two minutes left in the game. The joy of the Oakland go-ahead touchdown was now erased, replaced by a sickening feeling that the Dolphins were going to get us again.

Grimes was not at the desk next to the walkie-talkie when I got back up to the press box, but I easily found him, standing behind *Oakland Tribune* sports editor Bob Valli, who was sitting in the front row of the press box seats.

"The touchdown was 72 yards, and Branch caught it at the 27-yard-line," I reported, though all the life was gone from my voice. Grimes nodded and then followed me back to the workstation in the press box. Before I even completed the three-step climb from the lower to the top row of press box seats, I could hear an unbearable burst of static coming from the walkie-talkie.

"Uh-oh," I said, "LoCasale told me not to leave that walkie-talkie."

"Is that him yelling?" Grimes asked. The squawking actually made the instrument move on the table. The sounds blaring out were so ominous, I didn't want to touch the thing. I looked to Grimes for assistance.

He picked it up and tried to respond to the rants coming in. "We can't understand you," he said, while pressing the speak button located on the side of the instrument, which was about the size of an egg carton. "We can't make out your words," Grimes said in a second attempt to get a dialogue going.

An astonished look appeared on his face as he spotted LoCasale down on the field, yelling into the walkie-talkie. He was looking up at the press box while swinging his briefcase in one arm and holding the walkie-talkie up to his mouth in the other.

Finally, Grimes and I could understand a couple of the harsh sounds coming up from the field, "You're fired, Ranahan. You're fired, Ranahan. You will never work another game, you little shit. I told you to guard those phones. Where were you? Where were you? You're fired, Ranahan."

Grimes looked at me with a reassuring glance. "He's a little excited."

He tried again to get LoCasale's attention, "Al," Grimes said. "Al," he said again, but to no avail. LoCasale's theatrics didn't lose steam, and most of his words could still not be understood. Grimes held the walkie-talkie up where LoCasale could see it and with a very clear motion, showed the man yelling from the field that he was turning off the communication on our side.

The move caused silence from the walkie-talkie in the press box but inspired an even more vigorous reaction from LoCasale on the field. He was now yelling even louder into a communication device that had no listener on the other end. What he was missing while flailing to us in the press box was the drive Ken Stabler was engineering behind him on the field.

It was a classic.

In the final two minutes, Stabler completed all five of his passes, and Clarence Davis had gained one yard on a run early in the drive and six more yards to the Miami 8-yard line to set up a first and goal with 40 seconds left on the game clock.

LoCasale was still looking at the press box and yelling into his muted walkie-talkie when Stabler avoided the rush enough to get off a wobbly pass into an area that had three Miami defenders and the Raiders Clarence Davis.

Davis made the catch, and Oakland regained the lead with 26 seconds remaining in the game. The NFL Films crew caught LoCasale spinning around in contortions. To this day, that scene is always used when the play that became known in NFL lore as the "Sea of Hands" is shown. Even local television stations used LoCasale's antics caught on film for years when promoting Raiders football—thinking it was only a show of enthusiasm over a Raiders win when in fact, his incoherent rant spiked his spastic contortions.

The victory erased the abandoned walkie-talkie infraction, and my fourth-quarter firing was never mentioned again.

– – – – – –

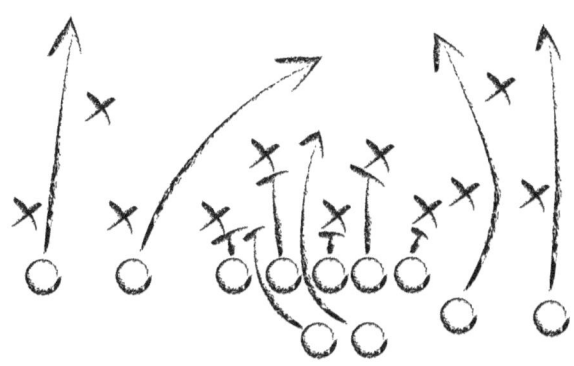

Chapter 26

Motivational
Leak

I WAS STILL IN BED AT MY ALAMEDA APARTMENT when the phone rang. I was watching the Sunday morning game between the Pittsburgh Steelers and Buffalo Bills on a 13-inch color television propped up on a chair.

"How ya doin', young man?" a cheerful voice said. It was Al Davis, and the euphoria of yesterday's win still glowed in his greeting. "Looks like O.J. may be coming to Oakland next week."

"Oh no," I quickly retorted. Even though the Bills were currently leading the Steelers late in the first quarter at Three Rivers Stadium, 7–3, I saw no way they could beat Pittsburgh in this AFC divisional playoff game.

Davis laughed—cackled might be a better description of his response. In his uncharacteristic light mood, he added, "Well, whatever."

On Monday morning, Tom Grimes arrived at the Raiders office about 20 minutes after I did. He had the morning papers under his arm and said, almost under his breath, "Not a very good idea."

The joy of the weekend was shifting to the focus for the upcoming AFC Championship Game, and Grimes had been talking to Joe Gordon, public relations director of the Pittsburgh Steelers, from his home before he arrived at the office. The Steelers had posted in their locker room after their 32–14 win over Buffalo a quote from John Madden, where he had said the game between Oakland and Miami was for a date with the Super Bowl.

"Not very smart," Grimes said. "Seems that the Steelers think they are still in the running, and our coach just provided them with a rallying cry to galvanize their efforts."

"Does that really matter?" LaRue asked.

"Not very smart," Grimes reiterated grimly while typing game notes for the media kit we were preparing.

"So what exactly did he say?" LoCasale said, entering the office.

"He said it to Don Shula with the media in earshot," Grimes reported to LoCasale, "and it hit the wire and was printed in the Pittsburgh papers this morning."

"What exactly did he say?" LoCasale said, still looking for clarification.

"He said that he was glad they we're playing this week so neither he nor Don would end up having to coach the Pro Bowl." That duty was given to the loser of the conference championship game, and one that Madden and the Raiders staff had performed after losing at Miami the prior season.

"So he didn't really say the winner of Saturday's game was headed to the Super Bowl," LoCasale looked to confirm.

"Doesn't make any difference," Grimes retorted. "The media picked it up and ran with it like he had. That is what the Steelers press got ahold of, and that is what they are running with. Nothing we can do about it."

"But he didn't really say Saturday's winner was headed to the Super Bowl?" LoCasale repeated, still holding hope the damage could be minimized.

"Al," Grimes said while stopping his typing and looking directly at LoCasale, "what matters is the Pittsburgh media has reinterpreted it to be like we thought beating the Dolphins was tantamount to winning the AFC. The Steelers are picking up just as much as they can from that. It's not good. Joe told me this morning that it is the buzz in the Pittsburgh media."

"Why does he have to make it tougher on us?" LoCasale said, turning toward me. He didn't expect me to have an answer.

We all sat in silence for a period of time, and then LoCasale got up and said to me, "I need a ride to the hotel."

Two hotels close to the Raiders Oakport Street offices were regularly used by the organization. The Edgewater was on Hegenberger Road just off Highway 17, while about a half mile up toward the Oakland Airport was the Airport Hilton Hotel. Visiting teams stayed at the Edgewater, while the Raiders utilized the Hilton facility for the team on nights both before home games and after-game parties.

The Dolphins had stayed at the Edgewater, and the Steelers would be arriving there on Friday night. We had also blocked off two suites at the Edgewater to serve as media rooms, and LoCasale, who did not drive, wanted to see the setup LaRue had arranged with the hotel.

Even more media requests were made for the AFC Championship Game against the Steelers than we had received for the prior week's contest against Miami. Among those requesting credentials was National Football League Commissioner Pete Rozelle. On Sunday, I was assigned to escort him and his new wife, Carrie, to their seats on an aluminum riser that gave the commissioner a clear view of the field over the heads of the media in front of him and the fans on the other side of the glass.

The adrenaline of ending the Dolphins two-year run as Super Bowl champions the prior week left the Raiders emotionally flat for the Steelers. But John Madden had identified the problem at halftime as one of X's and O's.

Even though the score was tied, 3–3, Pittsburgh was controlling most of the action with a consistent ground attack. Madden and his coaches had identified that most of the 82 yards Franco Harris and Rocky Bleier had gained on their 23 carries were through a hole in the line that should have been plugged by defensive lineman Art Thoms. At halftime, Madden addressed the problem head-on.

"Art," he called with a raised voice, "what's going on out there?"

"Well," Thoms said in defense of his first-half play, "I knew Horace had banged up his knee early in the game, so I was trying to cover his position too."

Madden had a colorful way of getting his point across, and sometimes his phrasing was invented in the heat of his passion for winning.

"Art," Madden blurted, "don't worry about the horse being blind. Just load the cart."

The coaching advice might have been insightful, but it was not enough in the second half to prevent Madden from losing his fourth championship game in four tries. The Steelers defeated Oakland on the Raiders home field, 24–13, outscoring the silver and black 21–3 in the fourth quarter.

The Steelers advanced to their first Super Bowl, a win over the Minnesota Vikings, and Madden led his coaching staff back to work against the NFC in the Pro Bowl.

– – – – – –

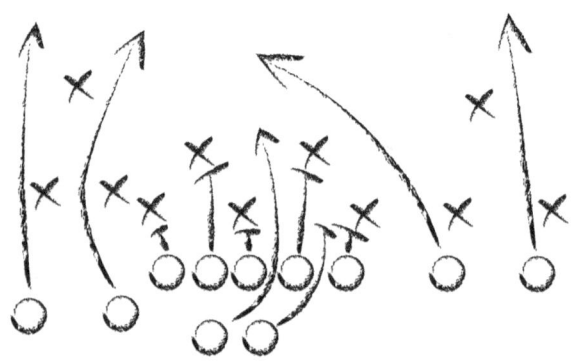

Chapter 27

Grammar
Lesson

Two weeks and two days after the Pittsburgh Steelers beat the Minnesota Vikings in Super Bowl IX, 16–6, the NFL conducted the 1975 draft. The Raiders communications with the NFL draft center consisted of a pair of scouts, Roy Schleicher and Kent McCloughan, on a speakerphone from New York, where the NFL was staging their annual allotment of college talent. In Oakland, Madden was again positioned at the head of the slate-black table in the Raiders conference room. The speakerphone was positioned between him and Davis, who sat to Madden's right in a silver chair.

Nearly an hour before the start of the draft, a conversation between the Raiders east and west connections was interrupted by the familiar voice of Howard Cosell. "And here I am with the brain trust of one of the truly great organizations in all of sports, the Oakland Raiders. Are you there, Mr. Davis?"

"Is that you, Howard?" Davis said.

Cosell didn't answer Davis directly but rather sprang into a rambling but accurate appraisal of the Oakland franchise. "The Raiders, one of the most successful franchises in professional sports. An elite football team leaning on the periphery of the elusive Super Bowl championship, which now stands as the lone accomplishment remaining to elevate Madden and the Raiders to Lombardi's Packers, Shula's Dolphins, and current champion Pittsburgh with the unflappable Chuck Noll."

"When we win it, Madden and the Raiders will be considered the best of all time," Davis interjected while smiling toward the coach on his left. Also in the room was Ken Herock, who was in line to move into the Raiders player personnel director position if Ron Wolf, who had been contacted by Hugh Culverhouse of the expansion Tampa Bay Buccaneers, was chosen to be their first general manager.

Cosell was aware of those behind-the-scene facts too. "Might this be the last time the man behind the Raiders astute player acquisitions for more than a decade is available to contribute to Oakland's success? If the Raiders are to leap over their final hurdle and end a season shielding their eyes from the glare of Super Bowl winning cameras, it needs to begin here, today, in the NFL draft of 1975. Will the organization fill the need for defensive backfield help or add to their potent attack spearheaded by Most Valuable Player, Ken Stabler?"

"Okay, Howard, who should we take?" Davis asked.

"WHOM should we take," Cosell yelled into the phone. "An English degree from Syracuse, and still you fail to grasp even the most fundamental footings of the language you call your first."

"Sorry, Howard, you got me. Whom should we take?" Davis said.

"Who shall it be? I only hope your picks today are superior to your command of the English language," Cosell said while fading out of listening range.

"He's gone," Schleicher reported, and the room went back to the duties at hand.

Cosell was right about the Raiders needs. Davis, Madden, Wolf, and Herock had determined in preparation with scouts and coaches that the defensive backfield was a top priority. They spent their first- and second-round picks on defensive backs Neil Colzie and Charles Phillips of Ohio State and the University of Southern California, respectively.

"If you just want a great physical specimen, we've got one right down the street here in Wasick out of San Jose State," Ron Wolf said while paging through scouting reports. It was the fifth round of the 17-round draft, and most of the players the Raiders had on their draft board were already selected, leaving Wolf and Herock in the best position to make recommendations Davis trusted.

"If you think he can be a player," Davis said.

"I think he is the best available," Wolf said.

Davis took a thoughtful look at his player personnel director, and, after a pause, said, "You're telling me he can be a player?"

"He's got the physical attributes to contribute in this league," Wolf deadpanned.

Davis then gave his approval. "Make Mr. Wasick a Raider."

"I don't think he is a good pick," I jumped in. I was sitting in the corner of the room on a lowly stool.

"What do you know?" Davis inquired.

"I know Dave Wasick personally. He was the boyfriend of Pam's roommate in college," I said. "He's just a jock. In fact, that's what everyone calls him. He's not somebody that is going to make it in the NFL."

A huge grin appeared on his face, and he directed his attention to Wolf. "The kid's got a firsthand scouting report there. I like it; let's find somebody else."

Wolf already had, suggesting Nebraska quarterback David Humm. He had great value for a skill position player in this round.

"Have you met Mr. Humm?" Davis asked me in an upbeat tone, and I said, "Not yet."

"Well, let's make him a Raider so we can all meet him," Davis said.

"Roy," Wolf said in the phone on the table, "David Humm, quarterback, Nebraska."

"It's in," Schleicher confirmed moments later, and my heart shifted into a faster gear as I experienced the pang of responsibility.

"With their fifth-round pick, the Oakland Raiders select David Humm, quarterback, Nebraska. The Minnesota Vikings are on the clock."

— — — — — —

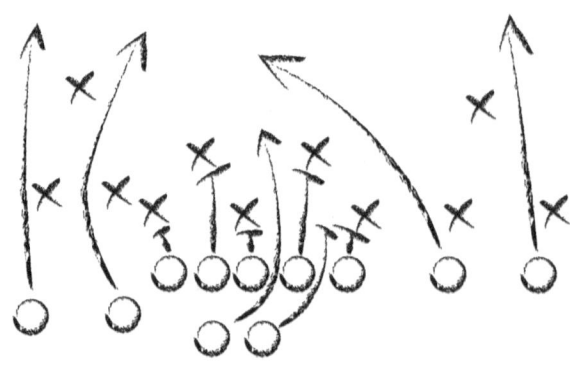

Chapter 28

Franklin

Aʟ Dᴀᴠɪs ᴡᴀs ᴇɴɢʀᴏssᴇᴅ ɪɴ ʟᴇɢᴀʟ ᴀꜰꜰᴀɪʀs once the draft ended. Ron Wolf completed his negotiations and moved to the Tampa Bay Buccaneers, taking Ken LaRue with him. Davis was focused, though, on a higher battleground—against Wayne Valley for control of the Oakland Raiders.

Valley had gone to Munich and attended the Olympics in 1972, and while he was gone, Davis negotiated a contract with the other majority owner, Ed McGah. The deal had a revolving clause that for each year served for the first ten years, another year would be added to the agreement, essentially guaranteeing Davis employment with the Raiders for 20 years if he continued to run the franchise effectively.

The contract was a very, very sweet deal for Davis financially, and even more important, as managing general partner, he had complete

authority on decisions by the Raiders at league meetings. Valley opposed
the deal on the grounds that, as a majority owner, he should have been
consulted before any changes on a new contract were made. The suit
was on the court calendar to begin in May 1975. As soon as the draft
was complete in February, Davis worked with a stable of lawyers in
preparing for his "war" against Wayne Valley.

That's because, as dynamic as Valley and Davis were in partnership during the 1960s, they were now bitter enemies. The Raiders
franchise hung in the balance as these two bigger-than-life men
squared off.

When Valley first filed the suit, William Orrick was handling
Davis' case. But he had been appointed a judge in 1974 and had turned
over the case to one of his firm's most respected lawyers, Richard
Lucas.

That winter and spring, I was almost always with Davis, driving him
between appointments with lawyers and to and from the airport. I was
in the lobby outside a meeting Davis was conducting with his lawyers
in San Francisco when the six-man team emerged from a conference
room during another marathon session.

"Why don't we all go out and eat?" Lucas said, motioning for me
to join their group.

Lucas' office was located on an upper floor in the recently completed
TransAmerica Building. After Lucas invited me for dinner, Davis said,
"Listen, we don't need to take the time to go out to dinner. Why don't
we just have Dennis pick us up something and have a working dinner
here in the office?"

I could tell the idea was not to Lucas' liking. I'm not sure meals
were often eaten in this plush office setting that had the smell of a new
building. But he agreed. "We could do that, too, if you want."

"Do you see an advantage in staying on top of this?" Davis said. His forceful statement rocked the poised Italian lawyer somewhat, and he leaned back on his heels. "There are a lot of good spots for food we can bring in that are within walking distance."

Amid the babble of possible suggestions, Davis' voice came through loud and clear.

"Is there a Doggie Diner in the neighborhood?"

Lucas was willing to deliver to the client what he wanted. "Not in this neighborhood. But if Dennis wanted to drive, I could give him directions to one not too far away."

Mr. Cox, a criminal lawyer Davis had hired, roared with laughter. "We are going to go out of our way to find a Doggie Diner?"

"Do what the fuck you want," Davis said. "I'm more concerned about our case than what we're fucking eating for dinner."

"There are a lot of good places in the neighborhood," Lucas said.

Davis ignored this suggestion. "This should be enough for anything you find," he said, peeling two hundred-dollar bills from a silver money clip he carried in his front pocket.

"Here are some twenties, so you don't have to use the big bills if you don't need to," Lucas said, handing me six of them.

I had just been handed half of my month's pay to fetch dinner for Davis' legal team. I did find an Italian restaurant about four blocks from the TransAmerica building that allowed me to take out, after some negotiations. I returned with more than $200 in change. The six of us ate dinner in the conference room.

"You married?" Lucas asked me while we ate.

"Engaged," I said, surprised that Lucas was showing interest in me. "Getting married on June 7."

"That's not long after the trial begins," Lucas said. "You are going to miss some of the proceedings." Then he added, "Well, I guess if you're getting married, you won't really miss the proceedings . . . but you won't be there."

I tried not to smile, knowing Davis was never pleased when I had anything to do other than be at his beck and call.

"My wedding was planned to not conflict with the season, draft, or rookie camps," I added. "But I do hate that I'm going to miss some of the trial."

"You could cancel it," Davis said in reference to my wedding.

I thought he was kidding, but before I could ask to make sure, Mr. Cox asked if there was any more butter.

Six weeks later, with the trial only days away, the same group met in a suite and adjoining room Davis had secured at the Lake Merritt Inn in Oakland. It was lunchtime, and I was in charge of taking their orders and providing lunch.

Davis had worked with his legal team night and day for almost two months, and their comments behind his back respected both his commitment to every detail and wonderment that anyone could maintain such a demanding pace.

"Does he ever come up for air?" Cox asked me while out of earshot of the men in the next room.

"He's here to win," I said with pride.

"I've never been so prepared to win," Cox said, "and I've fought for men's lives in the courtroom. Your boss is one committed son-of-a-bitch. You like working for him?"

"Love it," I said honestly.

Three days before the trial was set to begin, Davis took a moment away from trial preparation to have lunch with Franklin Mieuli, owner of the Golden State Warriors. The Warriors had just won the National Basketball Association championship, and while Davis had season tickets for the team and occasionally attended a basketball game during the football offseason, the victory by the basketball team was, in some ways, a bitter pill.

Davis prided himself on being a genius and running the most dynamic organization in professional sports. But now, even in his team's hometown, he was the only professional franchise without a league championship. The Oakland A's had won three consecutive World Series titles and had just opened their 1975 season in search of a fourth consecutive World Series win. Now the Warriors had won an NBA championship while the Raiders were still without a Super Bowl title.

Mieuli was everything Davis wasn't. The Warriors owner was personable and fun with a penchant for attending parties and celebrating with his team and staff. He showed up wearing his trademark deerskin cap and a hippy-looking wardrobe, in stark contrast to the image Davis cultivated. The Raiders owner did not socialize with staff, even at league parties or media events, and his demeanor was hardly what anyone would consider personable and fun.

These two mismatched men nevertheless enjoyed each other's company, and Davis had agreed to the lunch just prior to the start of his trial against Valley as an acknowledgment of Franklin's huge win over the Washington Bullets in the NBA finals.

I heard Mieuli's high-pitched voice greet Kris when he arrived for his meeting with Davis. I got up to welcome him, and Kris buzzed Beverly to let Davis know his lunch date had arrived.

A few minutes later, Davis came down the stairs, and Mieuli greeted him with the words, "Hey Al, I finally figured out how to win a championship and thought you might be interested."

Davis smiled and said, "How's that, Franklin?"

"Hire someone that knows what they are doing and let them do their job."

The comment blindsided Davis, and he nearly tripped with two stairs left on his descent from upstairs. Mieuli had hired Dick Vertlieb the year before, and his general manager had been named NBA Executive of the Year. But while Mieuli was a hands-off owner, more concerned about his next sailing journey or advertising sale than the running of the Warriors, Davis prided himself on being the final word on every aspect of the Raiders operation.

Davis winced at Mieuli's recommendation, and I turned away to hide my spontaneous smile. Once the swinging glass door shut and the two team owners were outside, headed toward Davis' black Cadillac, Kris turned to me and said, "Was that the funniest thing you ever heard?" We shared a smile.

"Was he mad?" Kris added, having not seen Davis' reaction from where she sat.

"He didn't look happy."

— — — — — —

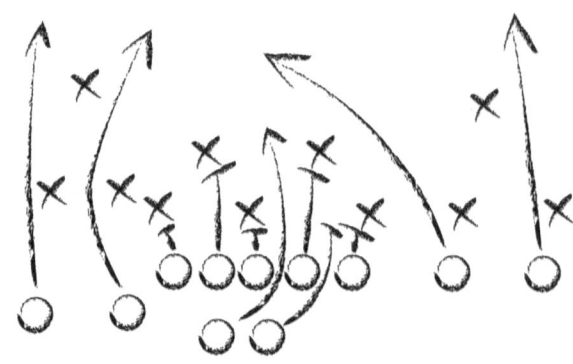

Chapter 29

Mismatch

"I GOT MY SWIMMING POOL LAPS IN THIS MORNING," Gladys Valley said to me as I met her on the stairs in front of the Oakland courthouse the day the trial opened. Wayne Valley, who was walking just behind her, turned away, keeping a cold distance from me, based on my association with Davis. But Mrs. Valley, who had always been approachable during our past meetings at games or on road trips, seemed unaffected by the war her husband and Davis were waging.

I didn't say anything, but kept an eye out for Davis, whom I had dropped off in front of the courthouse. When Davis left his house, he shouted back to his wife, Carole, "Got a little game to win in court today. Wish me luck." He winked at me while Mrs. Davis emerged from the back of the house to wish her husband good luck with a kiss on his cheek.

Davis was loving this conflict. It was like another game day for him.

While I would be married and on my honeymoon before the trial was complete, the days I spent in the courtroom showed clearly that Davis' willingness to do whatever it took to win was going to carry the day.

Opening arguments from Lucas on behalf of Davis were clear, precise, and a perfect balance of legal precedent and the contention that the state of the Raiders under Mr. Davis' leadership was evidence he was entitled to everything negotiated between him and Ed McGah.

The Valley case centered on the contention that as one of the three general partners, Mr. Valley should have been consulted before any contract was agreed upon. Valley's lawyer kept contending, after testimony showed Valley had been apprised that McGah and Davis were negotiating a new contract, that he thought the negotiations were just a "trial balloon" to set the parameters for a new agreement.

As the trial progressed, that contention became less and less powerful. While Davis and his legal team had prepared for all possible arguments, Valley and his lawyer had done little more than hope the "trial balloon" argument would win.

Any possible recovery for the Valley defense hinged on the testimony of Ed McGah, who had coupled his 45-percent voting share with Davis' 10 percent to consummate the contract without Valley's signature. If McGah could be found incompetent, since the once-athletic and powerful businessman was in failing health at 75 years of age, Valley could argue that Davis took unfair advantage of his diminished capacity.

McGah was sometimes confused on the stand during his testimony, often looking up to the judge or around the room for answers that only he could supply. Davis winced as McGah struggled for answers that should have been less difficult.

"He was a lot more stable a few years ago," Davis said at lunch regarding McGah's testimony. "I sure hope he can hold it together under cross-examination."

That afternoon offered a chance for Valley's lawyer to attack McGah and expose his diminished capacity. He could have probably destroyed his longtime business partner on the stand and created a reasonable argument that Davis had preyed on his advanced age to take advantage.

Valley called his lawyer, Robert Burnstein, to the table and had a private exchange. His attorney needed to lean in to hear what was inaudible for the rest of the courtroom. After the exchange, Burnstein addressed McGah in a different tone.

"So you're saying that you allowed this contract to be written because you considered Davis good for the Raiders?"

"I did," McGah said with a smile. Then he looked directly at Judge Staats and added, "We weren't winning before he got here, and we've been winning ever since."

Burnstein looked back at Valley, and the man that had brought Davis to Oakland nodded, motioning with his hand to end the cross-examination. His lawyer cocked his head and said to the judge, "No further questions for this witness."

Valley did not go for the jugular. He did not destroy McGah to win the case. Instead, he went back to the "trial balloon" defense while leaving his most viable argument out of the proceedings.

As I witnessed the exchange, I realized the compassion Valley had demonstrated probably cost him any chance for a verdict in his favor, and I surmised it was a concession Davis would not have made.

I suspected that Davis viewed Valley's compassion as a weakness.

- - - - - -

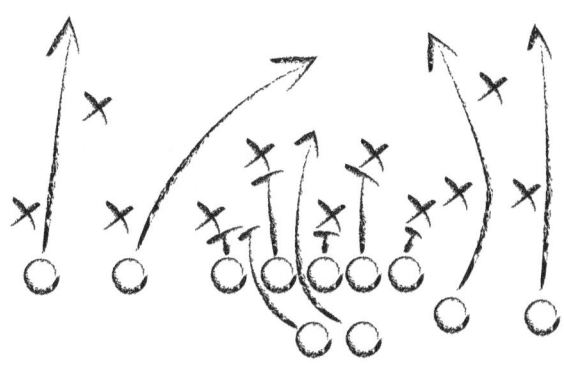

Chapter 30

Hawaii

Aʟ Dᴀᴠɪs ᴡᴀs ɪɴ ᴀɴ ᴜᴘʙᴇᴀᴛ ᴍᴏᴏᴅ on the first Wednesday in June. The trial was going extremely well. He and his lawyers were dominating the action in court. The greatest concern, Ed McGah appearing incompetent, had been averted.

The prospect of winning triggered an even more intense attention to detail, and Davis kept Lucas working past midnight before the Thursday proceedings. I spent more than four hours sitting in the waiting room outside Lucas' San Francisco office. Davis had excused me after dropping him at the TransAmerica Building with the instructions to be back by 9:00 p.m. to pick him up.

I had taken that opportunity to meet Pam in my Alameda apartment and have her bring me up to date on our wedding plans for that weekend. My parents were hosting our rehearsal dinner at Trader Vic's in Emeryville on Friday night, and the wedding was going to be held in Orinda the next day. I had arranged Friday off work to attend to all the details I needed to handle, while Pam and her parents were doing almost all of the wedding preparations.

"How long have you been here?" Davis asked when the door to Lucas' office opened just after 1:00 a.m.

"A few hours, sir," I said dutifully.

"So, how do you think it is going?" Davis posed in a rhetorical tone while we were driving to his Oakland Hills home.

"Very good, sir," I answered.

He made a call and then said, "I need you to pick up today's court transcript at this address in Berkeley after you drop me off at home. And bring them to my house tonight."

I knew, from the time on the clock, that he meant bring them back to his house this morning. It was past 2:00 a.m., but I agreed to his request without any debate.

I knocked on his door at 3:23 a.m. after retrieving the dailies from a mailbox at the Berkeley address he provided. While looking at the first sheet he pulled from the manila envelope, he said, "Be back at seven."

That meant I'd get home sometime after 4:00 a.m. I needed to sleep, take a shower, shave, and be back at his house in less than three hours.

Court was scheduled to begin at 9:00 a.m., and on other court dates, I would pick him up an hour before that time. While driving to my apartment, I pondered this question: Why, on this day, he would move up the starting time an hour? Perhaps because I was off on Friday, he was grinding extra hours out of me. Maybe because the trial seemed so conclusively in our favor, he was pressing not to allow anyone to take anything for granted.

In any case, even for Davis, this time request seemed too demanding. Still, I would be certain to knock on his door at exactly 7:00 a.m.

I'm not sure I ever really fell asleep, but I had showered, shaved, and arrived at his front door on schedule. I knocked on his door and got no immediate response.

Rang the bell.

Nothing.

After another knock, Davis opened the door barefoot, with a sky-blue pair of bell-bottom pants that had appeared to be worn on another day and a white T-shirt. His hair wasn't combed.

"I was working in my office," Davis said with clenched teeth.

"It's 7:00 a.m.," I said without revealing that I could see he just got out of bed and thrown on those clothes.

"Wait for me here," he said, pointing to the white couch in his front room. He headed to the back of the house to shower and prepare for the day in court. I sat on the white couch, smiling. I had just outworked Al Davis. He couldn't even keep the schedule he gave me.

That night, on our ride from the courtroom and his evening meeting with Lucas, Davis reviewed papers he had pulled from his black briefcase. "I'll need you at 8:00 a.m. tomorrow."

"I won't be here tomorrow," I said, pretty sure he already knew that. "I'm getting married on Saturday, and I'll be picking up my tux and taking care of other stuff tomorrow."

"Aren't you going to miss being with me for the rest of the trial?" Davis asked.

I tried to figure out if he was serious or kidding. "Ken Bishop will be driving you," I said, letting him know that his needs would be covered in my absence.

"Won't be the same," Davis said under his breath.

He offered no other comment, but I figured I would see him on Saturday at the wedding.

I didn't.

While some of the coaches—not John Madden—and most of the front office people came to the Santa Maria Church in Orinda on Saturday, Davis did not. I was surprised. I figured that the time I had spent with him over two years, and the dedication I had shown him in long hours of work and availability, would be reason enough for him to attend my wedding.

It was not.

Del Courtney, who had become a good friend, would have attended the wedding, but he was on vacation in Hawaii with his third wife, Nalini. Pam and I were going to Hawaii on our honeymoon, and Courtney had set up a time to meet when we were both in Maui.

Nalini was an attractive lady, not that much older than Pam or me, and Del acted so much younger than his 65 years when he was with her. He had on a blue Hawaiian shirt with white slacks when he greeted us in the lobby of the Westin Kaanapali. Nalini was wearing a Hawaiian one-piece dress with a plunging neckline that offered anyone looking an ample view of her substantial breasts.

Pam was already tan from our two days on the beach; her Italian skin was as comfortable in the sun as my Irish complexion was challenged. I had gotten burned our first afternoon in the sun, and had spent most of the second day of our honeymoon in our beachfront room at the Royal Lahaina.

"Does that hurt?" Nalini asked while eyeing my red face.

"I'm fine," I said, not wanting to be drawn into a conversation about how red my back and chest were.

"You look beautiful," Del said to Pam while giving her a hug and kiss on the cheek.

"Mai tais for all of us?" Del asked while a waitress waited to take our order. Pam laughed and proceeded to tell the story of our first night in Hawaii, when we both got hammered on mai tais.

"Where do you go from here?" Del asked.

"Two more days here in Maui, then the last three days of our honeymoon in Honolulu," I said.

"Oh," Del said, shaking his head. "For a honeymoon, you don't want to spend any time in Oahu. That's just like another big city. You need to go to Kauai. I've got a friend there."

I wasn't offended that Del didn't approve of the honeymoon itinerary I had set up, but I didn't know if our flight could be changed and I could cancel my reservations in Oahu without a penalty.

Del did seem to know.

"No trouble changing reservations," he said. "This is Hawaii. I'll make your reservations with John, my friend, at the Coca Palms. You'll love it. It is where Elvis Presley filmed *Blue Hawaii*."

I turned my attention to Pam. "What do you think?"

"Sounds pretty good to me," she said. "Are you sure we can change our flights and still make our connection home on Monday?"

"That'll be easy," Del confirmed.

"Okay," I agreed, "let's do it."

The Royal Lahaina was perfect and would have been the highlight of our honeymoon if we hadn't changed our plans. Del's friend John met us at the entrance to the Coco Palms, and Pam and I were treated like royalty. Our first night there, after a welcome cocktail party in the center of the resort, we attended the dinner show on the grounds.

The featured singer, who was not Don Ho but sounded a lot like him, had a quartet of beautiful Hawaiian dancers. At one point, while Pam and I sat at a table right next to the stage, he announced that a member of the Oakland Raiders was in attendance tonight, enjoying his honeymoon. "Where are you, Dennis and Pam?" he asked while extending his hand in a welcoming manner.

I sheepishly waved while rising a bit but not fully standing. The entertainer looked at Pam and said, "You have a beautiful wife, and we would like to do this song for you with our hopes that this is the beginning of a wonderful life together."

Pam had a broad smile on her face as he reached out and touched her hand during the song. When it was over, I nodded a thank-you just as a waitress came to our table, holding out a piece of paper and pen.

"You're an Oakland Raider," she said while handing me the paper and pen. "Can I have your autograph?"

"I just work in the front office. I'm not a player," I replied.

"Oh," she said, abruptly grabbing back her pen and paper. "How disappointing."

She turned away without another word. I looked at Pam and burst out laughing.

She remarked, "That was a bit rude."

"She wanted a Raider," I said while still laughing. "She probably only thought I was a player because I was with a lady as attractive as you."

"I think he introduced you as a Raider player from the stage," Pam said.

I glanced around the entire scene. "Well, maybe that is why they are treating us so well."

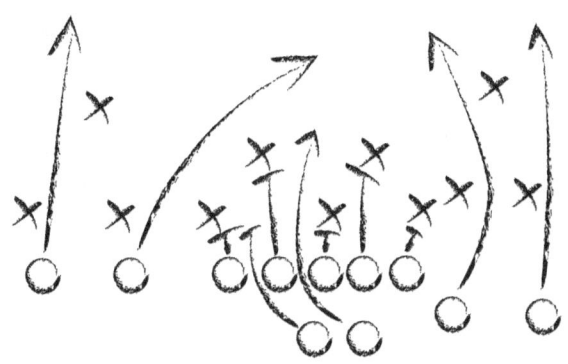

Chapter 31

Sign Him

Aᴛᴛᴇʀ Rᴏɴ Wᴏʟꜰ ᴀɴᴅ Kᴇɴ LᴀRᴜᴇ ʟᴇꜰᴛ for the expansion Tampa Bay Buccaneers, the Raiders organization had two openings: player personnel director and business manager. Ken Herock, who had once played for the Raiders and had served as Wolf's assistant, was hired to replace him. Jim Otto, who was forced by injuries to end his Hall of Fame playing career with the Raiders, was brought in to replace LaRue as business manager.

Tom Grimes, head of the public relations department, even while assisting the coaches and working with Wolf, wanted to move from his position to the scouting department. He had come to the Raiders from the Miami Dolphins and was willing to interview for a player personnel position with both the Raiders and in Florida with Wolf.

Grimes and I were working on the media guide when Beverly buzzed our office and said, "Dennis, Mr. Davis and Ken would like to see you in his office."

"They're asking for Denny now?" Grimes shook his head and said, "What are they going to do now, make you player personnel assistant?"

"I don't know," I remarked, understanding his impatience. Grimes had not yet gotten an answer to his request to meet with Davis about the opening in the player personnel department, and Wolf appeared to be going in a different direction in Tampa.

The door to Davis' office was open at the end of the upstairs hallway, and I stopped before being motioned in by Herock. Davis was behind his desk on the phone.

"We've got something for you to do," Herock said as Davis completed his call. He emerged from behind his desk to join us at his round glass table with a chrome frame. Davis took over for Herock: "I'm telling you, this is an opportunity to see if you've got what it takes to move to the football side of this business."

"There is an offensive lineman we'd like to sign who lives down in San Diego," Herock said.

"Think you're up to it?" Davis adds.

I had flown to Southern California several times to hand-carry contracts for players to be signed at Howard Slusher's office, but those deals were already complete, and I was little more than a messenger. This was going to be a negotiation, and I was given parameters for the contract: numbers for a signing bonus and the maximum amount I could offer on a one-year deal.

"Listen," Davis said, "I know you can do this. What you want to do is get the player in a vulnerable place. Get him thinking he's got to prove himself to you. Challenge the fuck out of his ego. Find a weakness and attack it."

When I didn't respond, he asked, "You want to do this?"

"Yes, sir," I said. I didn't fail to notice that Davis had accomplished with me what he had challenged me to get done with the athlete.

"The Cowboys, Patriots, and Chargers have already all made a run at him, and nobody has signed him yet. Mr. Davis is not authorizing any big bucks to attract him, probably not any more than those teams offered. But see what you can do." Herock handed over the personnel file on offensive lineman Don Buck.

"Listen," Davis said, "you can go as high as a $3,000 signing bonus, which is good for an undrafted rookie, and a standard first-year deal."

On the PSA flight to San Diego, I studied Buck's college stats and measurements along with his time in the 40-yard dash. He had good size for an offensive lineman, and had been named to a number of league all-star squads. But his posted time in the 40-yard dash was 5.8, which was slow even for an offensive lineman. So, I had found a weakness and could use it to our benefit.

Buck was not difficult to spot at the gate as I departed the plane, although he would never have imagined I was the representative from the Raiders he was picking up.

"Don Buck?" I said, extending my hand. He nodded his head while registering surprise. I was so young, only a year older than him. "I'm Dennis Ranahan," I said. "I'm here to see if you want to be a Raider."

He seemed unimpressed, even disappointed that someone so young had been sent to offer him a contract. I remarked, starting to walk away, "Did you have your shoes?"

"What?" he asked, now having to hustle to keep up with me.

"Your shoes?" I said over my shoulder while walking fast toward the airport parking lot.

"What?" he said again, not understanding what I meant.

"When you ran the forty for our scouts, did you have your shoes?"

Finally, he caught up to me and kept pace on my right side.

"Yeah," he said in a somewhat befuddled tone.

"Damn," I said. "Was it raining that day?"

"No," he said, finally registering that his time in the forty was a strike against bringing him to Oakland.

"Damn," I growled. "I was hoping for some reason why you ran so slow that day. Fuck," I said, "are you sure it was as good as you can do?"

"I've been working out. I'm in good shape," Buck quickly put in.

"Say, what's the best restaurant in town?" I asked as Buck took the driver's seat of his 1969 Datsun.

I ordered escargot as an appetizer and recommended the same for him.

"It's snails, right?" he asked, wrinkling his forehead.

"The best snails you ever ate," I assured him. "You should try them."

He didn't know how to work the utensil to hold the snail steady, and he shot one across the table and under the lit candle. In most cases, I would have laughed and told him about the first time I had tried the delicacy. But this time, I didn't. I let him retrieve the snail shell on the table and struggle with the pliers-like tool and small fork. In the meantime, I went to his stats and pulled out a contract.

"Why do you think you can make up for your lack of speed?" I said without looking up.

"All I need is a chance," Buck pleaded. He took the snail shell in his chubby hand.

"You understand that the greatness of the Raiders has always been anchored by a superior offensive line," I told him. "Coach Madden thinks the front line on offense is the most important position on the field. You get all the advantages of a rich history with the Raiders. Let me tell you something, even if it didn't work out with us, if you couldn't crack our roster, all 25 other teams are looking for athletes the Raiders release to add to their roster."

Buck was nodding to everything I said. He seemed eager to prove himself.

"I suspect other teams have offered you deals," and he nodded yes. "But if you go with another team and don't make their roster, you're probably done. Here, if you make it with the Raiders, you're in. You're with the best organization in all of the sports."

Buck's head was nodding up and down like a bobblehead in the back of a '57 Chevy.

"The Raiders are your launching pad. You either play with the best offensive linemen in the game, or you get another opportunity with a team looking for the players that don't make our roster." I had him fully engaged even before our main course arrived.

"We've got a choice here," I said, becoming more deliberate. "We can get this thing done, make you a Raider, and enjoy dinner when it arrives as teammates. Or you can take your stats, and that goddamn time in the forty, and see if you can get a better offer from someone else."

"Do I get a bonus for signing?" Buck asked.

"Undrafted players don't usually get a bonus," I said. "I'd have to sell that to Al Davis. He'd be aware of your screwed-up time in the forty, and probably wonder if you had your shoes or it was raining that day."

Buck's head dropped, and he clenched his fists. "I'd really like to prove myself. I can play."

"You had the prime rib medium rare," the waiter confirmed while placing my dinner in front of me. "And you, the rib eye medium," he said to Don.

"Oh, that's good," I beamed after taking my first bite of the meal. "This was a good suggestion for a restaurant, Don. Good job."

"Okay," Buck stated, "I want to play for the Raiders. But the Patriots offered me a bonus to sign."

"That's because they have to," I remarked. "They don't have anything else to offer except money. How's your steak?"

"They offered me $1,500 to sign," Buck persisted.

"Did you meet with the Cowboys?" I asked.

"Yeah," he confirmed.

"Did they offer you a bonus?"

"No."

"Because they are offering you the Cowboys, just like I'm offering you the Raiders. When you're a great team, you have more to offer someone like yourself. Get cut by New England and you're finished. Get released by Dallas somewhat, and Oakland for sure, and your career in the NFL could just be starting."

Buck was silent.

"Listen," I counseled, "you just got out of college. A little money right now would probably really help. Right?"

Buck nodded.

"Tell you what I'm going to do. I'm going to give you the best of both worlds. I'm going to raise the Patriots bonus offer and have you become a Raider. Would you go for that?"

He choked out an emphatic yes while swallowing a mouthful of food.

"A two-thousand-dollar bonus and a contract with the Raiders," I offered, turning my attention from the food to the contract I carried in a manila folder. Buck signed before dessert arrived.

The next morning at the office, Davis was pleased that I accomplished the objective of signing Buck and got the deal done for two-thirds of the bonus money I was given to negotiate.

"How did you get it done?" Davis requested while Herock checked over the signature and terms.

"I took your advice, sir. I focused on his weakness, his time in the forty."

"Fuckin' kid has got it," Davis said.

When I walked into the PR office, Grimes said without looking up from his typewriter, "So you got the kid signed. So who are you now: Mr. Davis' golden boy or my assistant?"

— — — — — —

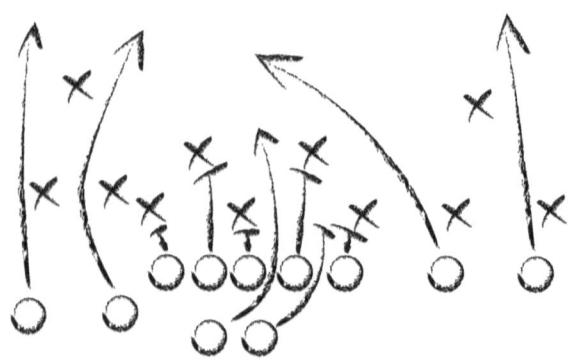

Chapter 32

Monday Night
Dolphins

THE RAIDERS WERE SCHEDULED TO OPEN the 1975 season on the road against the Miami Dolphins and then play the second week at Baltimore.

As early as April, when Grimes and I attended the National Football League public relations meetings in Tampa, Madden had decided he wanted to keep his team on the East Coast after the Dolphins. Grimes and I scouted the University of South Florida campus for a possible site to house the Raiders and their practices.

"There are a lot of young distractions there," Grimes noted. "At least there was when Denny and I visited the campus last month." Madden brushed ash off his plaid coaching pants from a Chesterfield cigarette.

"That was during the school year. If we stayed there the first week of September, though, it would be before fall classes started," Grimes went on. "I understand you wanting to get the team out of Miami and on to their next game site on a standard travel schedule."

"That's what I want," Madden said while flicking another cigarette ash toward the wastebasket at the foot of my desk.

The Miami Dolphins were two-time Super Bowl champions and hadn't lost a home game in three years, an all-time record 27-game home winning streak. The Raiders had snapped Miami's unbeaten string in 1973, ended their reign as Super Bowl champions in 1974, and now were forced to open on the road to kick off the 1975 *Monday Night Football* schedule against Don Shula's squad. Yet this year, the Dolphins are different, and presumably not for the better.

In the biggest deal of the fledging World Football League, three key offensive players, Larry Csonka, Jim Kiick, and Paul Warfield, had ditched the Dolphins and the NFL.

"They couldn't be more focused on beating us than any team in the league," Al LoCasale put in. He had, for his part, located a private school in Alexandria, Virginia, that offered the Raiders housing in an unoccupied dormitory. After more scouting, LoCasale turned down the living accommodations there in favor of the facilities available at the nearby Marriott. He did, however, rent the field and locker room at the private school for the week leading up to our bus ride to Baltimore.

On Wednesday before the season opener, Grimes headed for Miami to deal with the media, and I went to Virginia to ensure the practice field, housing, meals, and transportation for the Raiders stay were all set up properly.

I called Larry, the owner of the company that supplied the vans to carry the luggage from the team flight to the Marriott. I called him at

2:00 a.m. on Monday morning, as we had agreed, and he answered the call. "This is what time your vans have to be at the airport tomorrow for the arrival of the team from Miami," I informed him.

"I got it," he replied, adding, "you know, you can trust me. This is not my first rodeo."

My concern was Al Davis and his football team would be arriving in the middle of the night, and they would be tired for certain, and in a foul mood if they didn't beat the Dolphins. "Everything matters" had been drummed into me by Davis, and a smooth trip from the airport to the hotel was essential to set up a productive week.

"I just want you to know that this is the Raiders, and it has to be perfect," I reiterated.

"I got it," Larry said, sounding amused at my thoroughness.

When I arrived, the field and locker rooms LoCasale secured were smaller than the Raiders were accustomed to. The showerheads were at a height for the size of an average young man, and the Raiders would have to lean over to wash above their chest. Plus, the field was tucked between dense, mature trees, with dimensions that didn't appear to be regulation.

Afterward, I took a drive around the area and spotted the freeway exit sign for Laurel, the Maryland city where George Wallace had been shot a few years earlier. I took the turnoff and found the shopping center where it happened. When I got back to the Marriott, just after 5 p.m., I took the elevator up to my room, and two gentlemen in suits were talking about the Monday night game.

"I hope they kick the Raiders ass," one remarked, and his friend agreed, "I hate Oakland. Can't stand them."

I smiled as I stepped off the elevator. It was not yet 6 p.m., with more than three hours before the Monday night kickoff. I was used to the Pacific Time zone, where the *Monday Night Football* game kicked off at 6:00. I ordered room service—a steak sandwich with fries and a Coke—before turning on the television to catch a sports report. The sports coverage was interrupted by a special news bulletin announcing that President Gerald Ford had been the victim of an assassination attempt in San Francisco.

A few weeks earlier, I visited the site where Kennedy was assassinated in Dallas while we were in Texas to play the Cowboys in a preseason game, and Lynette Fromme took a shot at Ford. Now I went by Laurel and he got shot at again. I made up my mind then not to visit any more assassination sites, for Ford's sake.

Howard Cosell was flanked by Alex Karras and Frank Gifford as the *Monday Night Football* crew set up the season-opening game. Much of their pregame patter was focused on the changes the Dolphins were forced to make after the defections of their three star players.

Once the game started, it was clear that the Dolphins offense was overmatched by the Raiders defense. We scored the first 17 points of the game before Miami finally got on the scoreboard with a touchdown late in the first half. The only score in the third quarter was a Mark van Eeghen touchdown run. Miami countered with a Norm Bulaich TD dive on the first play of the fourth quarter to cut the lead back to 10 points. Harold Hart then returned the ensuing kickoff 102 yards to push the lead back to 17 and the Raiders never lost control of the contest on their way to a convincing 31–21 road triumph.

We did lose one player for the season with a knee injury. Kelvin Korver, a second-round draft choice in 1972, wasn't on the Raiders flight to National Airport that evening. Instead, he flew to Los Angeles, where Bob Rosenfeld would examine his knee the next day for possible surgery.

During the game in Miami, the weather in Virginia had turned nasty, with torrential downpours and high winds. I decided as soon as the game was over to head for National Airport and make sure the buses and vans were in place for when the Raiders flight arrived.

The United charter was scheduled to taxi to a facility away from the main terminal, a loading dock area mostly used for cargo. I confirmed with one of the workers on-site which way the plane would taxi in to make sure the buses were on the same side as the ramp the players would use to exit the aircraft.

"Haven't seen rain like this in a long while," he said while shielding his eyes. The downpour was moving almost sideways in the wind. "The luggage comes off on that side," he motioned, "the passengers on this side. Are your vans here for the baggage?"

Just then, Larry came sloshing through the rain and announced he had a problem. "One of his vans had a blowout and slipped into a ditch in the mud."

"So now what?"

"Well, because you made such a deal of no mistakes during last night's call and all, I had another driver and van on standby to make sure we didn't have any problems. But in this weather—and I just got ahold of him—I'm not sure he is going to be here before the flight lands."

"But he is coming," I confirmed.

"Yep," Larry said. "Glad I took the precaution of having a third van standing by."

"If he gets here on time, perfect," I said. "But if he arrives after the flight, what will we do?"

"What can we do?" he queried. "I'll wait for him, and we'll load all we can onto my van as soon as the plane stops and get the rest when he arrives."

"How long is this plane scheduled to sit here after we arrive?" I asked the airport representative.

"It's your charter," the worker said. "I don't think it will be moving out of here anytime soon, given it won't be here until 3:40 a.m."

"I can get the stuff off the plane and wait for the van if we need to," Larry confirmed.

"But in this rain? I want the bags going right from the cargo bay to inside your van," I insisted.

"You're right," Larry nodded.

An hour later, moments before the Raiders charter taxied up to our location, the three buses were in place and the extra driver had arrived.

"We're all set," Larry announced.

"Great job," I told him. "How do you like working for the Raiders?"

"You guys run a tight ship," he assured me. "It's because of that boss of yours, isn't it?"

"You don't want to tell Al Davis that you missed something."

Just before 4:00 a.m., the players filed off the plane in near silence and immediately took a seat on the waiting buses. Many looked like they did not want to wake up from the sleep they got on the flight out of Miami. I stood there with pride as the rain continued to pour.

"Everything okay?" Tom Grimes asked me as I stood with an umbrella at the bottom of the ramp the players were using to leave the jet.

"All good," I confirmed to him.

But Davis heard my response and inserted, "It's not all good. We lost a player tonight. We've got to fill that hole."

He was not celebrating the win over the Dolphins. He was focused on the next challenge, which included finding a defensive lineman to fill the roster void created by Korver's injury.

The following afternoon, I got instructions to pick up Korver's replacement on Wednesday morning at National Airport. The Raiders had made a deal to acquire Dave Rowe from the San Diego Chargers.

Rowe was easy to spot coming off his plane, and I extended my hand, welcoming him to the Raiders.

"Kind of all happening pretty fast," he said with a smile.

"You got luggage to get?" I asked as we walked from his gate.

"All I've got is in this bag," he said, lifting his carry-on.

Moments later, we slipped inside the rent-a-car that a guard had allowed me to park on the curb at the arrival area.

Rowe was in extremely high spirits for someone who had just been traded and taken a red-eye flight to Washington that began with a leg from San Diego to Los Angeles.

"I feel great," Rowe confirmed. "I'm with the Raiders. On Sunday, my team lost 37–0 to the Steelers, and now I'm on the team that beat the Dolphins in Miami. Although I don't think Coach Prothro enjoyed our last meeting."

"Why?" I asked.

"He calls me into his office after practice yesterday and says, 'I've got some bad news. You've just been traded to the Raiders.' To which I replied, 'What's the bad news?'"

— — — — — —

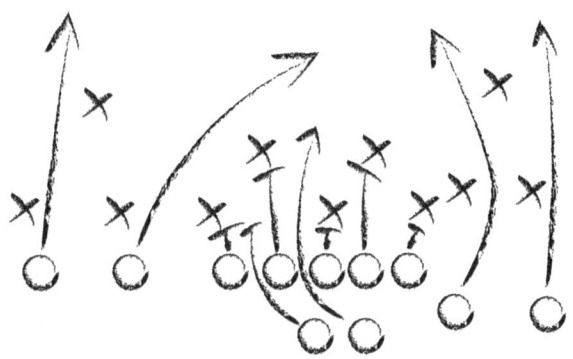

Chapter 33

Doors
and Tunnels

Madden wanted to keep on a normal week's schedule as much as we could while living in a hotel and practicing on a strange field. On Friday, we had our last practice at the boys' private school, mostly working on special teams, and checked out of the Alexandria Marriott. The Baltimore Hilton was about 50 miles from our hotel in Virginia, and the trip was expected to take a little over an hour.

After practice, I put on dress pants and wore a coat and tie. That was how I traveled with the team on the airplane, so I thought Madden would appreciate my efforts to have this be as much like a normal Friday trip as possible.

"You didn't have to dress up for the bus ride," Madden laughed upon seeing me. "For Christ's sake, it's a goddamn bus ride."

I didn't tell him I had done it for his benefit, but did say, "This is how I always dress for a Friday travel day."

We arrived at the Baltimore Hilton after a caravan of three buses took nearly two hours to complete the journey. Tom Grimes had rented a car and was already waiting. Tables were set up in the lobby with envelopes that included a player's room key and the itinerary for the weekend, which ended with the words, "WE GO TO WAR," at the designated game time on Sunday.

"Here is your per diem for the weekend," Jim Otto said while handing me an envelope that contained two bills, a fifty and a twenty.

The players had been served a late lunch before we left Virginia, and the dinner was scheduled for 8:30, about 90 minutes after our arrival in Baltimore. They also had a Friday night curfew imposed at 11:00.

"I want you on the floors now," Madden instructed while I stood in the hallway outside the room that was beginning to fill up with players arriving for their meal. "I want you patrolling their floor now until curfew. I want a quiet Friday night."

"Sir?" I asked, thinking I might have misunderstood him.

"If you stay on top of it now, while the players are down here and the girls are looking for them, they won't be able to get in their rooms," Madden told me.

"You want me to guard their rooms now until curfew at 11:00?" I clarified, still hoping I had heard wrong.

"Right," Madden said as he turned and marched into the dining room.

A herd of young girls with heavy makeup had been positioned in the lobby when we arrived, and they mingled with the players while they were picking up their keys. Even though the athletes had been warned not to let anyone stay in their room while they weren't there, a few of them might well be watching TV or whatever while waiting for a player to return from his dinner.

Dick Romanski spotted me eyeing the girls.

"You don't want any of that stuff," he said on his way to the team meal.

I shook my head, used to seeing the litters of women the players were exposed to and seemingly having their pick. With that in mind, I asked Romanski, "Do all of the players screw around?"

Romanski took measured aim at my question and answered it definitely and in a very serious tone, "Cotton Davidson didn't."

Baylor graduate Cotton Davidson played for the Raiders from 1962 to 1969, and he served as a plum line for living a straight-lace and principled life.

As I walked down the hall, I could hear and smell them.

Both the sixth and seventh floors had areas that reeked with the thick smell of perfume. I first took the elevator to the seventh floor and used the stairways on the far end of each hallway to change between the sixth and seventh floors for my round trip, which took about ten minutes.

I was about to start my fourth tour of the player rooms when I considered knocking on the doors that I heard the noises coming from and asking any person that wasn't with the Raiders to leave the floor.

Instead, I decided that I would confront any ladies outside the rooms, but honor that if they were already in the room, they were probably an invited guest of a player, and I wouldn't bother them. Three times I spotted ladies that didn't belong on the floor, twice at the elevator and once when three young girls were wandering the sixth floor.

About a quarter to eleven, the players started arriving at their rooms, and they seemed somewhat subdued. Whether that was because we had been on the road for a week or they already had girls waiting for them in their rooms, I'm not sure. But not too long after 11:00, everyone was accounted for, and Ken Bishop took over my guard duties.

"Go get something to eat," Bishop offered. "I'll watch the floors."

The dining area the Raiders had used was all cleaned up. No food, not even a bread roll, was left on any of the tables. The doors to the kitchen were locked, and I went out to the lobby to ask the hotel's concierge where I could get something to eat.

Strikingly attractive, she looked like a young Sophia Loren. She took the time to check for any food available in the hotel before acknowledging that there was not this late. "But there is a sandwich shop across the street," she offered. "Just be careful; this is not a good neighborhood."

"Is it worth the sandwich?"

"It's a good sandwich," she confirmed, "but keep your eyes open."

Baltimore had a light rainfall in the afternoon, and the streets were still glistening in the streetlights. A streetcar ran on tracks between the two lanes headed west and the two lanes headed east. I let it go past before darting across all four lanes just after a cab went by. I jumped over a puddle near the gutter on the other side of the street and slipped without falling in my black dress shoes on the wet sidewalk in front of the sandwich shop. My clumsiness got the attention of two Black guys standing near a garbage can and smoking cigarettes.

They followed me into the sandwich shop, and when it came time to pay the $2.14 for the sandwich, Coke, and chips I ordered, I realized I had two bills in my pocket, the fifty and the twenty. I hoped that the one bill I pulled out of my pocket was the twenty.

It was.

The person with the white apron that made my sandwich struggled with how much change I should get.

"Do you have anything smaller?" he asked while looking in his cash register.

I wished he hadn't said that. I didn't want my money to become an issue in front of the two possible thugs. "No."

He found a ten under the cash tray and counted out my change. Only he lost track partway through and needed to start over. I felt like a bull's-eye for these two stalkers salivating over the prospect of separating me from my cash. I put the change in my pocket, said thank you, and headed for the street.

The two guys rushed out of the sandwich shop and positioned themselves between me and the front door of the Hilton. Fortunately, I knew of a side door that I had used at least two times earlier while moving stuff from Dick Romanski's truck into a storage area.

I reached the door while they were trotting to run me down. I put my hand on the side doorknob, and only then did the chilling prospect of pulling on a locked knob occur to me. Sure enough, it was solidly locked. My fate appeared sealed.

I turned away from the door, hoping to part only with the money and not getting beat up or worse. The guy on the left was wearing old soiled pants and shirt but with brand-new tennis shoes. "Whacha doin', buudddy."

I focused on him, although his partner, also dressed in dirty rags with a new pair of white tennis shoes, became more of an immediate threat. He held up his hand while making a claw. He was lunging for my neck when the locked door suddenly flew open. My friend Henry Lawrence, all 6' 4", 270 pounds of him, filled the doorway.

"Do we have a problem here, Dennis?" Henry asked. His question prompted a quick retreat from my adversaries. As they scampered away, all we could see in the dark of night was the bottoms of two pairs of white tennis shoes. I turned to Henry in thanks. "Not anymore."

We shared a smile, and I added, "That is the best curfew you ever broke. Please enjoy your evening out with my blessings. Thank you, thank you, thank you."

"You shouldn't be out here," Henry said, putting his hand on my shoulder as we began walking to the front of the hotel. "It's a dangerous neighborhood."

"Then you take care of yourself," I replied. My silver-and-black knight jumped into the back of a cab parked outside the front door of the Hilton and went off to who knows where.

Maybe to see a relative.

The next day, the Raiders had an early afternoon practice on the Colts home field, Baltimore Memorial Stadium. I was standing on the sideline with Tom Grimes, who had an appointment with the NBC broadcast team to bring them up to date on player news and depth charts.

"We need a few more programs and flip cards," Grimes noted, requesting that I go back into the locker room and fetch them from the box he left in the coach's office.

I was on my way to get the materials when a voice got my attention.

"You're getting those for me. Let me go with you." In a flash, I knew who he was; it was Johnny Unitas.

As a kid, I grew up thinking the word "unitas" was a common noun. It meant what a person needed to do in order to be a perfect quarterback. Not until I was 10 did I realize Unitas was actually someone's name. Johnny Unitas played a pivotal role in the growth of football in the '50s and '60s. NBC had broadcast the NFL Championship Game between the New York Giants and Baltimore Colts in 1958, a contest that included a Unitas-led fourth-quarter comeback and an overtime win. The game was credited for the birth of the popularity now enjoyed by football on television.

In 1975, Unitas was again connected to NBC, this time as a color commentator on the network. His broadcast schedule included tomorrow's contest between Oakland and the team he led to those championships, the Baltimore Colts.

"You don't need to do that, sir," I said while holding up both hands.

"Nonsense," Unitas replied, "I'll walk with you."

"My name is Dennis, Mr. Unitas," I said while extending my hand.

After he grabbed it, Unitas remarked while pulling me toward him, "You don't have to call me mister. I'm John."

"I know as a staff member, I'm here to be professional with you and make sure you have all the materials you need," I said, almost out of breath. "But I just want you to know that while I'll get you anything you need, I'm really just an awestruck fan of yours."

"Well, you can be that, and we can still get the programs together," Unitas laughed. "Just make sure you call me John."

We went into the locker room through the long tunnel that had been a staple at Memorial Stadium for almost twenty years. Its significance didn't hit me until we were coming back out of the locker room. Through that tunnel, Johnny Unitas so often ran in on his way to play those historic games. The realization that I was walking through this tunnel with Johnny Unitas overwhelmed me. I wasn't about to faint, but I certainly felt lightheaded and needed to stop.

"Okay," I told him. "This is where my fan is taking over. I'm walking from the Colts locker room and down this tunnel at Memorial Stadium with Johnny Unitas. This is the greatest," I said, catching my breath with both hands on my knees.

"No big deal," Unitas said with a twinkle in his eye. I could tell he appreciated my admiration for him.

"Pretty big deal," I managed to say as I regained my composure.

— — — — — —

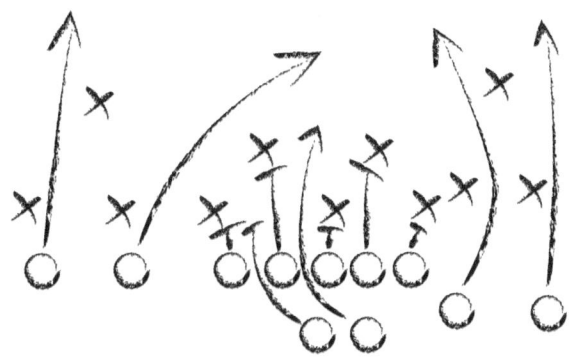

Chapter 34

Cincinnati
in Bed

In 1974, THE BALTIMORE COLTS HAD WON only two games, costing head coach Howard Schnellenberger his job. He was replaced by Ted Marchibroda, and in his first game, the Colts had beaten the Bears in Chicago, 35–7. They were still decided underdogs against the Raiders, though.

Sleeping all week in a hotel and using unfamiliar practice facilities often add up to a recipe for a poor outing, and that's not counting the emotional win against the Dolphins. In the first half, the Raiders were out of sync and flat against the undermanned Colts. Baltimore led at halftime, 13–10, but Oakland scored three second-half touchdowns to churn out a 31–20 road triumph.

The next Sunday, Dave Rowe was back in San Diego to challenge his old Charger teammates, and the Raiders scored only two field goals, but that was enough to edge Prothro's winless squad, 6–0.

The following Sunday, Madden was able to crack a smile in the postgame press conference even after his team was beaten, 42–10, by the Chiefs at Arrowhead Stadium. "We almost killed Warpath," Madden said in reference to the Chiefs horse, which circled the field each time the Chiefs scored.

I also took note that David Humm, the fifth-round draft selection that Wolf had recommended after I suggested to Davis that we not take Dave Wasick, saw action in the fourth quarter and threw our only scoring pass of the day, a nine-yard completion to Cliff Branch in the final minute. As I could have predicted, Wasick, who was drafted by Kansas City, was not on the Chiefs roster.

Four weeks were done, and only one more week on the road remained before the Raiders would finally open their home schedule for 1975. The team had not looked sharp since the opening Monday night win, and the Cincinnati Bengals posed a real threat in week five.

It also ended up posing a personal problem for me. Steve Ballard, who worked in the accounting office with the Raiders, had relatives in Cincinnati. He had never been taken on a road trip with the team but had been promised he could come when the Raiders visited the Bengals. The problem was, he made the mistake of showing his enthusiasm to go on the Monday after we got clobbered by the Chiefs. After a loss, Al LoCasale always demanded a solemn demeanor from everyone.

"I haven't been back in six years," Ballard told Kris outside the public relations office. "I'm going to spend Saturday with all my cousins, and then on Sunday, I've got a couple of tickets to share."

LoCasale overheard Ballard as he walked from his office down the hallway. "I don't think there is room on the flight for you."

Ballard didn't say anything, and I raised my head to see his reaction. He looked like a kid that was just told Santa Claus wasn't going to visit his house this Christmas. He didn't argue the point but instead sheepishly turned away and headed up the back stairs to his desk.

"Steve has been looking forward to this trip for months," I told LoCasale while he thumbed through the mail on Kris' desk.

"Unless you want to give him your seat, there is no room for him," LoCasale said shortly.

I checked with Tom Grimes to see if he and Ken Bishop could manage the duties the three of us perform on the road. I also voiced my opinion that it was shitty LoCasale would crush Steve's one opportunity to take a trip and visit relatives.

"I'm not sure you want to make yourself expendable," Grimes cautioned but agreed to cover for me in Cincinnati if that really did allow Ballard to make the trip. "Think about it overnight before you do anything drastic."

"I'd love for you to be home this weekend," Pam confided that night at dinner. "But don't you want to go?"

Pam had started working as a registered nurse at Merritt Hospital in Oakland, and as a new hire, she began her career on the night shift. She left our Alameda apartment for work around 10:30 p.m. and usually got home before 8:00 a.m. On most evenings, I got home by nine so we could have dinner together before she left, and on some nights, I would go back to work when she headed to the hospital.

We hadn't seen a lot of each other during our first few months of marriage. Actually, we hadn't seen too much of each other since I went to work for the Raiders while she finished up her last two years of college. I always thought how fortunate I was to have met her at San Jose State because the schedule I worked with the Raiders would never allow me to start a relationship now.

Also, as much as I enjoyed traveling with the team, this was our fifth straight week on the road, and spending a weekend at home seemed like an attractive alternative.

On Tuesday morning, I knocked on LoCasale's open door before entering his office. He motioned me in, and I dropped into his black leather couch.

"I really feel for Steve," I said. "He was really looking forward to this trip. He has relatives in Cincinnati."

"No room for him on the flight," LoCasale said without looking up.

"Well, I've talked it over with Tom, and he has agreed that he could manage without me on this trip. I would like to give my seat to Steve."

That shocked him. In an instant his glare registered both surprise and contempt for me taking him up on his offer to give up my seat.

"That would be stupid for you to do," he said. "What if Al needs you? What if John needs you? You really want to just not be there?"

"No," I said. "I want to be there, but this trip is a once-in-a-lifetime opportunity for Steve. I know how much he was looking forward to it."

"You're stupid," LoCasale repeated. "If Mr. Davis wants you and you're not there, you will have to pay a price."

"I'll be at the airport when the flight leaves if I'm needed, and I'll be there on Sunday night when you get home."

"Ranahan of the Raiders wasn't strong enough to make five straight trips, huh?" LoCasale said in a condescending tone. "Okay, you're off the manifest. Your call, Ballard goes."

The Raiders charter to Cincinnati departed the Oakland Airport on Friday afternoon, and on Saturday morning, I woke up in our Alameda apartment before Pam got home from work. It was the strangest feeling. Davis and the team were gone, and the phone was not going to ring to tell me to meet someone at the airport or pick up something at the office or Davis' house. Other than my honeymoon in Hawaii, I couldn't remember a time when I felt so detached.

I liked it.

Pam had been telling me for weeks that she wanted a shade in our bedroom so she could sleep better during the day. Now I knew why. The curtains were closed, but hardly blocked any of the sunlight pouring into the room. That afternoon, while she was sleeping, I installed a pull-down shade. As quiet as I tried to be, I did wake her, and she smiled while watching me first attach the brackets and then hang the shade.

"Wow," she said as I pulled down the newly installed shade and blocked the sun from the room. "It's nice having a man around to do things."

"It's nice to have time to do things."

"I switched weekends with Shirley," Pam told me. "So I'm off tonight."

"Super," I said. "I want to spend every moment with you this weekend."

That weekend in Alameda was better than our honeymoon in Hawaii. For the first day in months, I didn't go into the office. We ate out on Saturday night in Jack London Square without the threat of a call from Al Davis for me to do something somewhere. Even our time together in our own apartment seemed more pleasant, free from a possible call to go to work.

"I could get used to this," I whispered in her ear as we lay in bed after enjoying a bottle of wine and each other.

"I've missed you." Pam snuggled forward and dropped her head on my chest.

Two of the candles we lit the night before were still burning when we woke up. One other had burned down, and all that was left was the metal base and remaining wax around the black wick. The room was dark, the first morning we had woken up in this room without sunlight pouring through the window.

"What time is it?" Pam asked, lifting her head off my arm to check the alarm clock.

"I don't know," I said without opening my eyes.

"Ten twenty-six," she cried in a voice that was both louder and surprised.

"Oh, my God," I groaned, still not opening my eyes. "I missed the kickoff."

The Raiders-Bengals game was scheduled to kick off at 10:00. Yet I didn't leap up to turn on the television. Instead, I just lay next to Pam, enjoying her and my newfound freedom.

"Let's see what's going on." Pam crawled to the foot of our bed and turned on the portable color television on top of our dresser. There was no score, we had the ball, and Ken Stabler had just completed a pass to Cliff Branch for a first down at the Bengals 29-yard-line.

Pam was making coffee when, early in the second quarter, Clarence Davis dove over the right side for one yard and a Raiders touchdown. After George Blanda converted the extra point, we led 7–0.

That turned out to be our only touchdown of the game, and the Bengals scored one on offense in the second quarter and returned a Stabler interception 52 yards for another en route to a 14–10 home victory.

That night I felt like a pair of brown shoes waiting for a tuxedo when the players, coaches, and staff arrived at the Oakland Airport from Cincinnati. Only Grimes greeted me like I had not abandoned the team, but that was probably because he and I were headed to the office to do the stats and prepare this week's press release.

John Madden walked by like I was an opponent. Davis stopped, eyed me with disdain, and said, "Seems like you've got some decisions to make. You've got to decide what's important to you."

It was as if Davis sensed my enjoyment in being away from the team.

"Did you have a nice weekend?" LoCasale remarked in a manner grounded in accusation and contempt.

"I wish the team had a better one," was all I could reply.

– – – – – –

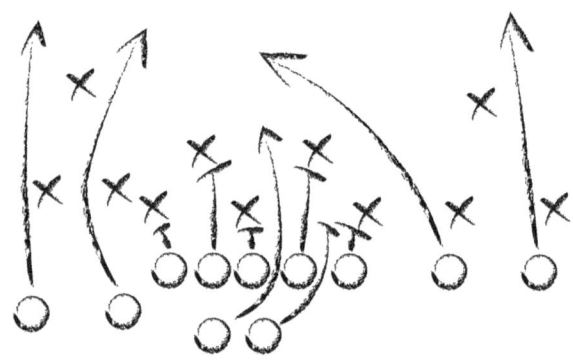

Chapter 35

Halftime

THE FOLLOWING SUNDAY, IN OUR HOME OPENER, we again held the San Diego Chargers off the scoreboard, and, this time, tallied 25 points for an easy win. The next week, though, the Raiders had a critical AFC West matchup against the improved Denver Broncos.

The Mile High crowd was sun-drenched on an unseasonably warm first Sunday in November. They also enjoyed the action on the field as the underdog Broncos battled Oakland to a 7–7 tie through most of two quarters. The partisan Broncos crowd was on their feet and cheering as Ken Stabler surrendered an interception to Randy Gradishar in the final minute of the first half to set up the Broncos in field goal range. Davis, sitting to my left, was at first upset with the lost possession. Yet he soon focused on what could be a much bigger setback.

"Don't be fuckin' hurt," Davis murmured at a volume only I could hear. On the field, trainer George Anderson and team physician Bob Albo were hurrying from the sideline after being motioned by Raiders offensive guard Gene Upshaw to attend to the quarterback. Stabler was lying on his back and rocking in pain while holding both knees toward his chest.

"Don't be fuckin' hurt," Davis said again.

With his arms out to the side, Stabler had one leg bent at the knee with his foot planted in the turf. His right leg was stretched straight by the doctor.

"He's not hurt," Davis cheered, as much in hope as could be immediately known from our perspective. His diagnosis of healthy gained credence as Stabler rose to his feet and was able to make it to the sideline under his own power. Snake declined offers of assistance from Anderson and Albo, who walked on each side of the reigning Most Valuable Player.

"He's not hurt," Davis reaffirmed as Stabler applied more weight to his right leg as he headed toward a seat on the bench.

"He'd be in the locker room right now if it was bad," Davis remarked.

I nodded in agreement without taking my eyes off Stabler. Dr. Albo held up his finger in front of the quarterback, asking him to follow it with his eyes. Meanwhile, the half ended with a successful Broncos field goal. Stabler was still sitting with Albo as the players headed toward the end zone and into the locker room behind it.

Even though Stabler appeared to be merely shaken up, Davis wanted to know what the injury was and if it would affect his second-half availability. "Go find out from George," Davis ordered.

Davis' request would force me to enter the Raiders locker room at halftime, sacred ground for John Madden. Even though I'd been on staff for three years, I'd been on the sidelines only a few times during a game, and never had I ventured into the Raiders locker room during their halftime ritual.

Everyone working the game wears a credential that allows access to their area of responsibility. Credentials are used to identify stadium workers, media, and team personnel that have legitimate business on the field, in the press box or locker room. Before I worked for the Raiders, I never knew what that tag was hanging off Madden's belt loop on game days. It looked like a laundry or price tag.

My credential allowed me access anywhere in the stadium, and while it was designed to be worn outside a person's clothing by a string looped through a hole punched on one side, I kept mine in the breast pocket of my suit jacket. Usually, I preferred that the guards get to know me by sight, but for this halftime trip, I attached the credential to my jacket button.

The most direct route to the locker room at Mile High Stadium is walking through the crowd to the first row behind the Broncos bench and jumping down five feet to the playing field level. I was just touching down when a pair of guards approached from either side.

I held up my credential and quickly erased their concern that I was trespassing. "I'm with the Raiders," I told them while they verified my credential. "I've got to check on something in the locker room."

Both nodded approval and allowed me to pass.

I made my way to a blue door in the back of the end zone. I pointed to my credential for the benefit of the security guard stationed at the locker room entrance and pushed the door open.

At the Oakland Coliseum, the entrances to the locker rooms are ten yards down a cement walkway, with the Raiders on the left and the visitors to the right. Yet once I stepped through the blue door at Mile High Stadium, I entered the Raiders locker room directly.

The opening door got more attention than I wanted. The first group I saw was the running backs sitting together to the left. Two were stretched out on the floor, two on a wooden bench, and the fifth, Clarence Davis, was sitting in a folding chair with his legs stretched out in front of him and his feet six inches in the air.

As he spotted me, his legs lowered to the ground, and he cocked his head sideways, trying to deduce why I had shown up. Dick Romanski was hurrying to fill the requests of equipment adjustments some players were requesting for the second half. When Romanski saw me, he was stunned. With a questioning look in his eye, he asked, "What are you doing in here?"

"Davis wants me to get Kenny's status from George," I replied.

"You're a brave man," Romanski commented. He pointed at Anderson, who was retaping wide receiver Fred Biletnikoff's left ankle on a training table positioned outside the training room, in full view of most of the locker room.

When I asked him, Anderson was annoyed by my question. All he said, though, was that Stabler was fine. I knew Davis wanted a more detailed report than that, and I pressed him. Anderson quickly satisfied my request to get me out of his hair. "He's not hurt. He'll play in the second half. He's fine."

I could see Madden beginning to move across the locker room in my direction.

"Tell him he's fine," George replied, this time explaining that the injury was more of a cramp than anything else. He hadn't seen Madden moving our way as he recommended, "You better get out of here before John reams your ass."

I could no longer pretend not to see Madden. As he came closer, I gave him a meek look that told him I understood this was his domain and I didn't mean to intrude, but I was just following orders to get an update on Stabler for Mr. Davis. I could see Madden was near a boiling point. With necessary information gained from Anderson, I turned as calmly and unassumingly as possible, stepped over the scattered bodies and equipment that littered the floor, and beat a retreat out of the locker room.

I made it through the door without a confrontation, but I knew Madden was seething. I decided to take whatever he wanted to dish out now as opposed to avoiding the conflict and allowing his anger to fester. Once outside, I positioned myself by the door where I could be seen by anyone leaving the locker room. A few minutes later, the door swung open and a parade of players made their way back onto the field.

A few of them patted me on the butt on their way by, acknowledging my bravery. The last person to exit the locker room was Madden. I didn't look at him but stood there ready to take his wrath.

I don't think he looked at me either. We stood side by side gazing out toward the playing field.

Madden did all the talking. "You mother-fucking cocksucker, waltzing in here for whatever you need is just straight bullshit. You don't ever fucking fuck with my halftime locker room again. I don't give a rat's ass who is telling you to do what. I'm the coach of this team and don't want any fucking interruptions from you or anyone else. You keep the fuck away, you fucking little prick."

I didn't move, I didn't say anything. I let him get it out. Maybe that made him madder, but that was not my intention. I just wanted the punishment to be over.

Madden called me a prick and asshole one more time before he walked away to take his position on the sideline. I briskly headed back behind the Broncos bench and up a set of stairs I hadn't seen on my earlier descent that led from the field to the seating level.

Moments after the second-half kickoff, I delivered the "expanded report" Anderson had provided on Stabler's condition.

"Did you have any problems?" Davis asked, well aware of the peril he exposed me to by sending me into the halftime locker room.

"No, sir," I responded dutifully. I was pretty sure Davis had seen the exchange Madden and I shared outside the locker room, and I knew what he respected most was a person that got a job done without any blather about the process. Davis was only interested in the result, which in this case was getting the report from Anderson.

"Good," Davis said with a hint of a smile.

Despite my intrusion into the halftime locker room, the Raiders drilled the Broncos in the second half, turning a 10–7 halftime deficit into a 42–17 romp victory.

That evening, as we boarded the charter flight home, Clarence Davis pulled on my jacket to get my attention and flashed a big smile. "We saved your ass."

I don't know how Madden would have responded if the Raiders had lost, but the easy win didn't totally dismiss his disfavor for my halftime appearance.

Shortly after takeoff from Denver, Madden asked me to surrender my seat across from him so he could meet with a couple sportswriters, Frank Cooney and Art Spander. I found a seat next to Phil Villapiano, who was wearing headphones while watching the in-flight movie, *The Getaway*, starring Steve McQueen and Ali McGraw.

Villapiano asked me, "Do you know McQueen married McGraw after they made this movie?"

I acknowledged that to the Raiders fourth-year linebacker.

"What a life, huh?" Phil said.

"Are you nuts?" I replied, laughing. "You play linebacker for the Oakland Raiders. You are so damn good-looking that my wife has already confided she would consider leaving me for you. And you sit here talking about how good McQueen's got it?"

Villapiano laughed in reply. "All I know is today I was banging on 250-pound linemen, and McQueen in his job was banging on Ali McGraw."

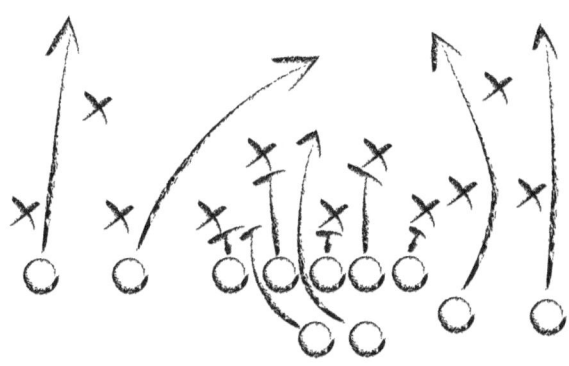

Chapter 36

Out in
the Cold

KEN STABLER WORE A CONFIDENT SMILE on his face. Even though a few key players were out with injuries—Fred Biletnikoff, Willie Brown, and Tony Cline—our star quarterback was certain we would beat the Pittsburgh Steelers in the American Football Conference Championship Game.

Perhaps the Steelers organization was aware the game was a major challenge, and because of a severe winter weather forecast, they chose to leave the field covered right up to the time when the players needed it to warm up on Sunday morning. That forced our Saturday practice from Three Rivers Stadium to the University of Pittsburgh. The AFC Championship Game for the 1975 season would be played on the fourth day of 1976.

"Looks like we're ready, doesn't it?" Stabler remarked to me.

I beamed with approval; this was as good as it gets for the Raiders. It was our turn, on their field, on this weekend.

John Madden had a reputation of falling short. He had coached in four championship games and never led the Raiders to a Super Bowl. He had been relegated to the AFC Pro Bowl coaching spot rather than wearing a ring.

But Madden couldn't lose this one.

This time his team was ready.

Oakland's defense was nearly as good as Pittsburgh's, which was among the best in history, and the Raiders outside speed offered an edge that Stabler was geared to exploit. He would need all the guns he could get against them. Mean Joe Greene, the best defensive player in football, and a Pittsburgh linebacking corps of three all-pros, Jack Ham, Jack Lambert, and Andy Russell, combined with a physical and talented defensive backfield.

"This is the field he did it on, right?" Pete Banaszak asked. "In November the kid from Pittsburgh ran for 303 yards against Notre Dame on this field."

"Tony Dorsett," Dave Casper filled in, walking toward the group, which included Stabler, Banaszak, Gene Upshaw, Art Shell, and Clarence Davis. Casper was keenly aware of the humiliation that had been visited on his Fighting Irish.

"That's a lot of yards," Stabler joked while whipping a pass to a streaking Cliff Branch.

"It was a lot of yards to give up," Casper replied grimly.

On Sunday morning, Tom Grimes and I had driven in his rent-a-car to Three Rivers Stadium. We arrived almost 20 minutes before the first wave of players and press. Joe Gordon, the Steelers director of public relations, had agreed to meet us early so we could double-check the seating assignments for the scheduled media and team front office personnel. Three Rivers Stadium, like the Oakland Coliseum, had limited press box space, and not everyone who wanted a seat inside could be accommodated.

Tom was walking in front of me and saw the field out the window of the press box first. "What happened here?" he said in an accusatory tone.

"The tractors were blown over in last night's storm and the tarp blew off the field," Gordon reported with a straight face.

"The tractors blew over?" I questioned. The exposed field glistened from all the ice and water puddles scattered throughout the artificial playing surface.

"Is that guy watering the freezing field?" Grimes asked. Steve, one of the groundskeepers we had met the day before, had explained why we couldn't work out at Three Rivers Stadium before the AFC Championship Game. Not only did we not get to practice at Three Rivers, but now he was deliberately altering the field conditions so they were weighted heavily in the Steelers' favor.

Pittsburgh's offense was designed to plow up the middle with Franco Harris, while our attack relied more on wide pass and run patterns that required firm footing outside the hash marks. What the overnight exposure didn't accomplish in eliminating the footing near the sidelines, the Steelers grounds crew was getting done now, watering a frozen field with outside temperatures in the minus degree sector.

"I guess they are trying to melt the sidelines for you guys," Gordon commented lightly while pulling from his briefcase the seating assignment Xerox copy that he handed to us.

"You've got to stop him," Grimes said, knowing what pouring water on the sidelines of a frozen field would do to both our passing and outside running game. "You've got to call down to the field and stop that guy with the hose," Grimes repeated.

"There's LoCasale," I said, spotting him walking behind the far sideline bench with his walkie-talkie in hand.

Grimes pulled his own walkie-talkie from his briefcase and soon was communicating his concerns with Al Davis' executive assistant.

The groundskeeper was six foot two and more than 220 pounds. LoCasale is not even five feet tall, and even though he was overweight, he weighed a good forty pounds less than the guy holding the hose. After his brief exchange with Tom, LoCasale confronted the man with the hose, waving his arms in dramatic fashion.

Yet he kept watering, looking over his shoulder at LoCasale without responding to his request. When the more physical presence of Jim Otto showed up to also request that the watering should cease, the groundskeeper was more compliant. He turned the nozzle until the water first went to a trickle, and then off.

"The guy is fucking nuts," LoCasale raged to Otto. "He thinks water on a frozen field is going to make less ice?"

"He knew what he was doing," Otto replied while eyeing the grounds crew with a look that had stared down many an opposing NFL linemen.

"They won't be doing any more watering," Otto reported to Al Davis as he and Pete Rozelle discussed the field conditions.

"This is fucking unfair," Davis complained to the National Football League commissioner as the Three Rivers Stadium head groundskeeper stood by.

Davis had disliked Rozelle for years because he had been selected over Davis as the first commissioner of the combined leagues, and the feeling was mutual. "It's the same field for both sides," Rozelle responded.

"It not only isn't the same for both teams, but the field conditions they have orchestrated is designed to benefit their strengths," Davis said in a fully agitated state.

"It's the same for both sides," Rozelle repeated.

The matter was closed. Despite the fact we were perfectly poised to beat the Steelers, Pittsburgh had rigged the field to change the odds. This outrageous behavior by their grounds crew would be matched in all of NFL history only by the snowplow used by the New England Patriots in 1982 to clear a spot for placekicker John Smith's game-winning field goal. My earlier confidence about our chances was already fading before the game had even started.

The wind chill factor was minus nine degrees, and the fans filling the stadium created a fog with each breath. A collective mass soon hovered over the growing crowd.

"I got a press box seat for you," Gordon told me about ten minutes before the scheduled kickoff. I had told him I understood the capacity problems in the press box, and I could stand in the back during the game if necessary.

"You'll like it," Gordon said with a wink. "It's all the way to the right in the front row."

He was right, I did like the seat. It was a balmy 65 degrees in the press box, and just a Plexiglas wall away, the seats were freezing cold.

Feeling very fortunate, I put down my briefcase on the table in front and hung my overcoat over the back of my chair. While the captains congregated in the center of the field for the coin toss, I went to grab something to eat from the press box lunch room.

I came back with two hot dogs, a bag of chips, and a Coke. I had already pulled the flip card out of the game program when I saw, out the Plexiglas window, just three feet away, Mrs. Davis in a winter coat with the collar turned up. Mr. Davis was sitting in the aisle seat to her right.

I opened my mouth off the hot dog bun, showing my teeth marks on it, and instantly stood up. This wasn't right. I put the program and flip card in my briefcase, and carried the food on a plate in one hand and my briefcase in the other. Once out of view of the Davises, behind the top row of press box chairs, I ate the hot dog I had started at my seat, and tossed the other one with the plate and chips in a garbage can.

"You can use that seat you got for me," I told Gordon before I headed out into the freezing cold. Sam Bercovich, a good friend of Al Davis, and his wife were seated in the section outside the press box too, and he greeted me as I sat in a chair a row behind Mr. Davis. He was standing with his hands in his overcoat pockets, bouncing on the balls of his feet to combat the gripping cold.

In front of the Davises were two executives from the Philadelphia Eagles, owner Leonard Tose and his general manager, Jim Murray.

Officially, the stadium temperature was 16 degrees, but with a 20-mile-an-hour wind from the west, we felt much colder than that. In the cove where Davis was sitting, the cement roof over the seats and the concrete floor with a Plexiglas wall caught the freezing wind and threw it back in our faces.

Midway through the first quarter, Bercovich handed me a cardboard box folded to form four layers. He instructed me to place it on the floor to give my feet a cushion from the frozen concrete. Just that layer of protection made a big difference.

Tose had an overcoat that was as thick and rich as I had ever seen, and Murray also had the outerwear to combat the elements. Mrs. Davis' winter coat had leather to offer additional warmth gained from extra layers at the collar and cuffs. Al Davis was wearing three layers of Raiders garb, some black, some white, some silver. The outside jacket was black, and he kept his hands in the jacket pockets—when not flailing them in reaction to plays that went both for and against the Raiders.

A week earlier, we had defeated the Cincinnati Bengals in Oakland under clear blue skies and conditions in the mid-60s. In Pittsburgh, our breath seemed to freeze before our very eyes. The mood among our group was just as chilly. Davis occasionally under his breath muttered what Rozelle had said to him earlier: "It's the same for both sides."

Late in the first half, Clarence Davis took a handoff and had an alley around the left side. But as he made a cut, his feet flew out from under him and what might have been a long touchdown the week before against the Bengals was limited to a five-yard gain.

Davis exposed his bare hands from his pockets as his running back lost footing, and said to no one in particular, "They've fucked us out of our fucking game plan."

Leonard Tose, growing more and more uncomfortable not only with the weather, but even to a greater degree by the agitated displays by Davis, nodded his head to agree with the unfair conditions.

At one point Davis glanced at me, seeming to want my opinion on the team's odds. Since that time three years earlier when I warned Davis that the Raiders were in trouble against the Chiefs, he had asked my opinion on an upcoming game 17 more times. I had never steered him wrong. Fortunately, in all but one case, I could tell him the Raiders looked ready and they went on to win.

This was another one of those times. I was as confident as Ken Stabler. This was our day. We were going to beat the Steelers in Pittsburgh and play in Super Bowl X. The day before at practice, I had assured Davis it was so, but with the field in its terrible condition, the balance of power has shifted dramatically toward the home team. I knew Davis wanted to see confidence in my eye, a nod, a knowing wink.

But I couldn't supply what he needed. This was a bad situation and we all knew it.

To our credit, we were battling the Steelers play-for-play on nearly equal terms. Unfortunately, the late second quarter drive that began with Davis' five-yard run ended at the 36-yard line when a Stabler pass fell incomplete to a wide-open Davis, who slipped on the field as the ball sailed over his head.

Tose turned in his seat again and again winced in agreement to the pain registered by Davis' contortion over the near miss. Ray Guy punted with 1:40 left on the first-half clock, and the ball sailed through the end zone to set the Steelers up at their own 20-yard line.

Two carries by Franco Harris gained 11 yards and a first down. Terry Bradshaw then looked to add to the 3–0 Steelers lead, by virtue of Roy Gerela's 36-yard field goal, with a pass to Lynn Swann with a minute left in the half. The ball bounced out of his hands in the cold, though, and linebacker Monte Johnson picked it off. It was the third time Bradshaw had been intercepted in the first half; Jack Tatum twice had picked the Steelers quarterback in the first quarter. The second, which gave the Raiders the ball at Pittsburgh's 29-yard line, failed to produce points when George Blanda was wide right on a 38-yard field goal attempt. This time the interception would have given Oakland the ball at midfield, but a 15-yard personal foul was called on Otis Sistrunk, and the Raiders drive began at their own 32 with only 45 seconds left on the clock.

Madden chose not to take any chances on the Steelers side of the field, and carries by Marv Hubbard and Clarence Davis ran the time off the first-half clock. The teams headed to the locker room with Pittsburgh holding the advantage.

A three-point halftime deficit would not normally seem like such a daunting prospect for the high-scoring Raiders, but today, in the January cold and the frozen field, the deficit felt nearly out of reach. The worry registered on Davis' face and in the empathetic glares from Tose and Bercovich.

"I'll get the halftime stats," I said while trying to flex my frozen bones as I stood up. I was as much looking forward to escaping to the warmth of the press box as collecting the first-half stat sheet.

"Only one fucking stat today," Davis said in an uncharacteristically dark game-day mood. "The fucking Steelers have scored and we haven't."

Both offenses had struggled in the conditions, but the halftime stats were clearly in the Raiders' favor with more first downs, 9–5, rushing yards, 70–27, and turnovers, 3–1. But Mr. Davis was right. The Steelers owned the only stat that mattered, 3–0.

"Come on, White," Davis said on the Raiders opening drive of the third quarter, summoning up his usual confidence and focus. But as the quarter wore on, and neither team added points to the scoreboard, Tose said to Murray that perhaps it was time to go. On the first play of the fourth quarter Bradshaw completed a 17-yard pass to Harris, and on the next play the Steelers All-Pro running back shook off an attempted tackle by Neal Colzie on the left side and broke free for a 25-yard touchdown run. After the extra point the Steelers led, 10–0. That was enough for the Eagles executives. Tose shook Davis' hand as he and Murray departed.

Amidst our desperate straits, trailing by two scores, seemingly an insurmountable deficit in these conditions, Stabler and his offense suddenly launched an unstoppable attack. Stabler went strictly to the air, hitting Dave Casper on three consecutive gains for first downs, and completed the Raiders' first scoring drive with a 14-yard touchdown pass to Mike Siani. Blanda's extra point cut the Steelers advantage to three points.

Davis surged to his feet, invigorated by the Raiders sudden offensive prowess through the air, and told his wife, "It's just us now. All the nonbelievers have cleared out."

Less than three minutes of game clock later, Davis' brief enthusiasm was erased by a Bradshaw pass to John Stallworth, extending Pittsburgh's advantage to nine points after Gerela's extra-point attempt was foiled by a bad snap.

"We can still do this," Davis vowed after the Steelers miss. "We fucking can still do this."

Yet a three and out that began with a play where a Stabler pass was almost intercepted by Mel Blount dampened our hopes. Our chances were shaken to the core as Pittsburgh then drove the ball on nine plays from their own 43-yard-line to the Raiders 19. With just over three minutes remaining on the game clock, and the Steelers in scoring position, Three Rivers Stadium was rocking with Steelers fans on their feet, waving yellow Terrible Towels. The noise was as deafening as the silence among the five of us.

Then, on first down, Rocky Bleier was separated from the ball and Sistrunk dove on it to end the Pittsburgh drive and light a flicker of hope among us. Yet three Stabler passes fell incomplete, and Ray Guy punted the ball back to the Steelers offense.

Again Pittsburgh seemed in position to end the drama with a first down in Raiders territory, but on second down with 1:38 left on the clock, Harris fumbled and Ted Hendricks recovered the ball for the Raiders at the 35-yard line.

On the ensuing drive Stabler passed 19 yards to Cliff Branch. Two plays later he hit Casper for 14 yards and a first down at the Steelers

32-yard line. On first down Stabler completed an eight-yard toss to Siani. Davis said out loud, "Kick the field goal now."

In sync, on the field, Madden called the Raiders' final time-out and sent Blanda in to attempt a 41-yard field goal. It was good, cutting the Steelers lead to 16–10.

"This is the Raiders. This is how we do it," I was thinking. While the entire day had an eerie dark cloud over it, we now had a chance to create another Oakland miracle. The noise from the Steelers fans was no longer celebratory but turned to concern as Guy's onside kick was recovered by Marv Hubbard near midfield.

Seven seconds were left on the clock. We had time for one play, one miracle to erase the sting of three years earlier on this field when a certain Oakland postseason win was stolen away by the *Immaculate Reception*.

Stabler got the pass off, and it was caught by Branch. While he gained 37 yards, the Steelers defense was positioned to stop him short of the end zone. Game over.

The Three Rivers crowd noise escalated into a warm roar for their hometown heroes, while the bitter cold of the day pierced icicles through our hearts. For a moment Al Davis said nothing. Then, while his supporting company stood silent, he muttered, "'Same for both sides.' Fuck you, Pete."

In all the years I had been with the team, Al Davis always had flown home with his Raiders. On a few occasions he had had business and hadn't met the team until Saturday night while they might have arrived on Friday.

But he always flew home with them.

The rule was broken on January 4, 1976.

I was standing in the bus circle outside Three Rivers Stadium, checking off names of the passengers loading the team and media buses, when I realized this. A black limousine was parked nearby. The driver in a chauffeur hat reached the car first, opening the door on the passenger side. Mrs. Davis was already sitting in the limousine when Mr. Davis emerged from the locker room. Several Oakland players had already boarded the bus, Steve Sylvester and David Humm among them. Neither had played in the game and they had cleared out while reporters filled the losing team's locker room. Davis glanced at me as he headed for the limousine. Ducking in the door, he asked his wife to scoot over. The truth hadn't dawned on me yet, but Davis was not just taking his own mode of transportation to the airport. He was headed in a completely different direction.

"I guess he won't be here," Jim Otto commented after confirming that everyone else on the manifest except Davis and his wife had boarded the aircraft.

"We can wait as long as necessary if he is coming," Stan Glazier said to LoCasale.

"I knew this was a possibility," LoCasale said, discouraged. "I don't think we need to babysit Mr. Davis. Let's get this flight on the way home. It's late. We're all done here."

John Madden had his eyes closed when I took my seat across from him.

What weighs on a man that has just lost his fifth championship game could only be known by the guy sitting across from me. Damn, I wished he had won. Life would be so cool right now if he had.

"Just a couple plays," Madden said, finally opening his eyes.

I didn't move, not a muscle. What was the proper response to a head coach that had won more games than anybody but never the big one?

Five championship games, five losses.

Every time, for good reason.

The Kansas City Chiefs got us while we were trying to beat them for a third time that season. In 1971, the Colts got us in Baltimore on a good day for Johnny Unitas; and the Miami Dolphins were better than us in 1973 and we had to play them on their home field. The loss last year came after the emotional win over the Dolphins, and the loss today was stolen because they froze the field.

Still, we could have won today. The Steelers turned the ball over five times, but they had more second-half yards and added to their halftime lead. They beat us by a field goal in each half.

"Sure would like to know how we would have done on a better field," Madden muttered while crushing a Dixie Cup he had been holding.

I still didn't respond, not wanting to say anything that would add to his despair.

I watched his knuckles turn white as the night flight from Pittsburgh hurtled down the runway. On most flights Madden's eyes would dart down the aisle, making eye contact with players and calling individuals up to our compartment for discussions. He never slept on a flight. His fear didn't allow it.

On this flight, at least by appearances, he seemed to be asleep. He remained that way for the entire trip from Pittsburgh to Oakland.

As I watched him, I couldn't help thinking that the Raiders were a 6½ point underdog. Which meant a bet on his Raiders won people money. It occurred to me that if I could pick any game, any team, each week, I would never have to lose. I knew when a team would likely play better or worse than their talent dictated, and I could pick any team I wanted instead of success or failure being pinned on the Raiders' result.

I had been thinking about leaving my job since my weekend with Pam in October while the team was in Cincinnati. I wanted more time with her, more time for a family, than I was ever going to have working for the Raiders.

The loss and Davis not flying home with us seemed like an appropriate time to leave the team. I was still thinking about that when Cheryl, an attractive stewardess that routinely worked the Raiders' flights, tapped Madden on the shoulder to request he fasten his seat belt for landing.

Madden leaned forward and looked out the window at the lights of Northern California on a clear winter evening. "Wonder how many of our fans will be here after today," he said while shaking his head. He gazed down the darkened aisle, where players and members of the press were straightening their seat backs and preparing for landing.

Glazier was the only person still standing on the flight, and he was talking on the phone in a recessed area just behind the cockpit. The call seemed important enough for Glazier to report its contents to LoCasale, who was sitting in the seat three rows back that Davis would have occupied had he flown home with us. I was struck by the urgency generated by this call.

After making his report to LoCasale, Glazier pulled out the seat that folded into the wall only a few feet from Madden and prepared for landing.

I mouthed the words without making a sound: "Is everything all right?"

"We'll talk," Glazier mouthed silently, which left me even more intrigued by what was going on.

The smooth landing earned a smattering of applause from players and staff. Landings were routinely rated by the players, oohing and hollering on the infrequent rough landings, and applauding the particularly soft ones. If the Raiders had played as well as Captain Silliman set down his 727, they would have won.

Madden didn't get up until all the players had filed by on their way into the terminal. He thanked them for everything they had done since July. This team had come so close, just not enough to clear the championship-game hurdle.

George Blanda seemed to avoid the moment of thanks with John, respectfully reaching out but then quickly moving on with only a grunt. He knew that if he had made that first field goal, the game could have been different.

Everyone knew it, but everyone also knew no one wanted to win more than Blanda.

"Coach, we'll get 'em next year," Phil Villapiano said in an upbeat tone. That was probably the first time Madden had thoughts about next season, the first time the reality that this season was over began to sink in.

I admired the rapport Madden had with each of his players. He had a special relationship with almost all of them. He rode a wide range of emotions, cheering those that chose to be upbeat and commiserating with those that couldn't hide their disappointment.

LoCasale and Glazier were talking just outside the airplane door on the jetway. I joined the conversation.

"It's probably nothing," Glazier told me.

LoCasale decided, "I'll tell John as soon as the players are through."

"It's something," I said to Glazier. "What is it?"

"There was a bomb threat, and the caller specified that John Madden was the target. Probably just some crackpot that isn't going to do anything, but we have to get him security before we go into the terminal," Glazier said. In the meantime, LoCasale moved into the seat across from Madden that I had vacated.

Only the two of them were left on the aircraft when LoCasale revealed the threat. Glazier and I could hear Madden's response.

"They're going to kill me over a loss? I don't think so. I'm sure a lot of our fans are upset, but I'm not going to be afraid that any of them are going to kill me over this."

He stood up and walked away, passing Glazier and me.

"Still, allow me to do my job and provide our best precautions," Glazier said while double-stepping to pull even with Madden.

Madden simply held up his hand, indicating that he didn't want any special attention.

Glazier insisted in an authoritative voice, "This is not your call, Coach. My job requires providing you security in light of a documented threat against you."

Madden was taken aback by Glazier's stern announcement, and he finally surrendered to whatever precautions Glazier deemed necessary. "There are four security guards waiting for us just inside the terminal. You will walk between them, one in front, one in back and one to each side."

Even though Madden nodded yes, he said, "I don't think this is necessary."

I was walking behind Madden with LoCasale, and I allowed LoCasale to go in front of me just as four men in matching gray blazers and dark blue pants circled the coach. As we walked into the main terminal, Madden was greeted by hundreds of Raiders fans, thanking him for the season and showing their loyalty to their beloved coach and team.

Madden was visibly appreciative of the turnout and support. He moved forward to part the guard to his left and the one in front to make himself more easily seen while offering a wave of thanks.

"We'll get 'em next year, Coach," a guy in a black T-shirt and a Raiders cap said while trying to reach out and touch Madden. His actions prompted the guard nearest to Madden to step between the fan and the coach.

"Let's move to the luggage area. It is private there," one of the guards told Madden. The coach followed instructions while fans continued to wish him well.

"We have to take every threat seriously, even though the vast majority are hoaxes," the guard remarked to Madden. "We want you safe, Coach," he added in a more personal tone. "How are you getting home?"

"My car is in the parking lot," Madden said, fishing his keys out of a bag in his hand.

"Walking though the parking lot alone is probably not a good idea," the guard replied.

"Maybe the bomb is on your car. You should be careful," LoCasale said in a way that seemed to reignite Madden's concern.

By this time, I was pretty much convinced that the threat to Madden was idle chatter, and before thinking it through, I said, "I'll go get your car, John. I'm not afraid."

"That's a good idea," LoCasale confirmed.

"What's a good idea?" I said, laughing. "That if a bomb goes off and somebody gets killed, it's better me than Coach Madden?"

"We'll miss you," LoCasale replied, laughing too.

"Give me your keys, Coach," I said. "I'll take the bullet for you tonight."

Madden handed over the keys to his black Chrysler Imperial. "I'll meet you on the curb out front."

While I left the terminal confident that the threat of a bomb carried no validity, as I approached the car, a shadow of concern overtook me. Before I inserted the key, I bent down on all fours and looked under Madden's car. I was not sure what I was looking for, but I figured if a bomb was attached to his car, I would see some wires or something hanging down.

I didn't.

The thought flashed in my mind: A loss wouldn't mean that much if I got blown up. Yet I turned his key to open the car door. The lock popped up and nothing exploded.

Before I twisted the key in the ignition, I had the fleeting thought: Is this really something I want to do? While pondering that, I turned the key.

The Chrysler started.

Nothing blew up.

I paid the $18.00 parking fee with a twenty and spun his car around to the terminal, where Madden, LoCasale, Glazier, and two of the guards were waiting. Madden said nothing to me but thanked Glazier and the guards for their concern while he put his bags in the back seat.

Twenty minutes later, I paid another $18.00 to get my car out of the parking lot. Driving home, I kept thinking: This might be the last road trip I'll ever take with the Raiders.

- - - - - -

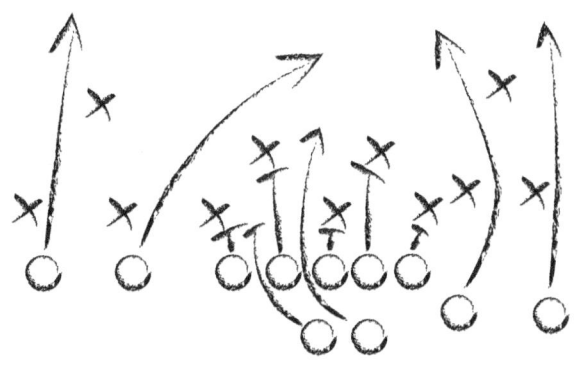

Chapter 37

Fatherly Advice

Everybody was telling me to do whatever I wanted to do except Al Davis.

My father was initially the most disappointed. He loved having a son working for the Oakland Raiders and was proud of me when my name appeared in the newspaper or seeing me on television sitting with Mr. Davis at a game.

Pam knew the real price of my job, the long hours and the lack of any personal time. But she, too, loved the fact that her husband worked for the Oakland Raiders. "I want you to do what you want to do," she said.

"Dennis, you have a very good job and work with an influential person," my dad pointed out. We were sitting in his den while we discussed my decision to leave the Raiders. "I think you should consider your advantages." Dad popped open a beer and leaned back in his desk chair. "Don't you want to work through the organization and stay in the business?"

"I want to have what you have," I told my father.

He squinted, trying to understand. "What do you mean?"

"How many Christmas Eve dinners at the Wharf have you missed in more than 30 years?"

"None," he admitted. I knew that he could not imagine a work obligation preventing him from being with his family.

"I've missed three in three years," I told him. "Do you think that would change if I stayed with the Raiders, even if Pam and I had kids?"

Dad did not reply.

"I understand a career is important to a man, and I want to provide for Pam and the family I hope to father, but when I do, I want to be there." I added, "Like you have always been."

My father was always quick to credit others while seldom flashing the spotlight on his own accomplishments. I gave him reason to pause. He held Al Davis in such high esteem, he probably never even considered how much more I respected the life he had built. I wanted to follow in his footsteps, not Al Davis'. I wanted to be a family man, not a Raiders insider.

"What would you do?" Dad asked.

"I don't know," I replied without a great deal of concern.

That week I attempted to make a few appointments with Al Davis to announce my intention to leave the Raiders, but I said that it was not urgent. I told his secretary, "I just want to talk to him sometime when he is not busy."

After two weeks, I realized that I was never going to catch Al Davis when he wasn't busy. I decided instead to just knock on his door when he was in and request a few minutes of his time.

The door was open, and Beverly first intended to interrupt my progress to his door, but I shot her a look that convinced her I needed to approach Mr. Davis now. I knocked on his open door while requesting, "I just need a couple of minutes of your time, sir."

"Does it have to be right now?" Davis said while looking up from the yellow notepad he was paging through.

"It will only take a second, sir, but I'd like to have a private conversation with you now." As I spoke, I drifted into his office and toward his desk. My bold behavior prompted Davis to get up and walk to his door. He closed it before saying, "What is your announcement?"

"I've decided to leave, sir, and I just want to do it right."

"You want to leave? Do you think that's right?" Davis snapped. "This is a hell of a time to be pulling out of here. With Tommy wanting to move into the player personnel department and you the one I thought I could count on for publicity. You never took my advice to really get to know the media throughout the league, did ya?" Davis said, exposing a weakness.

"Would I be the public relations director if Tom went to work with Herock?" I asked, intrigued by the possibility.

"Tell you what," Davis continued without answering my question. "You show me what you've got, we get the media guide done, and then we'll talk about who is going to be the Raiders PR director."

I left his office less than five minutes after I entered, excited about the prospect of getting out the media guide and then discussing the public relations position.

"Does that mean you don't want to leave?" Pam asked that night at dinner before she left for work.

"I don't know. This could be an opportunity to be the head of the Raiders PR department before I'm 26 years old."

She merely looked down at her pasta dinner. I realized she really did have a preference, after all.

– – – – – –

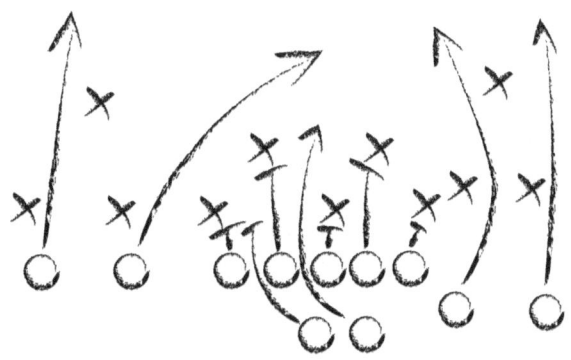

Chapter 38

Palm Springs

I HAD PICKED UP AL DAVIS at airports dozens of times, always making the journey to his gate to greet him as he stepped off his flight. He most often walked with a slow saunter that belied the quickness of his mind. He dragged his feet, looking more like a tired troop leader at the end of a long hike than a confident executive.

Yet on this mid-March evening in 1976, when I met him at the San Francisco International Airport, his demeanor was totally different. He was returning from Palm Springs and the NFL owners' meeting. He left the plane, pushing past other passengers with an impatience I had never seen. I offered to take the bag he was carrying, and he handed it to me while continuing to carry his overflowing leather briefcase.

He usually wanted reports on what was going on in Oakland, who was saying what, and the status of current projects. Not tonight, though.

Instead, he launched into an animated recounting of the events that took place at the owners' meeting

"They are no fucking better than baseball owners," Davis said loud enough for people not interested to hear. "You know what I mean, don't ya?"

I did. He considered some of his fellow National Football League team owners assets to the game, while every baseball owner, except George Steinbrenner of the New York Yankees, no more than a used car salesman. He often said baseball owners were men that made money in other businesses, such as selling cars, and then acquired teams and ran them like playing with a toy.

"This is a fucking business," Davis said, animated as we walked toward the luggage carousal. "And we've got guys like Bidwill, Adams, and Mecom thinking that what they do doesn't really matter."

Bill Bidwill was the majority owner of the St. Louis Cardinals, a team he had handed to him by his father, Charles, who purchased the franchise in 1932. Bud Adams, a self-made man that earned his fortune in the oil business, was an original owner in the American Football League; along with Lamar Hunt, he had announced the formation of the new American Football League on August 3, 1959. Both men established franchises in Texas, Hunt in Dallas, and Adams the Oilers in Houston.

John Mecom Jr. was both an owner and president of the New Orleans Saints, a franchise added to the National Football League in 1967. He had a number of interests outside football, including a passion for racing cars and boats. Davis considered him too much like a baseball owner.

"Well, are you with me, now we got a fucking group of used car salesmen making decisions for our league," he said with disdain. "Do you know what they did?"

Davis started off his diatribe with Carroll Rosenbloom, who owned the Los Angeles Rams. "Carroll announces yesterday that he is looking into moving the Rams from the Los Angeles Coliseum to Anaheim." I was surprised that Davis was criticizing Rosenbloom, since he had always indicated to me that Rosenbloom was one of the owners he admired most.

"Adams interrupts and says, 'None of us should be allowed to move a franchise without league approval.'"

Davis continued talking as we reached the baggage claim area. "And Carroll tells him that the Rams are his team and he will do whatever the fuck he thinks is best for his franchise. Imagine lightweight owners dictating what Carroll can do with his fucking team."

I just nodded, hanging on to every word he spoke.

"Then Bidwell says, 'Yeah, that's a good idea. I say we require 100-percent approval,' and fucking Adams agrees with him."

Pete Rozelle then interrupted the call for 100-percent approval because he was concerned about antitrust exposure. He suggested a majority of two-thirds or three-fourths for approval of any franchise move.

"I don't need any approval to move my team across town," Rosenbloom countered. "I'm operating within the 75-mile radius that we already allow."

He was right. The NFL had a rule that an owner could shift his stadium site within 75 miles of his previous home, a distance considered within an established fan base area.

"I think we need to deal with the possibility of other franchise shifts, those of more than 75 miles from their current home. I think the league should have the power to determine if the move is in the best interest of the league, which is all of us," Adams said in response.

"I'm fine with two-thirds or three-fourths approval to allow a franchise to move," Mecom conceded, and the other owners agreed. A vote was taken. The first one that included the two new league franchises, the Tampa Bay Buccaneers and Seattle Seahawks. The count was 26 in favor of the league having the power to approve a franchise shift, one against, Carroll Rosenbloom of the Rams, and one abstention, Al Davis of the Raiders.

"Then you know what Bidwill said after the vote?" Davis related with clenched teeth and his bottom jaw jutting out. "He fucking said, 'What does it matter? No one is going to move anyway.'"

Davis became even more animated, moving closer to me. "Let me tell you something, Dennis. Don't ever settle for making rules only strong enough if no one challenges them. Are you with me, you've got to make rules that can withstand the toughest test."

Davis grabbed his bag off the carousel and then locked his gaze with me one more time. "I'll tell you something, young man. These fucking guys need a wake-up call. They're down there passing rules because they think no one is going to challenge them. I tell you fucking something else; I'll challenge their fucking asses. I'll move the fucking Raiders."

I took the bag out of his hand, and we headed for his car, parked on the curb outside the PSA arrival gate.

"You think that would get their fucking attention, if I was to threaten to move our Raiders?"

— — — — — —

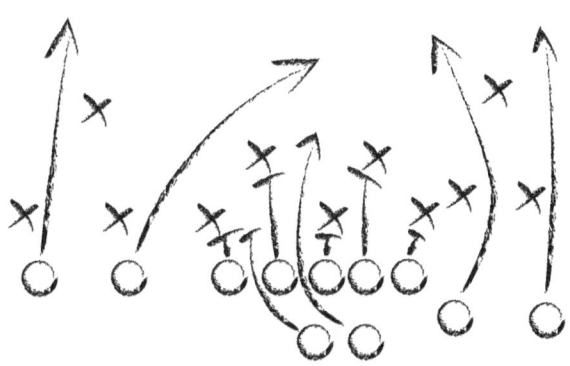

Chapter 39

Inmates

The MEDIA GUIDE HAD NOT YET BEEN PRINTED, and Davis had already enrolled me in getting the first *Pro! Magazine* published, the National Football League's home game program, before I left the team. The job included selling local advertising, layout, and design.

Art Snyder had called me at home the week before, the first time I had ever communicated with him outside the Raiders press box or a team social function. He told me he had something for me and wanted to know if I would be available on Wednesday night at 8:30.

I knew we had a rookie camp scheduled to start on Friday, but Wednesday night I would be available.

He knocked on the door of my Alameda apartment right on time. I answered and Pam greeted Snyder over my shoulder. She had met him at the press party to release the 1975 Highlight Film a week earlier. She asked him if he would like a cup of coffee or something else to drink.

He asked for tea. After serving it, Pam excused herself to get ready for work.

"I understand you are thinking about leaving the organization," Art said.

I was surprised he knew. I shrugged my shoulders without really answering.

"You know, things aren't working out with Ken Herock," Snyder said, divulging inside information on the Raiders organization that I wasn't sure how he got or why he was sharing with me. Herock had been named player personnel director for the Raiders when Ron Wolf moved to the Tampa Bay Buccaneers, but his relationship with Davis had been rocky from the start.

"He is going to be out, and Tom is moving to the player personnel department," Snyder went on. I knew Tom Grimes wanted to shift into the player personnel department with either the Raiders or Buccaneers. If Herock was fired, there was a very good possibility that Grimes would move over to the personnel side with Oakland. That meant his public relations position would be open.

"Do you have something else to do in mind?"

I immediately found myself uncomfortable, not knowing really who Snyder was, who he worked for, or why he was showing this interest in me.

"I've got the media guide to finish, and I'm going to get at least the first *Pro! Magazine*," I replied.

"Oh," Snyder said, taking a sip of tea, "I understood your mind was made up."

Once again, I didn't know where he gained his knowledge, but he seemed to be fishing for more answers. While I was contemplating how to respond to his line of questioning, the phone rang. Pam entered the kitchen dressed in her white nursing uniform and answered it on the second ring.

"It's Mr. Davis," she announced, holding out the phone.

"Dennis," he said in a manner that sounded like he was calling from a party. "I need ya to come over here. To the house, and drive Herman and me up to camp."

Herman Masin was the editor of *Scholastic Coach* magazine and one of the few people I had seen Davis interact with as if they were friends. Both Masin and Davis were from New York. He was the first to publish articles Davis had written on his "vertical offense" football strategies.

Those articles, I was told by Grimes, were what first brought Davis to the attention of Sid Gilman, who then hired him with the Los Angeles Chargers when the American Football League was originally formed. If Al Davis had any one person to thank most for igniting his meteoric rise in professional sports, Herman Masin was probably the man.

The call from Davis provided a good excuse to end my uncomfortable exchange with Snyder. After he left, I took off even before Pam left for work.

Mrs. Davis greeted me with her customary broad smile and a welcoming gesture, inviting me into the house. Davis and Masin were laughing about something, and both had a drink in their hand. While I had suspected Davis occasionally enjoyed an alcoholic beverage, I had never seen him with one before this night.

The coaches were scheduled to check in to our Santa Rosa training facility on Thursday and have meetings at the camp before the rookies and invited players arrived on Friday. Davis decided to arrive early and had called ahead to have two suites for him and Herman made available a day before they were originally scheduled.

Both men had obviously had more than a few drinks. As the three of us drove across the Richmond/San Rafael Bridge, they were telling stories and laughing like teenagers on a road trip.

"That's where we could have our old-timers' game." Davis gushed with laughter while pointing out the San Quentin Prison, located on the Marin side of the bridge. Davis was sitting in the front passenger seat next to me; Mason was in the seat directly behind me.

"That's terrible, Al," Masin said.

"We could save on travel expenses," Davis added. "I think we could field a full team with inmates that used to play for us."

They both roared with laughter.

The Raiders had no first-round draft selection in 1976 but spent a pair of second-round selections on players that might be the reason the relationship between Davis and Herock soured so quickly. Herock and the coach had determined that if kicker Chris Bahr was available when their pick came, he would be selected as a possible replacement for aging George Blanda.

Bahr was available when the Raiders' second-round selection, the 34th overall pick, came up. But Davis had second thoughts about spending that high of a draft choice on a special teams player, despite the success of first-round pick Ray Guy three years earlier.

The pre-draft work was erased when Davis emerged from his office after viewing a film on a defensive end out of Texas Southern. "I think I just found the next Buck Buchanan."

Buchanan, a mammoth defensive presence in the Kansas City Chiefs line, had just announced his retirement. Davis was looking to add to the Raiders' size and strength up front to compete with current Super Bowl champion Pittsburgh. He thought he saw those skills in Charles Philyaw.

While Davis was enamored with the kid's size and strength, what the black-and-white 8mm film didn't show was his lack of intelligence. I recalled how Davis gushed over meeting Henry Lawrence the day after the Raiders made him their first-round pick in 1974, and how disappointed the coaches were to meet Philyaw this year.

One of the veterans invited to participate in the Raiders camp this week was Mark van Eeghen. Philyaw was watching him run the ball while standing next to me on the sidelines. In a dialect that sounded as if he had a mouth full of marbles, he asked, "Why does he get to have his first and last name on his jersey?"

"What?" I said, not sure to what he was referring.

"Him," Philyaw said, "van Eeghen."

Later in the only draft Herock conducted as player personnel director for the Raiders, Oakland still had a chance to grab the kicker they coveted. Bahr was still available with the Raiders second pick in the second round, the fiftieth in the draft; and while everyone in the Raiders upstairs conference room was celebrating the fact that the player listed at the top of our board was still there, Davis made another surprise announcement after viewing a film in his office.

"This kid could be special," Davis predicted, choosing an athlete that had not been under serious consideration until his declaration. Herock looked pissed, dropping his head and lacking the poise Wolf traditionally maintained despite the draft-day pressure.

"We've got available who we want," Herock said, challenging Davis.

"We may miss a quarterback, someone who could run our team, for a fucking dime-a-dozen kicker," Davis spat in Herock's direction.

"I thought we were going to go for the kicker," Madden said, more timid than I'd ever seen him. Then the coach suggested, "Why don't we just let Cincinnati pick and if they don't take Bahr, we will?"

"Let them dictate who we take?" Davis growled. "Take this fucking quarterback," he said, storming out of the room.

The player Davis had identified was Tulsa quarterback Jeb Blount. "Why am I even here?" Herock snarled as Blount was announced in New York. The Cincinnati Bengals immediately followed that pick by making Bahr the 51st selection of the 1976 draft.

Blount, a bright-eyed, rosy-cheeked kid that always had a smile on his face, turned out to be someone you might like to go to a game with, but not an athlete that could run an offense or lead men on the field. He survived Raider cuts longer than his talent dictated because Davis was attempting to justify his pick.

He lasted longer than Herock, who quit before the Raiders opened their rookie camp.

When I got home from camp, on Sunday night, a message was waiting for me on the phone. It was from Art Snyder, and he said he had forgotten to give me his surprise.

He didn't say what it was, nor did he leave a number so I could call him back.

The Raiders were scheduled to open the preseason at home against the Dallas Cowboys on July 31, and that was also my last day with the organization. Frustrated that I was doing all the work of a public relations director after Grimes was named director of pro personnel and yet not given the title or raise, I had given my final notice before the summer training camp opened in July.

The next night I heard from Snyder. It was the first time we had talked since he left that message on my home phone weeks earlier. "Are you available to talk?"

It was almost 10:00 p.m., Pam had just left for work and I was reading a *Sports Illustrated* article about the Pittsburgh Steelers.

"Of course, I'm available to talk," I said with a smile. "I answered the phone."

"No," Snyder said, "I mean, are you available to talk in person?"

"Sure," I replied, uncertain if he wanted me to meet him somewhere or whether he was coming over to my apartment.

"I'm at the Oakland Airport, just arrived from Los Angeles, and I was thinking about you. Can I buy you a drink?"

"Sure," I said, "where do you want to meet?"

"How about the Hilton?" Snyder suggested.

He was already in the bar when I arrived, and I spotted him through the smoke and dim lighting in a room that smelled like cigarettes and calamari. He stood up as I approached the table.

"Sorry for the late notice. Glad you were available," he said as we shook hands. "What are your plans?" he asked while motioning for a waitress. He already had a non-alcoholic drink when I arrived, and I ordered a gin and tonic.

"Sir?"

"You're leaving the Raiders, right?"

"At the end of the month," I confirmed.

"Do you have something else lined up?"

"Only ideas. Nothing concrete," I admitted.

"What are you thinking?"

"I want to stay in sports. I have always had an interest in handicapping football, and I thought maybe I could find a way to develop that into a business."

"How?" Snyder questioned.

"Talking about the games on the air, maybe doing a newspaper column."

"There are people who would pay a lot of money to someone who could provide them winners," Snyder said, shifting to a cold business tone. His gaze was fixed on me, suddenly sending chills down my spine.

Our relationship had just taken an abrupt turn.

"I can pick winners," I said with bravado.

"How can you pick winners?"

I launched into a long explanation of motivational factors that I had developed while picking games with my dad as a kid, refined during college, and supplemented with the firsthand knowledge gained while working with the Raiders.

I pointed out that Madden regarded only the coaching side of a game as important, while I was certain that motivation plays an even more important role than the game plan. "You think John is naive because he feels only X's and O's dictate who is going to win on Sunday," Snyder remarked. "What you miss there," he went on, "is that John is taking responsibility for the only thing he has control over. That is why he is successful. If he worried about his opponent winning or losing last week, making it tougher to win this week, he would be wasting time on factors he can't control."

"But I get to use those factors in my work," I pointed out. "I don't have to rely on the Raiders winning to be successful. I can win every week with whatever team, with the point spread added to the under-dogs I choose."

"Yes, you can," Snyder said with a slight smile. "I think maybe it is time for you to sit down with Mr. Dom."

Two weeks later, Al Davis had his secretary schedule a meeting with me for Friday afternoon, the day before the Raiders hosted the Cowboys.

"Do you mind if I eat lunch while we talk?" Davis asked as I entered his office. He had me shut the door, and I sat down on the familiar black leather couch. Pulling a chair up to the glass table, he opened a sandwich wrapper, poured a bag of Cheetos on top of it, and popped the top on a Tab.

"Okay, I think you've done well," he said without preamble. "I'll give you the money you've requested and the public relations director title."

"It's too late, sir," I said without considering his offer.

"Well, what the fuck were you negotiating for?" Davis barked with a hint of anger.

"If you had made the offer sooner, but now—"

Before I was able to finish the sentence, Davis interrupted. "Let me tell you something, young man. When you are in a negotiation, know what you're negotiating for, and when it shows up, take it."

He waved his hand in dismissal. "That deal is done. We are finished. But let me tell you, the next time you're negotiating, don't lose sight of what you are negotiating for. I don't know what you are negotiating for now—your feelings, some acknowledgment from me? You shouldn't let emotions adjust your demands. Here I was, offering you everything you said you wanted, and you turned it down."

I realized then how much my feelings were tied to my decision to leave the Raiders. I felt used, taken advantage of, and now that I could have the pay and title to match my responsibilities, I was leaving.

"I'm not the sentimental type," Davis said, finishing another bite of his sandwich, "but I'm going to tell you, it was special having you around. Wheeling me from place to place in my car. I'll miss you."

He took another bite of his sandwich without taking his eyes off me. "You want out of the football business, huh?"

"I remember watching an episode of *Columbo*," I replied.

Davis looked at me as if I was speaking a foreign language. "*Columbo?*" he said, not knowing what I was talking about.

"The TV show with Peter Falk," I said. "Anyway, there was this episode with Robert Culp where he was the owner of a football team and then got caught murdering someone." I could tell Davis had no idea where I was going with this story, but he let me continue. "Anyway, I was thinking at the time—this was about a year before I started here—how would someone who worked in professional sports need to kill anyone? Wouldn't they just always be happy?"

"I'm not sure what you mean by that," Davis chuckled, "but I can see it means something to you. What are you going to do now . . . you're not going to write a book, are you?"

Snyder's surprise for me, which he had neglected to bring to my apartment but did hand over after our meeting in the bar, was a tape recorder. He had told me I should record my experiences with the Raiders and write a book.

"I can barely get through writing the articles for *Pro! Magazine*. I don't see how I could ever tackle a book," I honestly replied to Davis. "I do know this: I want to spend more time with Pam and start a family."

"Well, make sure you do that, then," Davis nodded. "I know too many men who think they need to cut back their work schedules to be with the family and then end up going out and partying when they could be with their wives and kids."

"Sir?" I questioned. I had never before heard him put any emphasis on family.

"I'm saying this." Davis leaned toward me. "If you put an emphasis on your family, you should do two things: work hard and spend the rest of your time with your family. A person dedicated to a home life needs to always be one of two places, at work or at home." With that lesson imparted, he moved on. "So, what are you going to tell people about the Raiders now that you are no longer a part of us?"

"What people most want to know is about you. 'What's he like?'"

"And what do you tell them?"

"I tell them about how focused you are, how dedicated you are, how you taught me that you can bend any negotiation your way if you are willing to stick at it longer than the person you are negotiating with."

"Do you believe that?" Davis asked.

"I've seen it. I know it," I flatly replied.

"I'm going to miss you, Dennis," Davis said with a trace of a smile. "But know this: Once you are out of the organization, you are out. You are on your own. There will be no help for you coming from this office."

Just as he finished saying that, before I truly grasped what it meant, a knock at his door interrupted us. The summer intern for that year came in to deliver a copy of the program for tomorrow night's game against the Cowboys.

Davis looked it over, pausing as he scanned the cover. "Now, that looks like a Raiders program."

NFL Properties produced major sections of the game-day magazine, and each local team could add their content and local advertising. The league also printed seven regular season, three preseason, and postseason covers for *Pro! Magazine*. For the first preseason game, we had the option to use a league-provided cover or produce our own. I explained to Davis why I had chosen the pictures and printed the cover in all silver and black.

"See?" Davis said. "You do good work. Like I said, we're going to miss you."

"It was easier to work here when I cared about nothing else."

He seemed to take that statement to heart. "One hundred percent is easy, total commitment is absolute. But ninety-nine percent is a bitch. That one percent will rear its ugly head and blur a person's focus. It creates inner conflict that throws a person off his game."

We ended up talking for almost two hours. Just before 3:00, Al LoCasale opened Davis' door. "The driver downstairs needs to know where to deliver the programs at the stadium," he said, glancing at me. "Do you have a key for the storage area at the Coliseum?"

"I do," I said. "It's in the top drawer of my desk."

"Well," LoCasale said, "you're going to have to give that key to me before you leave tomorrow. For now, could you go with the driver downstairs to deliver the books?"

"We're done here," Davis announced, turning his back on me while carrying the program to his desk.

I had started out the door when I overheard LoCasale say to Davis: "You like the cover I did for the magazine?"

Davis looked over LoCasale's shoulder at me, and I winked in reply. Davis said, "Nice job, Al."

- - - - - -

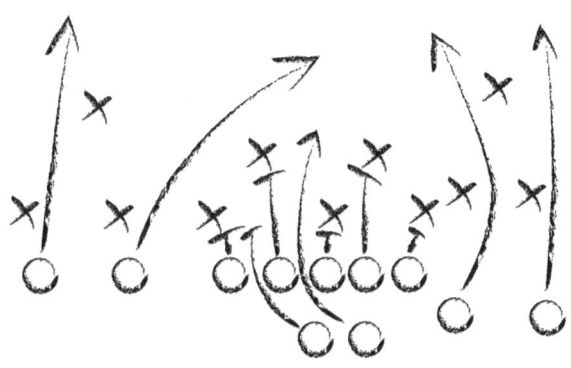

Chapter 40

Outside

I WORE MY FAVORITE SUIT TO OUR GAME against the Cowboys, my last hurrah. Most of the friends I had made in the local media had two questions for me that night: "Why are you leaving?" and "What are you going to do now?"

"I'm just done being a Raider guy," I told *San Francisco Chronicle* writer Art Spander and went on to relate a recent story. "A couple of weeks ago, I was taking Morris Bradshaw to the airport in Oakland. We were running late, and I walked right by everyone waiting in line for the helicopter to San Francisco, pushed the glass doors open as the chopper was revving their engines, moments from leaving the tarmac. 'Stop that helicopter,' I yelled at a worker who was motioning to the pilot that all was clear. Upon my request, he suddenly waved to abort the flight. The helicopter settled back down, and I said, 'Thanks, I need to get Morris on that flight.'

"The guy directing the takeoff knew who I was, knew who I worked for, and knew Morris played for the Raiders. That is, no doubt, why he granted my request. He had the attendant on board push the door on the helicopter open and Morris thanked me with a wave as he boarded."

"So, what's wrong with that?" Spander said.

"When I walked back by the line of people waiting for the next helicopter, one guy in a suit stepped out in front of me and lowered a shoulder that halted my walk. 'Who the hell do you think you are, asshole?' the guy said. He was angry that I could delay the flight while he needed to wait in line."

"What did you tell him?" Spander said with interest.

"I said nothing. But when I got back to my car, I put my head on the steering wheel and asked the same question of myself, 'Who the hell do I think I am?'"

"Sounds like you were the kind of guy Davis likes having on his payroll," Spander remarked.

"I didn't even see the people waiting when I hurried by and stopped that helicopter," I said. "I think I have become an asshole. Someone who thinks rules don't apply to me because of my position with the Raiders is more important than whatever anyone else is doing."

"I enjoyed working with you," Spander said. "Don't be too hard on yourself. You did what you had to do."

"But I don't have to do it anymore," I said, relieved. "I'm looking forward to waiting in line with everyone else."

"That will wear off soon," Spander said with a laugh.

On the field, George Anderson and Dr. Albo were attending to defensive lineman Horace Jones, who was in obvious pain, while they measured the damage to his injured knee. A few minutes later, I got a call from the field on the press box phone. The injury to Jones was serious, and his knee would almost certainly require surgery. He was probably lost for the season.

I went to Davis' box, two sections over from our makeshift press area because the field was running in a different direction than a regular-season game. The stadium was still in a configuration to accommodate the Oakland A's baseball team.

"Fuck," Davis said upon hearing the severity of Jones' injury. Then he added, "Well, okay, we'll just have to find another player. A better player."

Injuries, particularly serious ones, are always a concern for a team. The sting seems even greater when a starting player is lost while participating in a meaningless preseason game—in Jones' case, the first one of the season.

"How bad is it?" Spander asked when I returned to the press area.

"He's probably done for the year, most likely surgery," I replied. Al LoCasale overheard my report to Spander and jumped in. "We don't know how serious it is yet." He then led me to the back of the press area and lectured me. "We don't give out injury reports. I don't care if the guy is dead. It gives us no benefit to report someone is seriously injured."

He was livid that I could be so casual in revealing the seriousness of the injury, not adhering to the Raiders' code of secrecy. His harsh words didn't move me, however. I was on the clock for only a few more hours, and then I would be free.

After the Raiders won, I headed to my car in the players' parking lot when I unexpectedly ran into John Madden.

"So this is it," John said.

"Good luck this year, Coach. Go win it all," I said, extending my hand to shake goodbye.

Six weeks later, I had the opportunity to do what I had envied others doing for the previous four years: tailgating in the parking lot before the game and going into the stadium as a fan. So often, I would pull into the Coliseum parking lot in my suit and tie hours before a game and smell the grills firing up and fans preparing for their tailgate ritual before Oakland home games.

On September 12, I was the guy in the parking lot, along with Pam and two of our best friends, Tom and Donna Roberts. I had missed their wedding two years earlier because we were playing the Philadelphia Eagles in a preseason game on the night they were married.

No regrets, no pangs of wishing I was back in the press box.

Pure joy in the stands watching the Raiders play the same team they had met in my final meaningful game on staff, the Pittsburgh Steelers.

I had made my first bet since college, driving to Lake Tahoe on Friday and putting $44 on the Raiders plus one point to beat the Steelers. It seemed like an easy choice; they should have won the prior year in Pittsburgh and gone on to meet the Dallas Cowboys in Super Bowl X, a game won by the Steelers.

Now they were getting a point on the spread at home in a game they were almost certain to win. Maybe I didn't have to get a job. I could make it betting on winning football picks.

"Do you miss it?" Pam asked while I tried to locate friends in the press box through my binoculars. I shifted my gaze from the magnification of the binoculars and stopped at Pam's beautiful brown eyes. "I'm right where I want to be," I said, pulling her closer.

Pam was about to say something nice, but she was interrupted first by the sound of a human collision and then the roar of the crowd.

Tom yelled at me over the deafening noise, "Atkinson just laid out Swann." Tom then held up his rather muscular forearm and demonstrated how Atkinson drilled the unsuspecting Pittsburgh receiver. The hit was on a play when the ball was not thrown in Swann's direction. "He coldcocked him," Tom said loud enough for me to hear over the crowd noise.

The Raiders tallied first, and the teams were tied at halftime. In the second half, the Steelers offense made steady progress toward the end zone our seats were located in; and early in the fourth quarter, everyone around me saw Theo Bell break wide open before catching an 11-yard touchdown pass from Terry Bradshaw, opening the Steelers lead to 21–7.

"This is just Raiders football," I noted to Pam during a brief time the Raiders crowd was somewhat subdued. I found Al Davis in my binoculars, sitting with both his elbows on his knees. His mouth was moving while talking to no one. I thought I knew what he was saying and smiled.

"How's our investment look?" Tom asked. Half of the $44 I placed in Tahoe was his.

"I just told Pam," I shouted over the crowd, "this is just Raiders football. We'll win."

A Stabler to Biletnikoff pass pulled Oakland within seven points, but the Steelers countered that Raiders score with a Franco Harris run for a touchdown late in the fourth quarter.

I was surprised. This sure did look like a Raiders win on my books, but it was going to take a monumental comeback now as Oakland trailed by two touchdowns with just three minutes left in the game.

Yet miracles in Oakland are common, as Curt Gowdy said. A Stabler to Casper strike cut the Pittsburgh advantage to a touchdown margin, and a Stabler run evened the score at 28–28. When Oakland got in range again, I was thinking about the Raiders draft the April before when two opportunities to get the kicker they wanted to replace George Blanda had been derailed by Davis' last-second changes. Blanda had been released and retired shortly after I left the team, but Chris Bahr was not our new kicker. Instead, the guy Blanda had beaten out the prior season, Fred Steinfort, was lining up for a field goal that could complete the Raiders' come-from-behind victory.

Steinfort's effort was enough. The Raiders had turned a recovered fumble and interception in the final three minutes into 17 points and another historic comeback victory, 31–28.

"That investment looks pretty good now," Tom said, grinning.

The Raiders would meet the Steelers again in 1976. On the day after Christmas, they renewed the rivalry that had now grown more and more intense during the decade. This time, again in Oakland, the two teams squared off, and for the third straight season, a Super Bowl berth awaited the winner of a Raiders-Steelers Championship Game.

I was working in the promotions department with the Golden State Warriors, having been hired by Bob Bestor and Scotty Sterling. Both men had worked with the Raiders, and Bestor was well known for the best impersonation of Al Davis on the planet. Bestor once called George Glace, the Raiders ticket manager, using his Al Davis voice while on a road trip in Denver. Bestor observed how intoxicated Glace got in the hotel bar, and gave him about 15 minutes to get comfortable in bed after seeing him stumble into his room. He broke Glace's solitude with a dire announcement that there had been a fire in Oakland and all the season ticket documentation had been burned.

"We need to take care of this tonight," Bestor said, sounding more like Davis than Davis himself. George sprang to life. "I'm down here with Scotty and Bobby in Bobby's room," Glace thought Davis said. "What's your room number?" Bestor yelled in his perfect Davis impression. "417," Bestor said in his own voice, and then reported that to Glace.

"We need to recreate these records tonight. Bring everything you have with you, and get down here to Mr. Bestor's room."

Glace was already out of bed and looking for his pants. He splashed some cold water on his face, tried it a second time, and then gave up on what he looked like. His shirt was half on and half off under his sport coat. But he appeared at the door with the few records he had with him in his briefcase.

It took Glace longer than it should have to realize that there was no fire, and it wasn't Davis on the phone. He did not see the humor when everyone laughed and slapped him on his back.

I was getting to know Franklin Mieuli better while working for the Golden State Warriors. Rick Barry was the star player on the team, and Keith Wilkes and Phil Smith provided enough firepower to win any night. But they were two years and a new front office removed from their championship season.

The men Mieuli hired and allowed to run it after Dick Vertlieb and Hal Childs had moved on, Sterling and Bestor, were running the operation while Al Attles and Bruce Hale were in charge of the basketball side.

The Raiders' return contest against the Steelers in 1976 was nowhere close to as competitive as the first meeting. Even though the defending world champions were favored by only a point in the opener, this coming weekend they were more than four-point favorites.

"You could be headed for the Super Bowl," Tom Roberts said while we ate dinner at our new home in Lafayette. It was Saturday night, the night before the game. I was staying up late, eating buffalo wings and drinking margaritas with friends, with nothing more to do the next day than roll over and turn on the television next to my bed.

"If the Raiders win tomorrow, we're all going to the Super Bowl," I announced. "You and Donna as guests of Pam and me. I would much rather be in the stands with you guys than working the game upstairs."

The next morning at 9:00, while CBS was broadcasting from Minnesota, where the Vikings were preparing to host the Dallas Cowboys, I rolled over and switched on our portable color television. Pam had already left for work. Because of a scheduling situation at the hospital, she had been moved out of nights to work the day shift for two weeks.

I didn't get out of bed until halftime of the Raiders game, past two in the afternoon. They are going to go to the Super Bowl, I thought as I headed out to check what was available to eat in the refrigerator. I felt a hint of disappointment that I had quit. If I had stayed, I'd be headed to the Super Bowl with them.

The second half secured the obvious result as the highly motivated Raiders continued to dominate the injury-riddled Steelers. They had almost completed their 24–7 win when Pam got home from work.

"How do you feel?" she inquired, aware of what I had lost.

Tears started to form in my eyes. Then, unexpectedly, I lost my temper.

"Why the fuck do they win it now!" I bellowed. I grabbed a sofa pillow and threw it as hard as I could at a chair across the room. Pam didn't make a peep, allowing me to vent my frustration. Just a few months after I left the team, they would finally return to the biggest show in sports.

And I was not with them.

"Should I have stayed?" I said while sitting up and putting my back against her legs.

"I'm glad you're here right now," Pam said as tenderly as she could with a person in distress.

"You're right," I declared with a burst of bravado, belying my outburst of only moments earlier. "We are going to the Super Bowl, and we are doing it together. Really together."

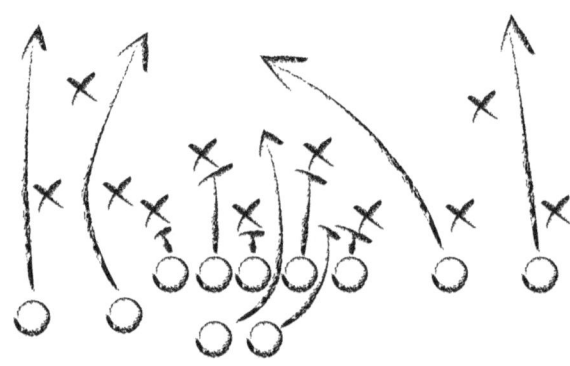

Chapter 41

Pasadena

IN ALL, I HAD ARRANGED for 14 Super Bowl tickets, located up high and near the 50-yard line at the Rose Bowl in Pasadena, the site of Super Bowl XI. On Wednesday, I had 10 of them fanned out on my desk, deciding who got what tickets. There were five pairs of seats and one group of four tickets together, and Norm Fisher, one of the top photographers for the Raiders, would give me those out of his allotment that he received from the team. Fisher was going to get those when the team arrived on Friday in Pasadena, and I was going to pick them up from him at the team hotel on Saturday afternoon. Those seats would be for Pam, Donna, Tom, and me.

I was figuring out how to divvy up the remaining five pairs. I could count out seven among family and friends. That left three tickets still available, and I thought it was wise to keep a few for people we might run into down south.

Penny, who also worked in the promotional department for the Warriors, buzzed me and said, "You have a call on line three."

I pushed the clear plastic button with a blinking white light. Before I was even done saying hello, I heard his distinctive voice. "Dennis," Mr. Davis said.

"Congratulations, sir," I blurted out instinctively.

Davis ignored the congratulations, moving straight to the purpose of his call. "Listen, young man," Davis said, "we'll have a lot to do down in Southern California next week, and I want to know if you'd like to be there with us?"

Before I thought about what to say, he continued. "I just figure you might want to be a part of this, and I'd like you to, you know, do what you always did. Drive me around, pretty much stay with me for the week."

I was amazed at how quickly he had me. Moments before, I was separating out the tickets on my desk and had my week planned to be with Pam, friends, and family. Now I felt close to accepting his offer.

"I just think you should be a part of this," Davis repeated after a few beats of silence.

"Sir," I said, eyeing the tickets on my desk, "thank you for the consideration. I really appreciate it, and I'll be at the Super Bowl, but I'll be with Pam in the stands."

"I was just thinking that you might be regretting not being here. Now I'm telling you that you can."

"Thank you, sir, I do appreciate it, but I'll be with Pam."

"You're telling me you don't want to go to the Super Bowl with the Raiders?" The tone of his voice had shifted from business charming to New Jersey thug. "I'm not waiting for an answer. If you want to do this, you have to tell me now."

I was wavering, but the sight of the tickets on the desk, reminding me of Pam and our friends, made me stay the course.

"Thank you, sir, and good luck. You're going to beat the Vikings. I'll be watching it as a fan from the stands."

The phone hung up.

No goodbye.

I sat there frozen to my seat. Scotty Sterling walked in and asked me what was going on.

"I was just talking to Al Davis on the phone," I reported. "He wanted me to work with him next week in Pasadena."

"What did you tell him?"

"I turned him down."

Sterling was glad to hear it. "Good for you. Davis always thinks everyone is just waiting to jump for him."

We planned to leave at 6:00 a.m. on Saturday, the day before the game. Tom and Donna would be coming to our house, and we would take the car Pam and I had bought a few months earlier, a red 1976 Pontiac Firebird with white interior and mag wheels. It was a very sweet ride.

In the middle of the night, Pam was sound asleep. We had gone to bed just after 10:00, earlier than normal, and I had only occasionally drifted off to sleep while thinking about our upcoming weekend. I had dozed off again when I awoke to the room rocking from a significant earthquake. I nudged Pam on the shoulder soon enough for her to feel the most significant movement from the jolt, and she lay there with a worried look in her eyes as the rumbling continued.

Earthquakes were common enough that the first movement was not always reason enough to take cover or jump for a doorframe to wait out the jolt. But this one was getting worse, and both Pam and I scrambled out of bed and stood next to each other in the doorframe. The rattling finally stopped.

"That was a pretty good one," Pam said while heading back to bed.

"I want to get going," I announced, not moving. "If we have the big one and we could have been in Pasadena because I hadn't left the Raiders, then that would have been a reason to stay with them."

"You're nuts," Pam said playfully. "Come back to bed; it's only 1:45."

"No," I responded. "We've got to get out of here now. I'm calling Donna and Tom."

They lived in Martinez, about 15 minutes away. They had felt the quake and were willing to move up our departure time.

"We'll be over in about an hour," Tom said, concluding our middle-of-the-night call.

We were on the road a little before four. The radio news reports were dominated by coverage of the earthquake.

"If you're in the East Bay, you may have been awoke by any of a swarm of earthquakes that have been rattling our Saturday morning," the announcer said on KCBS as I headed to the freeway. *"The most significant shock struck at 1:38 a.m. and registered 4.3 on the Richter scale."*

"That was the one that got us on the road early," I commented. Donna and Tom were leaning on each other in the cramped back seat, trying to get in some sleep.

The Raiders hotel for Super Bowl XI was in Newport Beach, and we pulled into the parking lot around 3:00. We'd been driving all day and looked a bit scruffy while wearing T-shirts I had made at Norm Fisher's office earlier in the week. Fisher had a new machine that allowed him to make color photocopies on almost any surface, and I had used the machine to make four shirts that had ten Super Bowl tickets fanned open and displayed on the front.

We were wearing them when we paraded through the hotel lobby. I used the white courtesy phone to call Fisher in his room. Laverne, his wife, answered and told me Norm was in their motor home parked behind the hotel. I had started across the lobby when I heard my name called. "Ranahan of the Raiders," Al LoCasale said. "It's too late for you to be here."

As we turned to greet him, he said hi to Pam, and I introduced him to Donna and Tom. Madden then appeared. The team must have been coming from a meal or meeting because, within moments, the lobby was filled with Raiders checking for messages at the front desk and milling about.

I was uncomfortable, not wanting to intrude. It looked like Madden was not happy to see me. I didn't introduce him or make eye contact as he joined our group, but Phil Villapiano spotted me and came over. "Dennis, I'm glad you're here. Glad you are going to get to see us kill the Vikings tomorrow."

His confidence irritated Madden, and the coach said, "We have to play the game first."

Villapiano laughed, hit Madden on the shoulder, and announced, "Coach, this one is in the bag."

Madden shook his head, not wanting to jinx his chances, but I thought he secretly shared his linebacker's confidence.

I headed for the door to meet Fisher in the back to collect our final four Super Bowl tickets. As I reached the exit, I heard my name again. "Denny," Tom Grimes called to get my attention.

I looked back, still holding the door open with my left hand, and Grimes said, "You could have been here."

I watched Pam heading off with Donna and Tom and looked back to Grimes. "I'd rather be here."

Norm was in his motor home, which doubled as a photography studio and office for him both in the parking lot at home games and now on location at Super Bowl XI. He offered the four of us sodas, and I thanked him for the tickets.

"I'm hungry," Pam said near the end of our visit with Norm, and he recommended the coffee shop in the hotel.

"They've got a great hamburger, and Laverne had the French dip and said that was good, too," Norm said. We all agreed to eat before continuing our trip to meet another friend in Long Beach. As we exited Norm's mobile office, I noticed Art Snyder near the back of the Raiders hotel looking my way. I hadn't talked to him since October. He had asked then if I had started documenting my time with the Raiders on the cassette tapes he provided.

I had made a number of tapes, most recorded while sitting in my office at night after Pam left for work. But I didn't want to share them with him. I didn't want to share them with anyone. I wasn't sure that writing a book about Davis and the Raiders, as Snyder had recommended, was smart.

"I talked to Mr. Dom about you," Snyder said after I told Pam, Donna, and Tom to go ahead and order me a French dip, and I would join them.

"What are you thinking?" I questioned, not sure I wanted Snyder representing me.

Yet he didn't pursue the topic. Instead, he asked, "So, who do you think is going to win tomorrow?"

"The Raiders," I confidently answered.

"Would that make the best show?" he replied.

I missed his point. "Show?" I ask. "What do you mean?"

"Dennis," he said knowingly, "remember when I told you John focuses on what John knows, and you think your motivational factors are trump?"

I nodded without speaking.

"Well, let me tell you what trumps both game plans and motivation: what makes the best show. Professional sports are entertainment first. How much of the game do you think is left to chance?"

"Nothing to chance," I said, though I knew better. "Everything relies on the athletic preparation and execution."

"Sure about that?" Snyder said in a flat voice. "How about the Super Bowl eight years ago when the New York Jets beat the Baltimore Colts?"

"Greatest upset ever."

"What did the league get done by having the Jets win?" Snyder posed.

The victory by the Jets legitimatized the American Football League after the merger was announced. If the Colts had blown out the Jets as the Green Bay Packers had downed the Kansas City Chiefs and Oakland Raiders in the first two games between the leagues, the perceived competitiveness between the AFL and NFL would have been pushed back for years.

"Do you see the advantages for everyone that the Jets won that game?"

What this man was suggesting ran counter to everything I believed about sports, but he did not waver in his contention.

"Want more evidence?" he said. "Who was the coach of the Baltimore Colts when they lost to the Jets?"

"Don Shula," I easily replied.

"And how have things worked out for him since he coached the Colts to a necessary loss in Super Bowl III?"

A year later, Shula was out of Baltimore, and in 1970 became head coach of the Miami Dolphins. The Colts won the Super Bowl the first year he was gone and beat Tom Landry and the Dallas Cowboys to complete the 1970 season. Then Shula led the Dolphins to their first

Super Bowl in his second season in south Florida and lost to Landry, who had been beaten by the Colts the year before.

The Dolphins played in three straight Super Bowls and had the perfect season in 1972.

"Do you think the league owed Mr. Shula?" Snyder said as if he knew these results were all orchestrated by more than simple competitive balance.

"Who was the quarterback of that perfect Dolphins team in 1972?" Snyder asked.

"Bob Griese," I responded.

"Actually, the guy who triggered most of the perfect season was Earl Morrall, who replaced Griese after he was hurt in the fifth game of the season. Morrall was the quarterback that missed all those open receivers for the Colts in their Super Bowl III loss. Think he got paid back?" Snyder posed.

"Even Lamar Hunt got what was coming to him," he stated while pointing out that his team, the Kansas City Chiefs, played in the first Super Bowl and won the last Super Bowl before the two leagues merged into the American and National Football Conferences in 1970.

"I don't believe you," I said, like a kid interrupting an adult who says there really isn't a Santa Claus.

"What's the best show?" Snyder repeated. "Where is the best entertainment value?"

I was involuntarily shaking my head no. This conversation left me with a sick feeling in my stomach.

"You ought to write that book," he recommended while walking toward the Raiders hotel.

The next day, January 9, 1977, I was standing near the top row at the Rose Bowl at the 50-yard line and thinking about my conversation with Snyder.

Was this just all a show?

If it was, it was a great one for the Raiders. They crushed the opposition all game long. The crowd rose in unison and Oakland fans cheered Willie Brown as the defensive back returned a Fran Tarkenton interception 75 yards. His fourth-quarter score iced the game for the Silver and Black.

When the final gun sounded on a Raiders 32–14 triumph over Minnesota, I was not cheering but rather saluting the years of work and struggles the Oakland organization had endured before gaining their first world championship. In a box not far from where I stood, Al Davis had his right hand up in a fist, beaming a smile that he had earned.

On the field, John Madden was being hoisted off his feet by his players. The torment of five championship-game losses and all those postseason disappointments had been eradicated in a final conquering moment.

From the radio booth, Bill King remarked as only he can: *"Madden's victory grin gives his head the appearance of a cracked watermelon."*

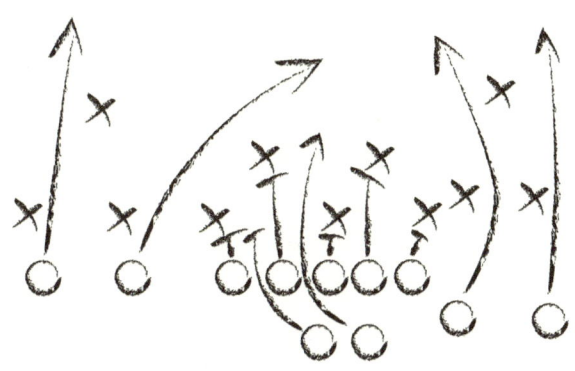

Chapter 42

Going South

THE RAIDERS WERE BACK IN THE PLAYOFFS IN 1977, while their reign as Super Bowl Champions ended in Denver with a 20–17 loss to the Broncos in the AFC Championship Game. By 1978, most of the key ingredients that had performed so well for the Raiders were gone. During their prime, Jim Otto, Willie Brown, Gene Upshaw, Art Shell, and a host of others were staples on a team that played in seven championship games during Madden's first nine seasons as head coach.

Now Oakland appeared in decline, and following a 9–7 season in 1978, Madden announced his retirement as the coach. He retired as the only coach in NFL history to win 100 games in a ten-year span, but his legacy was also tied to six championship-game losses. In his career, Madden won a single Super Bowl, while his replacement, Tom Flores, guided the Raiders to a pair of Vince

Lombardi Trophy winning campaigns in his first five seasons at the helm.

During Flores' nine-year tenure as head coach, Davis made good on the threat he voiced to me in 1976 following his exchange with Bill Bidwill at the NFL owners' meeting, when he sneered to me his disgust with fellow owners who were passing rules that they thought would never be challenged. He, Al Davis, would serve the NFL by challenging the league management and forcing them into running the NFL like a business, not a side toy for rich guys. Davis always viewed almost all baseball owners that way, and he was determined football owners would not sink to that level.

In 1980, the Raiders became the first wild card team to advance to the Super Bowl, and they won it in convincing style over the Philadelphia Eagles, 27–10. That would prove to be the last time the *Oakland* Raiders won a Super Bowl during Davis' life. His Raiders did win one more Super Bowl to complete the 1983 season, but that was after they had moved to Los Angeles.

By the time the Raiders had won their third Super Bowl in an eight-year span, Davis was spending more time with lawyers preparing for court than with his coaches. His contentious legal fight with the league, court battles he mostly won, coincided with the team's decline after their win over the Washington Redskins in Super Bowl XVIII. Historians will point to Davis' increased time in court battles with the league as a reason his team dropped from their high perch.

Flores never won another postseason game after capturing Super Bowl XVIII, losing in the first round the next two seasons and missing the playoffs in 1986 and 1987. After a 5–10 record in 1987, the worst the Raiders has suffered since Davis joined the team in 1963, Flores was replaced as head coach by Mike Shanahan.

The relationship between Shanahan and Davis was rocky from the start, and after another losing campaign in 1988 and losses in three of the first four games of 1989, Davis fired Shanahan and replaced him with one of the greats from the Raiders days of glory, Art Shell.

In his first two full seasons on the sidelines with Oakland, Shell led the Raiders to the postseason. He won a Divisional Playoff Game on January 13, 1991, over the Cincinnati Bengals, but the Raiders suffered the biggest loss of the day when star runningback Bo Jackson was dragged down from behind and suffered an injury that ended his football career. Oakland was pummeled the next Sunday in Buffalo, 51–3, and lost a wild card game the following season to the Kansas City Chiefs.

Another campaign without a postseason berth followed in 1992, and the once-proud Raiders organization seemed to be in freefall entering the 1993 season.

Attendance in Los Angeles had dwindled to where the Raiders, once regarded as the kings of *Monday Night Football*, were no longer scheduled for home prime-time games because the league did not want to show empty seats at an NFL game. Skirmishes in the stands became more violent than the action on the field as the Raiders hosted games at the sparsely populated Los Angeles Coliseum.

It was not what Al Davis had envisioned for his once-proud franchise when he manipulated the move from Northern to Southern California. He had anticipated that the Raiders would become another bigger-than-life Hollywood attraction. Instead, the organization was now a second-tier NFL franchise.

Although never agreeing to the terms Art Snyder and his associates proposed for opening a handicapping service, a year prior to the Raiders move to Los Angeles in 1982, I opened Qoxhi Picks. I derived the name from football letters, the "Q" for quarterback, "O" for offense, "X" for defense, and "HI" for what I based the method I utilized to locate point spread winners, motivational highs.

My assertion returning from Pittsburgh after the 1975 AFC Championship Game that I would "never have to lose a game if I could pick any team each week" was realized only once in my first 11 years of operation, but every season did generate more winners than losers. I built a healthy client base while also doing television, radio, and print.

Then, in 1992, I made the biggest mistake of my professional life when I started a handicapping newspaper that was in direct competition with my former publisher. While the paper content was what I wanted it to be, the distribution lagged well behind costs, and the lost income by turning a one-time employer into a professional enemy multiplied the problems.

Looking to add capital and expand distribution for the failing publication, I reached out to Mr. Davis in the spring of 1993.

- - - - - -

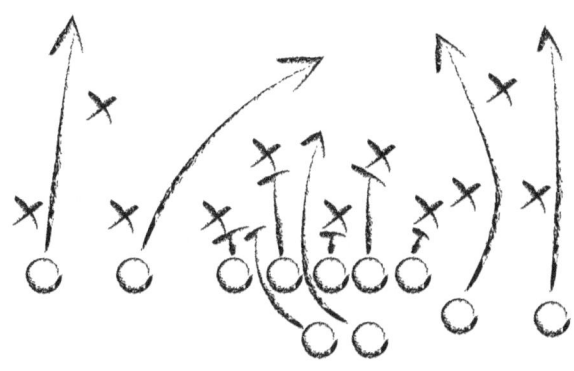

Chapter 43

Too Good

Pᴀᴍ ᴀɴᴅ I ᴡᴇʀᴇ ɪɴᴠɪᴛᴇᴅ ᴛᴏ Lᴀᴋᴇ Tᴀʜᴏᴇ by some friends to have the kids up to their cabin for the Fourth-of-July weekend in 1993.

I had been negotiating a deal with Al Davis to finance and expand the sports publication I had founded a year earlier, *Sports Stats Weekly*. The publication had done nothing but cost me money since I started the project on the naive proposition that a quality publication would find an audience. Beginning in 1992, I had dedicated nearly all my resources to what developed into a real attractive and information-rich tabloid newspaper. But, without adequate distribution channels or advertising revenues to sustain editorial and printing costs, I was left with a business that needed both a cash and management infusion to survive.

"I'm not saying I read or agree with anything printed in your publication," Davis said after I dialed his home number in June. I wasn't sure if he was referring to the gambling content included in *Sports Stats Weekly* or the two-part series I had written on him to launch the publication a year earlier. When I asked him, Davis said, "I'm not confirming nor denying anything you wrote about me. In fact, I can't recall for sure if I read it. But what are you calling for?"

Articles I had written about Davis had been nearly exclusively complimentary, as was almost all of the two-part series run in *Sports Stats Weekly*. Still, Davis distanced himself from being pinned down to what could be considered an endorsement, and he was setting the ground rules for our negotiations before I had even begun to explain any of the details in my proposition.

Still, from that icy business start, over the time of the call, Davis sounded like he was truly interested in working with me in the growth of *Sports Stats Weekly*.

It seemed too good to be true.

That is what I had been thinking before we talked next, four days after our first conversation. I had to make sure that my enthusiasm for working with Davis was not an illusion; the idea of an NFL owner involved in a gambling publication seemed a reach. Did he really know the content was mostly point spread and gambling information . . . or did he intend to turn the publication away from the information I required to be included?

Davis dismissed my concerns when he said, "Dennis, I know what the fuck we're talking about here, are you with me? Listen, this stuff exists; somebody is someday going to present it in a way that works for the league. That can be you." His statement elevated my enthusiasm to new heights.

I had the product, and he had the finances and influence to almost guarantee success.

The idea of having Al Davis with a vested interest in the success of *Sports Stats Weekly* was not only the breath of air I needed financially to survive, but the prospect of winning at every corner in order to get what we wanted.

Our phone conversation ended with him saying, "I'll call you on Sunday."

For a moment, I was going to tell him I wouldn't be back until Tuesday, but then, thought better of it. If he was going to be working on his birthday, I was certainly going to be available to him for what I considered the most important business opportunity of my life.

"That's your birthday, sir. Happy birthday in advance, and I'll be here so we can talk on the Fourth."

Davis made a sound that seemed to dismiss the birthday greeting as frivolous talk he didn't want to spend time on, and I suddenly regretted wishing him a happy birthday. Davis repeated, "I'll call you on Sunday," and his receiver hung up before I got a chance to say yes.

Pam wasn't happy about taking the kids by herself to Lake Tahoe, but she was supportive of my need to stay on top of this business venture.

I answered his call just after 6:00 p.m. on Sunday. His first words were, "What I need you to do—" Davis was speaking in his charming Southern accent, but moments later, was into his New Jersey street smart thug dialect, "—is go collect information on how these publications work. Listen, Dennis, are you with me? I need to know what works, what doesn't. I've got an interest in *Pro Football Weekly,* you know, although I'm not sure where my money went after I helped out Artie."

Davis had invested in *Pro Football Weekly* in 1974 while offering support to Art Arkush, who founded the publication a decade earlier. In 1985, the *Pro Football Weekly* Davis had propped up went out of print, saved by Jim Feist, who invested the capital needed to resume printing for the 1986 NFL season.

How ironic is it that the one year the Chicago-based football publication was out of print was the only year the Chicago Bears won the Super Bowl. Three years later, Feist, who had made a fortune in Las Vegas with various sports handicapping services and products that thrived on boiler-room tactics to buttonhole overmatched gamblers with picks for their credit cards, wanted to emphasize gambling in *Pro Football Weekly*.

The Arkush family balked at turning their publication from mainstream football news to an emphasis on handicapping and, in a well-managed business arrangement, parted ways amicably. This was both a tribute to all parties involved and a move that still left the door open for a publication that could both serve the serious gambler and not threaten the integrity of the NFL.

With that as a background, I could see why Davis wanted to partner with me and do something that had never been done—elevate gambling information on the NFL while enhancing the integrity of the league.

"Go to them all, Dennis," Davis said, "see how they run, learn their profit streams, and come down to Los Angeles and give me a report."

Two weeks later, I had completed my study while bending my American Express Card for airlines, hotels, rent-a-cars, and meals while meeting with publishers and employees of several of the best sports publications in the country. I was prepared to offer this information to Davis at his Los Angeles office when I was led to a room in the Raiders facility that had the feeling of half kitchen, half meeting room.

Not really the place I expected to meet Mr. Davis to offer my report from the road.

I was in the room for almost 10 minutes when the door opened. It was not Davis but rather one of his assistants, Amy Trask.

"Is Mr. Davis going to join us?" I asked politely, and Trask brushed off my question as much as she did me.

"Mr. Davis is not able to meet with you and has turned this project over to me on behalf of the Raiders. What have you got to show me?" Trask said while eyeing my briefcase.

Disappointed and without words, I reached into my briefcase and pulled out charts and graphs I had expected to be able to present to Davis. "I really thought I was going to meet with Mr. Davis personally," I said while handing over a few copies of *Sports Stats Weekly* along with the financials on the company and a bound book with charts and graphs from the research I had done following Davis' assignment.

My disappointment in meeting with her was apparent to Trask. She simply scooped up the materials I had brought and said, "I'll make sure Mr. Davis gets these."

I had waited longer in this room for the meeting to start than the actual time I spent with Trask. She walked out of the door in front of me, and I headed back to the airport and flew home on a flight four hours earlier than I had originally scheduled.

— — — — — —

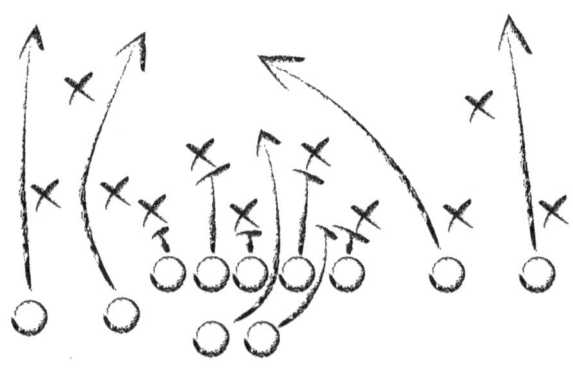

Chapter 44

Bus for One

On the plane ride home, I transformed the failure to accomplish any goals with Trask to again being tested by Davis to overcome any obstacle he would create to test my commitment to the project. This was not a time of loss but rather an opportunity to show Davis the level of my commitment.

I prepared a report on my meeting with Trask, reiterated my interest in working with him and producing something very special. On my third call to the Raiders office, I got him on the phone. Davis said, "I'll be up there for this weekend's game. We can meet then."

I decided to meet the Raiders plane and show Mr. Davis how interested I was in producing the best football paper in the world that dealt with the league's most compelling element: wagering on games. I was prepared to show numbers that has this activity growing from an estimated 500 million dollars a season during the 1970s to more than that each week today.

I drove a new sports car, and once it started, it ran well. But today, it is not starting. Instead of the purr of its turbo-charged engine, the disheartening click, more a tuc—tuc—tuc sound, indicated the battery was not providing the charge necessary to start the car. I have no idea why a new car would have a battery problem.

It should be working, but it's not.

Fortunately, I'm in San Francisco, and my car is parked heading down Webster Street. I figured the car would start if I popped the clutch before I got to the stop sign on Union Street.

It does, and the sound of its power charging into my mission to meet Mr. Davis at the San Francisco Airport on August 7th was in motion. As I pulled into an underground stall in a section that was painted bright yellow, I paused for a moment before turning off the engine. Better I park on the roof, I decided, and circled away from the spaces closest to my destination in the airport and drove up to where I could gain a rolling start if my battery failed again.

I confidently turned the key off after my selection of a roof parking position pointed at the down ramp at the San Francisco International Airport.

I had gotten the Raiders flight number and arrival time from John Otten, who worked for the team, but the flight was not listed on the arrivals board I was studying in the airport terminal.

The lady at the desk was most helpful after I explained I was here to see Mr. Davis, and he was on that flight.

"Well," she said freely, "the plane is on time; it's just touching down right now. But it's not going to any gate; it is going to load directly onto buses in an area off the runway."

"What's the best way to meet a plane that is unloading there?" I asked, reminding her again that Al Davis would want me to meet him coming off that plane.

"Well," she said, picking up a phone and dialing while still talking to me, "the only way we could get you with the people getting off that plane is to have a security person drive you out on his cart." A moment later, her eyes turned as she focused her attention on someone on the phone. Her conversation concluded by telling me to meet a security person at the door 57, which is located between gates 24 and 26 in the United terminal.

When I arrived at door 57, I was met by a man wearing a blue security guard shirt that introduced himself as Wally. He handed me a safety helmet I'd have to wear for our ride to the plane.

His vehicle was just a little bigger than a golf cart, but in contrast to where a golf cart would have fiberglass molding mounted on a frame, this truck-like cart was all steel reinforced. It had round molded iron fenders on front and back that were locked into place by a heavy metal frame and foot-wide tires to support the weight of its reinforced cage.

"You with the Raiders?" Wally asked while heading across an open area towards the Raiders arrival position.

"Used to be. Now I'm just working with Mr. Davis," I said while noticing the stairs that would allow the passengers to exit the Boeing 737 were still 10 feet to the right of the plane. The stairs were attached to a vehicle similar to the one I was riding in, and the driver pulling the ramp was wearing an orange shirt and had his leg up with his arm draped over it while he waited for the engines to rest so he could tow the stairs into place on the side of the aircraft.

"We better wait here until the buses are in place," Wally said while chauffeuring me to the Raiders arriving flight. The buses pulled up just after the stairs were docked and a stream of players, media, team personnel, and airline personnel emptied from the aircraft to the waiting buses.

I remained in Wally's vehicle, waiting to see Davis before moving toward the arrivals. The flow of passengers leaving the plane had slowed to an occasional athlete ducking his head out the door while carrying a silver-and-black duffle bag.

"You see him?" Wally asked as I handed him my safety helmet and thanked him for the ride.

"No, but I see some people I know. I'll figure out where Mr. Davis is later. Thanks again for the service," I said over my shoulder as I headed on foot to the buses from the opposite direction of those debarking the plane.

Al LoCasale was directing people to the buses when I asked him where Mr. Davis was. "He isn't on this flight," LoCasale said while asking me where I came from. I explained how I got a ride out to meet the flight, and he told me I was welcome to take one of the buses to the hotel. "But Mr. Davis will not be arriving until tomorrow morning," he reiterated.

LoCasale was one of the last of the arriving party to board a bus, and after he climbed on the second of the three buses on the tarmac, I headed for the third bus. The driver greeted me and I took a seat on the padded bench that faced toward the aisle with the driver forward and to my right.

"Looks like you're the last one," he said while the doors closed on the two other buses and we smelled their exhaust as they began a procession to the hotel. The driver pulled a lever and the door on our bus hissed before closing.

On the first bus were most of the players; it was full. The second bus had LoCasale, along with most of the Raiders staff on the trip and the bulk of the media traveling with the team. Next to LoCasale on the ride from the plane to the hotel was Dr. Bob Rosenfeld, the longtime Raiders team orthopedic surgeon. He is the man who introduced James Garner to the team after operating on the knee Garner had first injured as a running back at Oklahoma University and later as a soldier in World War II.

On the third bus was a driver named Gus and me.

Gus had paused while the first two buses pulled out of the airport secured area and toward the Burlingame Sheridan. That's why team equipment manager Richard Romanski and team trainer George Anderson were already standing on the curb when the third of the three buses hired by the Raiders pulled into the Sheraton circular parking area with just Gus and me aboard. I had thought about asking Gus to let me off at the corner so I could join the group without being seen arriving by myself on a bus.

But, while I was thinking of asking Gus to let me out early, he let out the clutch and we pulled in front of the hotel. The door opened with a sound like the hiss of a startled reptile. I was shaking my head and hoping for an entrance that did not bring attention to the fact that I was the only person on the last bus to arrive, but that relative anonymity was blown to bits by the loud, high-pitched voice of the Raiders longtime trainer, George Anderson.

"You've got your own bus?" Anderson yelled out with laughter while the attention of many people milling around the front of the hotel was drawn by his piercing voice to my solo arrival.

I sheepishly nodded with a smile and a wave with the arm holding my briefcase.

"I was thinking I was going to meet Mr. Davis on his arrival," I began to tell George before he interrupted me with the fact that Davis was flying in tomorrow.

Dick Romanski was standing next to Anderson when he announced my arrival but offered his comments to me in a much more serious and personal manner. Romanski is normally a very friendly fellow, but his greeting was in stark contrast to the bravado of Anderson; he asked me first what I've heard.

I didn't know what he meant. But I wanted to know what he thought I might already be aware of, so I said, "What have you heard?"

"It's not working down there," Romanski said in regards to the Raiders playing in Southern California. "It's not like when we were in Oakland."

I complained to Romanski how Amy Trask met me when I had scheduled a meeting with Davis in Los Angeles, and the Raiders equipment manager looked at me with a forlorn glare and said, "He's letting her do everything."

The subject of Trask and how her relationship with Davis was affecting the team led to Romanski confirming more details on Davis' flight plans.

"The man," Romanski said in reference to Davis, "is arriving tomorrow morning with Mrs. Davis."

"The problem is," Anderson interjected while still standing near where we were conversing and probably overhearing bits of our conversation, "everybody's asshole around here is tight as a frog's," the Raiders trainer said while both laughing and showing real concern for the team.

— — — — — —

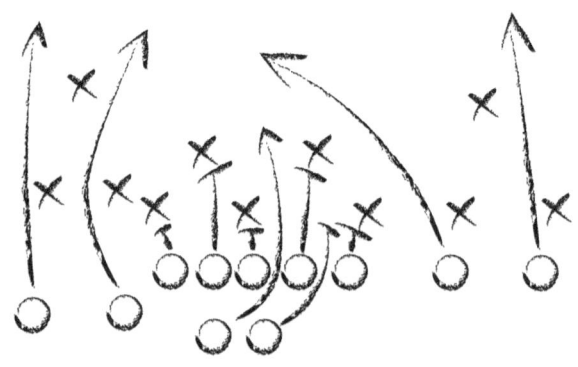

Chapter 45

Dinner for Ninety

"Ranahan of the Raiders," I heard shouted from five yards away. It was LoCasale, and he was inviting me to join him at the arrival meal the Raiders were holding in the hotel for the entire traveling entourage of players, staff, and media. I thanked him and accepted, but told him I would first have to make a phone call.

I wanted to check the Saturday preseason scores and headed down the hallway off the main lobby that included a gift shop and shoeshine stand. The row of pay phones was to the left halfway down the passage that led to a pair of elevators at the end of the hall. First, I heard Dr. Rosenfeld's voice, and then I noticed he was asking me a question while we were walking shoulder to shoulder in a crowd no doubt made much denser by the arrival of the Raiders.

Dr. Rosenfeld was a world-class orthopedic surgeon that worked with the Raiders from his Beverly Hills office while they played in Oakland. Since their move to Los Angeles in 1982, he had been able to dedicate his extraordinary skills to Mr. Davis' team in a geographically more advantageous arrangement. From my time of working with the Raiders 20 years earlier, I remembered Dr. Rosenfeld as a well-traveled, well-spoken, friendly guy who gave you a solid handshake and seemed genuinely interested in listening during conversations.

I always pictured Dr. Rosenfeld in a white Mercedes convertible with a tennis racket stashed behind his seat while he whisked along the Los Angeles coastline on the way to his waiting yacht.

That was not the man I got on this August afternoon in 1993. He was bewildered, overwhelmed by the mild chaos the throng of visitors who had come to see the Raiders had created in the front lobby. That crowd had now spilled into the hallway off the lobby Rosenfeld was trying to cut a path through, and when I made eye contact with him, he said, "I need to use the restroom. Is this the way I go?"

While asking me for directions, he was distracted by the commotion around us. He was headed in the right direction. The men's and ladies' restrooms were located on each side of the hall I was looking for that offered phones to check the scores.

"I don't know why I'm still doing this," Dr. Rosenfeld confided in me while shaking his head to indicate he wished he was somewhere other than on this Raiders trip. "I'm too old to be traveling with these guys," Rosenfeld said while adding, "It's not like 10 years ago when you were working with the team."

"I left 17 years ago," I said as much an acknowledgment of how fast time goes by as correcting the distinguished physician.

"That's too long," Rosenfeld said before entering the men's room while I headed down the short hall, about 15 feet deep, that had a bank of five phones mounted above a table that was attached to the wall off to my right. The entrance to the communication center was only about three feet wide, but four or five feet into the passageway, the area width expanded another couple of feet, which allowed for the Formica table braced to the wall below the phones. Five wooden chairs were positioned in front of the phone stations, and two of the chairs were occupied—the one closest to where I entered and the farthest from where I stood.

I used my phone credit card to connect with a scoreline that opened with an advertisement for a sports service called "Big Game Hunter." Once the sales pitch was over, up-to-date results were relayed through the recorded message. Because preseason games were spread over more days than the regular campaign, and most people didn't realize that there was a way to win in the preseason, I was not including National Football League exhibition games as part of the Qoxhi Picks season package. But, I still had clients who were interested if I had something, and I occasionally did.

I wrote down the current scores for the completed games and the few that were in progress. I also wrote a list of the games scheduled for the rest of the evening. I was thinking about those when I emerged from the phone bank hallway and came face-to-face with Art Shell, who was in his fifth season as Raiders head coach since taking over for Mike Shanahan after the fourth game of the 1989 season.

"Art," I said instinctively to a man I came to know and respect during my years in the front office of the Raiders while he was in the prime of his Hall of Fame playing career. I extended my hand as a greeting but he didn't take it, seemingly looking right through me without recognizing who I was.

Terry Robiskie, who was standing to his right, grabbed Shell's arm to nudge it toward my awkward handshake while saying, "Art, it's Dennis Ranahan, you know Dennis." I was already greeting Art by saying my name to jog his memory. I had remembered Shell as a most honorable and thoughtful man two decades earlier, and I had expected that his head coaching would reflect that character and find ongoing success.

But, this was not the bright young player I met in 1973; this was a man obviously overwhelmed. His eyes were sunken and distant, his handshake uninspired. I had a sudden and profound compassion for the man. Robiskie did more of the talking during our brief exchange of good wishes, and I walked away stunned by the stress Shell was wearing on his sleeve.

The Raiders meal was held in a conference room that had an accordion folding room divider that was pushed to either side to offer maximum area for the Los Angeles party. LoCasale was at the buffet line; I spotted him from the door I used to enter the dining room. "We are in the back," he said, pointing with a hand that was holding a plate of pasta salad.

"I'll put my stuff down and come back to get something to eat," I said while lifting my black briefcase and nodding my head.

LoCasale was on his way to the table when I passed him on my way to the food spread. He stopped me and said, "Did you know that Jim Finks had surgery yesterday? You know him, don't you?"

"I do," I said emphatically while bringing to mind one of my top ten football business heroes. I admired Jim Finks before I went to work for the Raiders 20 years ago. I had read about his career in Minnesota before seeing him in 1972 at Candlestick Park when his Vikings were playing the 49ers. He had been diagnosed with lung cancer the previous April, right after the NFL draft, and this recent surgery was an emergency procedure.

"He's listed as stable," LoCasale said in a solemn tone, seemingly not buying the prognosis while shaking his head with a look of despair for Finks' fate.

Finks turned the fortunes of three National Football League teams from the front office, first the Vikings, and later the Chicago Bears and New Orleans Saints. He had a seven-season playing career that began in 1949 with the Pittsburgh Steelers, and in his final NFL season was kept on the Steelers roster while they cut Johnny Unitas.

The Steelers didn't make the right decision in 1955 when they kept Finks and cut Unitas, but Finks proved to be as successful running a team from the front office as the great Johnny Unitas was moving a football squad on the field. I also flashed on that day in the summer of 1974 when he thanked me for my work during the Chicago All-Star negotiations.

"I'll say a prayer for him," I told LoCasale.

"He's going to need a lot of them," LoCasale said while breaking off our conversation and heading for the table in the back corner where I had propped my briefcase up on the chair next to where I wanted to sit.

I was lost in my thoughts while I picked up a plate and took a first glance at what the buffet table was offering. I didn't notice the man in front of me was James Lofton until he handed me a spoon after placing some pasta salad on his plate. I thanked him with a nod and scooped up some salad for myself.

Lofton was not dressed like the Raiders I remember. Instead of loose-fitting jeans and a pullover shirt, Lofton was wearing a suit seemingly worth a million dollars. I think it was brown, but it was darker than any brown I had ever seen and when he turned, it seemed to have a deep rich green color. His shoes were perfectly polished, his shirt crisp, and Lofton's silk tie was impeccably holding a Windsor knot and accented by a matching handkerchief peeking out of his suit jacket pocket. He looked more like he was ready to shoot a cover for a fashion magazine than traveling with a football team.

Particularly, the Raiders I knew in Oakland.

We didn't talk, although he twice handed me the serving fork for the next buffet item. I never met Lofton but marveled at his skills, from his college days at nearby Stanford University to his nine sterling seasons in Green Bay catching passes for the Packers and recent work in Buffalo that contributed to three straight Super Bowl appearances.

Lofton was in the Raiders camp for a second stint. He played in Los Angeles for two seasons after his career in Green Bay and before he helped spike the Bills to their consecutive AFC Championships. Now in his 16th NFL campaign, he was nearing the end of his playing days, but the Raiders thought their young receiving corps could benefit from his experience and leadership.

The room had 25 or 30 round tables that were big enough to seat ten but were set for eight to accommodate the Raiders. I joined LoCasale at the back table and took the seat, which offered a view of the entire room. The first thing I noticed was that Lofton was sitting at the table closest to ours, and he had it all to himself. He used the chair next to him to hold his open briefcase and started writing on a notepad that was bound in a brown leather cover.

His meal, on two plates, was off to the top left and right of his note-book, and his attention was being divided between what he was reading in his briefcase and recording on the pad in front of him. He looked a lot more like an investment broker than a football player.

I wondered, for a moment, what James Lofton was wearing and where his attention was focused when he played his rookie season with the Green Bay Packers in 1978. Actually, I realized quickly, it was more of an accusation than really a question.

"Do you have tickets for the game?" LoCasale asked while wiping his mouth with the back of his hand.

"I really wanted to meet with Mr. Davis," I explained to LoCasale, "but I wouldn't think he'd have any time on a game day for anything other than the game."

"I've got a ticket and can get you a parking pass if you want to come," LoCasale offered while pulling an envelope from his suit jacket pocket. He put the parking pass on the table while saying, "I don't have that many of them, so only take it if you're sure you're going to use it."

I wasn't sure if I was going to go to the preseason game in Palo Alto with my car not running right, and I didn't want to take the parking pass and then not be able to use it. I didn't take the ticket and left the parking pass on the table.

"Your loss," LoCasale said while scooping it back off the table and returning it to a number 10 size envelope that he slipped into his vest pocket.

- - - - - -

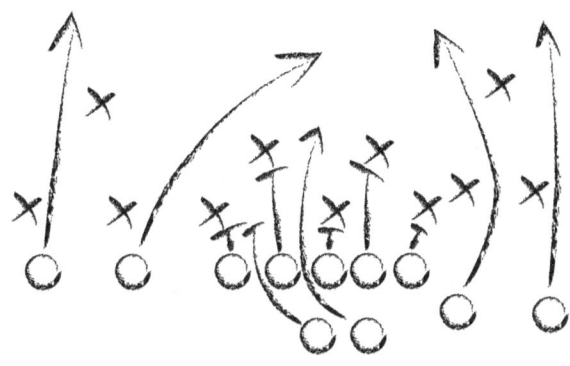

Chapter 46

No Parking

The hotel offered a free shuttle to nearby San Francisco International Airport, a much smaller bus than the one I had ridden on my arrival. I boarded it with five other passengers.

"United," I said when the driver, with a friendly disposition, requested my airline.

For me, it didn't really matter. I was only headed to the parking lot to retrieve a car that I left with what appeared to be a dead battery or some electrical problem. That concern was confirmed when I still had the car door open and put the key in the ignition. The buzzer to indicate an open door began with a sickly tone and quickly faded to nothing. Still, expecting no good results but needing to try, I turned the key in the ignition. The power from the battery only generated one click before total failure.

I was then appreciative of my decision to park on the roof, pointing at the down ramp with no cars in front of me. With the car in neutral, I needed to push my disabled vehicle with the window up on the driver-side door I had opened while gaining leverage with both arms to get it rolling toward the ramp. I noticed the steering wheel was difficult to turn without the engine running while gaining momentum toward the decline, but it wasn't until I jumped back in the car to begin my circular descent to a lower level that I realized the brakes were even more disabled than the steering wheel.

I was concerned about popping the clutch while going this fast in a narrow concrete alley, thinking my beautiful little machine might just kick out its rear end and hit the wall if the engine sprung into motion. Instead, I decided to just roll to the next floor before releasing the clutch in an attempt to start the disabled vehicle. As soon as I rolled onto the third-floor parking area, I released the clutch and pumped the accelerator; the engine roared into action while spewing an unexpected cloud of black exhaust.

While the car was running, it seemed everything was at full power and the battery gauge indicated it was charging. It ran like a dream from the airport to the Van Ness Avenue exit, which I took on my way to the Qoxhi Picks offices on Laguna Street.

The car had been running smoothly for almost half an hour, and in order to ensure maximum opportunity for the battery to charge on the drive up 101, I didn't listen to the radio or stereo. Didn't even turn on the headlights while pushing the period between light and dark without the benefit of artificial illumination. Still, at the first stop light, after I exited the freeway, the car died. The turn of the ignition key again only generated that sickly clicking noise. Once more, I was forced to provide all the power, and I pushed the car across Mission

Street and to a curb on the left side of a one-way street in front of a Goodyear Tire store.

Unfortunately, it was closed, so I fished through my wallet and pulled out my AAA card with the number for roadside help. I dialed it on my car phone . . . which fortunately had enough battery power on its own to operate independently of the dead car.

Within 20 minutes, a yellow tow truck pulled in front of my vehicle and a mechanic with a clipboard met me at the front of my car.

"Nice car," he said through the smoke from a cigarette lodged between his lips.

"I like this car a lot more when it's running," I said while he asked me to pop the hood.

"I can jump it, but if it dies and you're not getting a charge, you'd be no better off than you are now. I could tow it," he said while filling out a form on his clipboard with my AAA number and date of expiration. "But on Saturday night, I don't think anybody would be available to fix it until Monday morning."

"You're the second Gus I met today," I said while noticing the name sewed in cursive on the left breast pocket of his work shirt.

"Oh, I'm not Gus," the AAA towing representative said while pulling my copy off the form on his clipboard. "This is just Gus' shirt. I'm just filling in on the weekends. My name is Al."

"Well, you're the second Al I met with today too, but I was hoping for three."

"Where do you want me to tow it?" Al asked.

"I need to get this fixed now. Do you know of any garage open this late?"

"Not on a weekend," Al said while stepping out his cigarette in the street.

"I really need to get this car fixed tonight; I'm supposed to meet with Al Davis of the Raiders tomorrow."

"The football guy," Al said while raising his eyebrows and removing his newly lit cigarette from his mouth. "Let me try something," he said after I acknowledged it was the "football guy," and he retreated to the cab of his tow truck. I could hear him connecting with the AAA dispatcher and asking him for Andy's number.

"This guy's a big Raiders fan; if he thought he was doing something for Al Davis, he'd do it. And he owns his own shop and is a really, really good mechanic," Al said in a manner that had me believing him. "I can call him from my truck, but if you've got a car phone, this is his number and his shop is only about six blocks from here."

"Do you know Andy?" I asked the man recommending him to me.

"I met him once, when I was learning this route my first weekend with the company last October. The guy showing me the ropes made a call on a guy that was stuck on a Saturday night and was even willing to spend the night in the city just as long as he could get his car fixed on Sunday morning so he could get home to Ukiah or Eureka or something like that," Al said while hooking my car up to his towing bar.

"The driver I was working with that night called this Andy guy, told me he was a great mechanic. Andy said he couldn't do it Sunday because he was watching the Raiders game . . . so he helped the guy out by opening his shop on Saturday night and fixing the guy's car until like two in the morning or something. That's what made me think of him for you," Al concluded while I relished the thought that a great mechanic in the city was a Raiders fan and willing to work on a Saturday night. I now could only hope he was also available on a Saturday night in August.

"Do you want me to call him for you, or do you just want to talk to him?" Al asked while standing at the back of his truck as his towing equipment lifted the front of my car off the pavement.

"What do you think is better?" I asked Al while he pulled Andy's number from the pocket below the name Gus on his shirt. He had scribbled it on the back of the top flap of a Juicy Fruit candy box, and I asked him to clarify if that was a three or two after the four before I began dialing the number.

"I'll just talk to him," I decided while holding the phone I had removed from my car.

"Hope he can help you," Al said while on his hands and knees and checking the hookup between my car and his truck. To my disappointment, the rings rolled over to an answering machine before the phone was answered, and I put my left hand over the mouthpiece and said to Al, "I'm getting a message machine."

Al didn't respond while climbing over the back of his truck to check the rigging on the other side of my car.

"Andy," I began after the beep indicated it was time to leave a message, "My name is Dennis Ranahan, and you've been recommended to me for two reasons . . . you are a great mechanic and you might be able to get me out of a jam by getting me on the road tonight so I can make my meeting in the morning with Al Davis of the Raiders, who is in town for tomorrow's game against the 49ers at Stanford . . ." Before I finished that sentence, I heard a live voice interrupt the message machine.

"This is Andy; what's your situation?"

Andy didn't sound like a mechanic, whatever a mechanic is supposed to sound like . . . but struck me more like an intellectual, a college professor or something.

"I'm here near Mission Street and you've been recommended to me by the representative AAA sent over."

"Do you know what's wrong with your car?" Andy asked, seemingly more interested in what he might agree to fix than my location.

"All I know is that it is just shutting down on me. I've got no power, and have to start it with a push and clutch pop," I said before he got the make, year, and more information to determine what might be the cause.

"It could be electrical, which can be a major problem; sounds like it could be a solenoid, or you might just not be getting a good connection somewhere. I'd need to see it to know for sure, and you are in a hurry to get it done?" Andy asked.

"That is why you were recommended; the driver here had indicated you did something last October that got a guy back on the road in a few hours."

"Yaaah," Andy said in a drawn-out way for emphasis, "I've been known to do some crazy things to help people out."

"Can you take on my crazy situation tonight?" I asked with just a hint of pleading in my voice.

"You work for the Raiders?" Andy asked without confirming he was available to work on my car on such short notice.

"I used to," I said, "but tomorrow I'm supposed to meet with Al Davis and I was hoping my car could get me there."

"Let me talk to the driver; what's his name?"

"Al," I told Andy and handed the phone to the man who had completed his check on the towing apparatus and was ready to pull my car to Andy's if he would have us and could help me.

- - - - - -

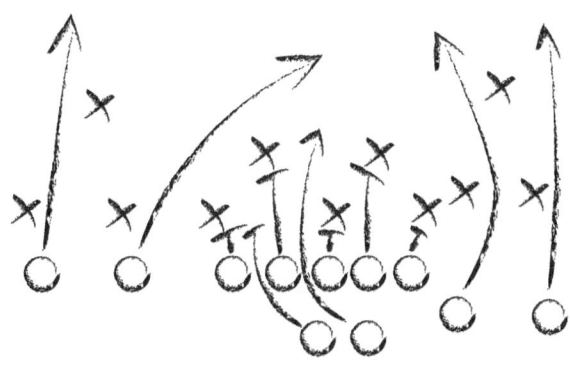

Chapter 47

Garage Night

As surprised as I was to first hear Andy's voice on the phone, I was even more thrown off-center when I met the man who was standing under a light on the right side of an open garage. In the light with a dark background, his white hair stood out like a halo on an angel. It was tied in a long ponytail, and his hands were hidden in the pocket of his sweatshirt. Before Al dropped my car from his truck, I jumped out to introduce myself to the man that was saving my life on a Saturday night by fixing my car.

His handshake was both strong and inviting.

"Think you can get your car fixed on a Saturday night just because you know Al Davis?" Andy deadpanned while pulling our handshake forward and tapping me on my right shoulder with his left hand.

"I do know him, and used to work for the Raiders," I confirmed. "But now I'm just trying to save a business deal with Mr. Davis, and you helping me with this car tonight would be a huge assist."

"When did you work for them?" Andy asked while overseeing Al maneuvering my car into his garage.

"End of Lamonica and best years of Stabler," I proudly announced for the time period I was with the Oakland Raiders, "'73 to '76. Great years," I reflected as Andy's eyes widened while recalling those seasons.

"Drop it across the street and we'll push it forward into the garage," Andy told Al while moving into the two-lane street and assuring no cars were coming from either direction. Al had unhitched his towing bar and pulled his truck parallel on the street before coming to give us a hand. "Get in and steer it," Andy instructed in my direction while he and Al pushed from the back. As we entered the garage, I realized why Andy didn't want me to help push the car, as it wouldn't have fit in the garage opening with the driver-side door open.

While Al was completing the AAA paperwork, the late-night mechanic asked me, "You got a Super Bowl ring?" Andy was enough of a fan to be aware that the Raiders won their first Super Bowl to conclude the 1976 season.

"I left five months before they won it," I said without regret in my voice. "If I would have stayed, I don't think I would have left the year after we won the Super Bowl, and I'm not sure what would have happened if I would have stayed with the team. Been married 18 years and have two great kids, boy and a girl. Wouldn't trade that for anything . . . certainly not a Super Bowl ring."

"First took my son to a Raiders game when he was 10; they played in San Francisco," Andy told me. "First at Kezar, and then at Candlestick. In 1962, Danny and I started our drives across the Bay Bridge for every home game at Frank Youell Field. The last thing we did together, just months before he passed, was go to Super Bowl XV in New Orleans and get to see the Raiders beat Vermeil's Eagles."

"I'm all done here," Al said while handing some paperwork over to Andy. I reached into my pocket and handed him a folded-up twenty to thank him for introducing me to Andy.

"You don't have to do that," Al said with his hand up but his eyes on the bill.

"I don't have to, but I want to. Thanks again, Al, you did great," I said while he accepted my tip and waved goodbye to Andy as he was pulling the chain to close the door of his garage. The aluminum door was on rails and sent a piercing sound through the garage as it rolled to a close. When it did, Andy pushed a lynchpin in place to secure the door was locked.

"Upshaw, Otto, and Shell up front; Freddie and Cliff wide; Stabler, Hubbard, and Davis in the backfield," Andy rattled off the top of his head, bringing to mind a team from 20 years earlier.

"They were all great guys off the field, too," I said while feeding his appreciation for those great Raider years.

Still thinking about how old Andy was, he didn't look to be much over 50. I was 43, and my curiosity was peaked on how he could have had a son my age. It prompted me to pry about his age by saying, "I was 10 in 1960, and my dad was 44. Now, he had me later than his other three kids, and we're spread over 10 years, but you don't look old enough to have had a 10-year-old in 1960?"

Andy laughed. "Well, if your dad was old enough, I was, too, because Danny was born when I was 36. I'm two years older than your dad."

"You're 77 years old?!" I asked, more surprised at learning the age of a person than at any time in my life.

"I'm 79, will be 80 next month," Andy said while loosening the bolts on the battery connections.

Again, for at least a third time, I was absolutely caught off guard and surprised by this guy willing to work on my car on a Saturday night. Even though I thought Andy was much younger, he told me his age with no need or apparent effort to mislead the truth. My first inclination was to find evidence of his advanced years, and noticed his hooded sweatshirt, while not pulled over his head, was bunched at the neck, covering everything from his chin down. What didn't make sense was his hair. It was white but not old, appearing to be that of a person half his age.

Neither of us talked for a few minutes while he focused on my car, and my mind ran on this guy being two years older than my dad and having a son my age, who was gone. And my dad being gone, he died in 1990, but Andy being here. What I didn't know, and couldn't know, was if it would be hurtful for him to share about his son. Or, would he appreciate the opportunity of talking about the son he lost more than a decade earlier? While I was thinking about that, Andy was working on my car. Before long, he had a part in his hand and was checking a catalog in search of a replacement number.

"As far as I can tell this little puppy is not pulling its weight," Andy said while holding up a piece of the car that was the size of a D battery. It had two connections coming out of the side. I could see from the way Andy was holding it in his left hand, and at the same time, he was turning pages with his right hand in the catalog opened on his work bench.

"How did you lose your son, Andy?" I asked respectfully, although no doubt more intrusive than most would have been on a first meeting.

"Leukemia," Andy said with a tone that indicated he still viewed the illness as his enemy.

"Beautiful kid," Andy said while turning his attention away from the parts catalog and toward me. "He had finished medical school, served three years in the Navy. Now he's home, and the first Sunday he is here we go see the Raiders play. Even though they lost to Seattle, we had a great time . . . his first game with me in three years."

My sense was Andy enjoyed having someone listen to his stories about his son, and my emotions had already crossed from curiosity to empathy.

"I remember leaving the game that afternoon; Danny got winded even while we were walking down the ramps at the Coliseum. I told him, 'You're a doctor, diagnose yourself.' I feel so bad about saying that even to this day," Andy confided, "because he was a doctor, and he could diagnose himself, and he was hoping to keep it from us until after the holidays.

"Can you believe that kid," Andy said proudly, "he's dying of cancer and he didn't want to burden us with that fact. Wanted us to have a nice Christmas.

"I'll tell you something, sir; we had the Christmas I look back with the fondest memories because we did know. We had only one more Christmas with him, and only two months before he died we were in New Orleans and at the Super Dome to see our beloved Raiders win it all. If you're going to go out, you might as well go out a winner," Andy concluded with a broad smile.

"My dad was a 49ers fan, and his last Super Bowl was when they beat the Denver Broncos, 55–10, three years ago. He went out a winner, too," I smiled at Andy while acknowledging both of our losses.

"Was your son married?" I asked Andy while he was paging through a personal phone book and seemingly locating the number he needed to dial.

"Never married," Andy said, "but had a great girlfriend. Ginger was her name, and everyone always said she was the sweetest of all the spices. They were right. We kept in touch with Ginger for maybe eight, nine, ten years after Danny died, but she eventually met a guy and got married. He got transferred; I think she lives in Scottsdale, Arizona, now. We haven't heard from her in three or four years. Too bad, I liked Ginger. Hope she's doing okay.

"If this guy tells me what I want to know," Andy said, taking his eyes off the catalog long enough to look at me for a moment, "then you are going to be outta here in a matter of minutes." Andy rested his arm on the vise attached to the end of his workbench. About two feet away from the attached vise was one that was portable, it had a large wing nut that allowed it to easily be secured on the edge of the table.

"I always wanted two vises next to each other," I said while looking past Andy and to the vise that lay on its side on top of the metal table. He looked at me, obviously not understanding what I was referring to, when his attention shifted to the phone. "KB9-LC45K," Andy said into the phone after greeting the person on the other end as if they were longtime friends.

"That's good news, they put all sorts of fancy numbers on their parts, but it is a simple solenoid and the one I've got will work," Andy said moments later. "Tell Rita hello for me, and thanks again.

"Fortunately," Andy said to me while hanging up the phone, "I've got one that will get you on the road as soon as I find it on this shelf and do a quick install."

He was standing on a wooden step stool, no more than eight inches off the ground, but enough to allow him to reach anything in the cabinet he had opened. The cabinet was gun-barrel silver, sturdy in both appearance and functionality. Each of the four shelves Andy had exposed with the open doors was clearly marked with small boxes positioned to expose their part number. His order reminded me of how Ron Wolf kept his personnel records on all those college prospects he charted. While Ron could find a future All-Pro in the eleventh round of the draft and a Hall of Fame member with earlier picks, Andy was able to find a blue-and-white box with the five letters and number he was looking for.

"Your system reminds me of Ron Wolf's personnel office with the Raiders," I told Andy. He looked at me, clearly not understanding what I meant.

"Broken down and kept in perfect order," I said to Andy in an attempt to explain the parallel I saw between the order on his shelves and the structure Ron used in the best player personnel department in football.

When Andy realized what I meant, he just shrugged it off with a disarming smile and wink. "The Raiders always were best when the field was stocked with draft picks made during Wolf's years. How is it going for him in Green Bay?"

"Ron told me that when the Packers were making the offer, Davis asked him, 'Why would you want to go there, they only have one star player?'"

"Sterling Sharpe," Andy accurately filled in.

I nodded that he was right while adding, "Now look at what's he's got. His quarterback, his coach, and a team that is getting really good in a big hurry. And the Raiders are dropping again without his counsel."

"What's Davis like?" Andy asked while removing the black rubber protection mat that was draped above the wheel well to protect my car's finish while he was working under the hood. Then, without getting my answer, he added, "Soon as I open this door, you can give your car a turn of the key."

"Fixed already?" I said as Andy surprised me again.

"We'll know when you turn that key," Andy said while pulling on the chain to raise the door after he had pulled the coder key out of the latch.

I turned the key harder than usual, prompted by the recent problems I had starting the car. But I didn't need to; the moment the key engaged, the car sprung to life. Because I was in Andy's garage and the test was not the engine, but the starting, I saw no need to step on the gas or let it run for more than a moment.

"Perfect," I said, stepping out of the car. "What do I owe you?"

"I'll be able to tell you that in a moment," Andy said while washing his hands with extra-strength soap in a basin that was near the bathroom on the opposite end of the noisy garage door.

"He's the most amazing man I ever worked for," I said to Andy in response to his earlier question. "Black and white. In or out. A hundred percent a hundred percent of the time. He made me, anyone that worked for him, better than they could be without him."

"I hated when he moved the team to LA," Andy said with a shake of his head.

"You know what the worst day for me was, and I was surprised," Andy continued, "the day they beat the Redskins in the Super Bowl. I was rooting for them even though I hated that they were no longer in Oakland, but when they won the Super Bowl and the television showed all the people celebrating in LA, I just felt sick. That's our Raiders.

"Well," Andy said with a smile and shrug, "LA's got their Raiders now; that was our Raiders that won the Super Bowl in 1983."

He handed me the yellow copy of a work invoice; it was for $83.61.

"What?" I said, "That doesn't seem like enough, given you opened the shop on a Saturday night and all."

"Parts, an hour labor, and Uncle Sam, that's what it equals."

"Well, it doesn't do justice for my appreciation," I said while handing him two one-hundred-dollar bills.

"Too much," Andy said, shoving one of the hundreds back into my hand. "I'll take this one and consider it a full appreciation tip, and I appreciate it."

"Appreciate this too," I said while handing him back the second hundred.

"Then I offer you a cold one if you'd like," Andy said while moving toward a refrigerator that was at least 20 years old and located to the left side of his workbench. He pulled out two Coors cans and popped his top after handing me mine. "Hard to work for?" Andy asked while enjoying his first sip.

"Not at all. Not for me." I repeated, "I liked the black and white. I got through school pretty much on charm and wit, but with Davis, no stories made up for not doing your job. He was exactly what I needed. Tough is doing a lot without succeeding. Knowing you are contributing to a winning team is inspiring."

"I've heard that he is committed to people for life," Andy said.

"Well, he's committed to people that remain loyal to him. But it is cold when he is done with you. We've always stayed in pretty good communication, but I've seen him absolutely ice people off the map.

"I'll tell you something," I said while finishing my beer, "when I was first working for the Raiders, I would have taken a bullet for the guy. This was the mid-'70s, Gerald Ford was getting shot at twice in a few months period; Davis was controversial, and could polarize people. He could have had a whacko out to get him just like John Lennon did a few years later. Anyway, I used to walk with him through airports and other crowded areas just looking for a gun in someone's hand, and if I'd seen it, I would have stepped between him and the bullet."

"That's a scary thought," Andy said.

"Got scary for me, too," I confirmed. "In 1975, I got married, and when I was with Davis the following September in Baltimore, I was thinking about Pam and how I couldn't leave her, have her husband give up his life for someone else."

"She gave you something important to protect."

Andy's comment stopped me for a moment. I hadn't ever thought of it in those terms. Maybe my life was more important than giving it all to my work . . . even if it was the Oakland Raiders. That's what I had decided on my own in 1976, but Andy gave me an "ah-hah" moment that stopped me talking.

"What are you thinking?" Andy asked while observing my reaction to his comment.

"I'm thinking I better call Pam and let her know what my plans are for the night. Last I talked with her, I was waiting for a Triple-A truck while stalled on the side of the road."

Andy turned the phone on the desk we were sitting at toward me, and I punched in my home number.

Pam was glad to hear my car was fixed and wanted to know if I was or wasn't going to the Raiders game on Sunday.

"Now that my car is fixed I think I will," I told her. She replied, "You need to drive Erin to the school parking lot on Monday morning because she leaves from there on a bus to cheerleading camp. And Tim Dantono called; he wants to know if you can ump the baseball championship game this week."

"On Tuesday?" I confirmed.

"I think so," Pam said while looking on the kitchen counter below the phone for the baseball Little League flyer that had the postseason schedule. "Yep," she said with the confirmation in hand. "Tuesday."

"He knows Kevin is playing in the game, right?" I asked Pam.

"Tim says he still thinks you'd do the best job."

"I don't want to," I confessed. "I'd rather just enjoy watching Kevin play. Can you call him for me and tell him I'll do it if he's stuck, but that I'd rather just get to watch Kevin."

"I'll call him. How did you get your car fixed so fast?" Pam asked.

"My new best friend here, a real Raiders fan and a great guy. His name is Andy."

"Well, tell Andy thank you for getting my husband off the side of the road. Get home safe," Pam said before hanging up.

"My wife says thank you for helping me out," I said to Andy before adding, "You really did do me a great service tonight. Thanks a lot."

"It's been my pleasure," Andy said while heading back to the cold box. "You want another?"

"Absolutely. Thanks," I said before he delivered my second beer.

When Andy sat back down, I noticed what appeared to be a bit of melancholy expression on his face as his bright blue eyes seemed to pick up a special twinkle during his second beer. I thought I knew what he was thinking about, and responded to that.

"I'm sorry you lost your son," I said with real compassion.

"So am I," Andy said while opening the third drawer down on the right side of his desk. "This is Danny," Andy announced while handing over an 8-page photo book that held 16 pictures of Danny. There was one of him as a baby with a much younger Andy proudly holding him at his waist. A shot of a young Danny running the bases in a Little League baseball game, and a number of pictures of Danny and Andy at football games and on special family occasions. There was a professional wallet-size photo of a strong-looking Danny in his Navy whites, and the last photo in the book was of a much thinner and pale Danny standing under a Bourbon Street sign in New Orleans.

"That one was taken the night before we beat the Eagles," Andy said while noticing what photo I had turned to.

"He died just a couple months later, on March 26, 1981."

The date had special significance for me. My dad died on that date in 1990, even though his death certificate and tombstone say March 27. Because Mom found him in their yard on the morning of March 27, but we could see by where Dad's projects had been left that he died on the evening of March 26. There was a can of beer almost full on his desk, the reading lamp was not turned on, and his television was tuned to Channel 8, a channel he only watched for a half-hour per night to get the race results. Mom had gone to bed early that Monday evening and last saw him about 7:00 p.m. when he was lying on the coach in his den. He was waiting for the downstairs bathroom carpet that he had cleaned to finish drying on a rope he had tied between his storage shed and a tree. Mom had told me about their last conversation.

"I think this area is going to be a lot nicer with clean rugs," Mom had said while looking into the bathroom just outside Dad's den.

"What time is it?" Dad blurted out while quickly moving from a reclined position to a sitting one. He rubbed his left arm and looked around in an attempt to get his bearings. Dad was still sitting on his couch, rubbing extremities to get his blood circulating, when Mom answered his question, "It's a little before seven. I'm going to bed."

"I need to be ready to get the race results," Dad said while moving toward his desk and changing the channel on the television from

ABC-7 to the independent station that came through on Channel 8. It featured local sports personality Sammy Spear recapping race results.

"The last thing I told my father was that I loved him," I fondly recalled and told Andy.

"I must have told Danny that I loved him a million times in his life, and so many times in his final year," Andy said while shaking his head and heading for another beer.

"You want another?" he asked, holding a can up that he just pulled from the old refrigerator with rounded corners.

"No, I'm going to be driving soon. Two is enough," I said while Andy poked his head down to see what else he might have in the icebox.

"You want a Coke or something like that?" he asked. "I've got diet soda or orange juice. The orange juice is good. I've got a client that a few times a year brings me a couple of pitchers of fresh squeezed from his trees."

"Not diet; I'll try the orange juice," I said while getting up to fetch my own glass. I expected plastic or even paper cups in the cupboard he pointed me toward, but was surprised to find four perfectly clean and lined-up drinking glasses resting on a fresh paper towel.

"Wow," I said. "Nice." I took one of the glasses out of the cupboard. Andy took it out of my hand and put it on the workbench before using two hands to carefully pour the juice into the glass. He didn't lose a drop before screwing the top back on the 48-ounce glass bottle.

"My wife, Anna, keeps that shelf clean and stocked," Andy said with a smile. "Says that is my company entertainment center. Guess she was right, 'cause you're company."

"Tell her I much appreciate her entertainment center, and am truly enjoying all the rewards it provides. This orange juice is great," I said after a second sip.

"Isn't it good," Andy said while shaking his approval of my review. "Seems like he must be adding something to make it taste so good, sugar or something, but he tells me it's all natural."

"It's all good," I offered while finishing more than half my glass with another sip.

"I'm refreshed, my car is running, and you've probably got a wife to get home to on a Saturday night," I said while nodding my appreciation and moving toward the driver-side door of my car.

"The best days were the late sixties and most of the seventies," Andy said while fetching himself a fourth beer.

"Those were the best, weren't they," I said with approval in my voice and on my face. "And I'll tell you this, even while it was going on, we knew this was something special," I said while pausing my push to get in the car.

"What years exactly were you there?"

"1973 to 1976, although I left at the start of the preseason the year they won the Super Bowl."

"Do you regret leaving before the Super Bowl?" Andy asked.

"The only day I regretted it was when they beat the Steelers in the AFC Championship Game because I had lost three championship games and dreamed of moving on to the Super Bowl in each of those years. But it didn't happen in the three years I was with the Raiders, and, quite frankly, I don't know if I would have left on the heels of winning the Super Bowl."

"Would staying be a bad thing?" Andy asked, interested in why I wanted out of the Raiders instead of enjoying the great joy it was.

"The Raiders was 24 hours a day and required that total commitment. I loved working in that black-and-white no-nonsense structure while I was totally committed, but when I wanted to commit myself to Pam and start a family, I could not see, as LoCasale stills refers to me, 'Ranahan of the Raiders.'

"When I think that I was willing to step in front of a bullet for this man when I was 23, and now I have a wife and kids and in no way would volunteer to leave them alone. They are so much more important than any job, and now that I have them, they're 15 and 13. I can't imagine trading them for a dozen Super Bowl rings."

"I'd give anything to have my Danny back," Andy said while sitting back down across from his beer.

"You and Danny went to a lot of games together?" I asked while Andy's expression seemed to indicate he was thinking fondly of a time spent with Danny.

"One of my favorite memories was the Heidi Game, Danny had just turned 18 and he had a girlfriend he wanted to take to the game to celebrate his birthday. I tried to find some extra tickets; Anna would have enjoyed joining us and making it a foursome. But, I couldn't find any tickets, it was sold out, and Anna didn't want to go to the stadium needing to count on buying tickets from a scalper.

"So, I told Danny to take his girl, I think her name was Jane, and we get into this big debate about how he doesn't want to break our tradition . . . and now he feels bad," Andy said while mocking a voice in a childlike pout.

Then, with a burst of laughter accompanying his words, he said, "The boy was mixed up because his hormones wanted the girl and his head was telling him not to leave the old man behind. How old is your son?" Andy asked while shifting the topic from his son to mine.

"Thirteen," I answered.

"Whoa," Andy said in a drawn-out way while shaking his head. "You've got it all in front of you. And you've got a daughter too?"

"Erin," I responded. "She's 15."

"You got pictures?" Andy asked as I walked away from my car and back to the table, stopping to grab a glass of orange juice on my way.

"I do," I said, reaching for my wallet and pulling out a plastic photo booklet that contained four pictures. Andy was silent with a smile on his face as he took in each photograph while I named the people pictured. "Norm Fisher, one of the best photographers the Raiders worked with, took that one," I said while pointing to a baby picture of Erin in a pink dress sitting on a blue pillow.

"Great-looking family," Andy said while handing me back the photos.

"But you were telling me about the Heidi Game," I reminded Andy while he shifted back to a facial smile while telling his memories of the week Danny turned 18. "His birthday is the 17th, same day as the Heidi Game, and he wanted to spend the day with his girl. He was a freshman at Santa Clara, and he was both going to introduce me to this girl and give her my beloved ticket to see the Raiders against Joe Namath and the Jets.

"Now and then, I can laugh at the thing, but god damnit I missed the Heidi Game, one of the biggest games in the history of football, and some girl who Danny probably saw no more than one or two times after that, got to see that game!"

His comment brought both of us to laughter, which was thoughtfully stopped when Andy instinctively uttered, "God, I miss him."

"What was your favorite game?" I posed to Andy.

"Loved lots of them," he said to the sky as he pushed himself back in his chair and took an extra long chug from his beer can. "The playoff win in '74 over the Dolphins."

"December 21, best game ever," I concurred while shaking my head.

"Danny was in his second year of med school, home for the Christmas holidays," Andy said while lifting his head as if he remembered something special.

"That's how that holiday season started," Andy beamed, "with the Raiders winning and Danny home for the holidays. That was the year we met Ginger, the one we kept in touch for a while but haven't heard from in three or four years."

"During that Raiders/Dolphins playoff game, I heard the funniest thing I have ever heard and got fired right before Stabler completed the pass to Clarence Davis," I said with a shake of my head and a chuckle in my voice.

Andy howled with laughter when I told him what Monte Stickles said, "Dempsey would have been in."

"So you liked working for him?" Andy asked, shifting the subject back to Davis.

"I didn't recognize everything I was learning until after I left," I confided to Andy. "I didn't know what 'context set' or 'clearly defined objectives' truly meant, and the real importance of attention to detail is still one I struggle with today. But with Davis and the Raiders in Oakland during the '70s, I was overworked, underpaid, and loved it.

"Everyone was better under the challenging eye of Davis. He inspired those willing to give it everything they had for the shared objective, and he had me convinced that I had as much to do with the Raiders winning on Sunday as Stabler, Biletnikoff, or Blanda. He showed me that doing my job with the media, travel arrangements, or whatever contributed to us winning on Sunday. Having the room keys set up correctly in the lobby was a contributing factor to Ken Stabler completing a touchdown pass to Cliff Branch.

"When I was willing to give it everything I had, it was inspiring . . . but, while 100 percent is exhilarating, 99 percent is debilitating."

"He had you guys working hard, huh?" Andy asked while showing an interest in my perspective on the Raiders.

"It wasn't so much as working hard, as much as it was a calling. Being a Raider was different than working for any other team. It was better because we worked harder and got better results. When a person can provide that environment for an inspired worker, then he's got your soul. The only work is doing everything for the good of the organization."

"Why did you leave?"

"Once I didn't have it all to give, once I decided Pam and starting a family was more important to me than serving Mr. Davis, I was done. Couldn't survive in a context of 100 percent without the willingness to sacrifice all for the organization."

"So you left," Andy nodded with approval.

"I'll tell you something, Andy, when I hear those players, coaches and executives of the league being inducted into the Hall of Fame and thanking their family for all the sacrifices to allow them to pursue their dreams, I know it's true.

"Geeze," I said while checking the time on my watch, "It's after 11, and I'm glad I have a family to get home to. I've got to get on the road."

"Well, I hope your car doesn't have to break down for the opportunity of visiting with you again," Andy said while extending his hand. I shook it while we promised to get together to talk more about football. While he was pulling the chain to raise the metal door on his shop, I felt the comfort of my leather seats and then the strength of the turbo-charged engine throttling into action with the twist of a key: a far better system than having to push it and pop the clutch.

- - - - - -

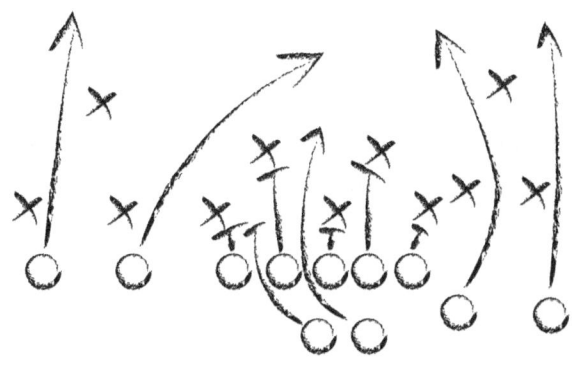

Chapter 48

No Time for Greatness

I WAS CURSING MYSELF FOR NOT TAKING the parking pass or ticket from LoCasale now that I was stuck in the public traffic and looking for a spot to park in a dirt lot blocks from Stanford Stadium. The game was a half-hour from starting when I arrived at the press gate and requested a media credential for the game, not wanting to ask LoCasale for something I had already turned down. A representative from the university didn't know who I was, and wouldn't accommodate my request, so I was left to either have them contact LoCasale or just get in on my own.

I decided to go it alone.

On my walk between the press gate and the ticket line, I was drawn to a short, dark-haired person who said to the group walking in front of me, "Need tickets?"

They nodded no while I said, "I need one."

"I've got a single on the 30-yard line halfway up," he said while fanning a handful of tickets like a deck of cards and thumbing for the single in a good location. Once he found it, he quoted a price ten dollars more than face value.

I offered five dollars less than the price printed on the ticket before we agreed on the actual amount.

He was telling the truth, the location of the ticket was near the 30-yard line and higher than the middle of the stands. It would have been a great seat to enjoy the game if that was what I had bought the ticket to accomplish. But, I had a different agenda. I was here for a meeting with Mr. Davis.

I was hoping the Raiders beat the 49ers, which I knew from experience would have a great influence on Mr. Davis' mood after the game. The Raiders had won the prior week in the annual Hall of Fame Game in Canton, Ohio, over the Green Bay Packers, 19–3. The 49ers were also scheduled for five preseason games this season and met the Pittsburgh Steelers in the American Bowl the previous week in Barcelona, Spain. The 49ers beat the Steelers, 21–14.

I straddled my black briefcase while standing for the national anthem. After the anthem was complete, I remained standing to use my binoculars to see if I could find Davis in the press box that was above my left shoulder. The reflection of the afternoon sun masked who was sitting in the press box, but I fully expected Davis to be there.

My hopes for a Raiders triumph were blunted early. New Raiders quarterback Jeff Hostetler, who had filled in for an injured Phil Sims three years earlier and helped guide the New York Giants to a Super Bowl win, appeared totally overmatched by the 49ers defense and his poor timing with Los Angeles receivers. His first pass sailed over Tim Brown's head, and his second, intended for James Lofton, was also overthrown and intercepted.

The 49ers turned the Raiders third first-half turnover into a 17–0 lead, and before halftime, the Los Angeles deficit was 20–0. Not exactly results conducive to a good meeting with Davis. On the field in the second half were a number of players who were not going to be on either the 49ers or Raiders roster in four weeks when the regular season opened.

The game was clogged in the middle of the field for most of the second half, with backups on both sides misfiring on offense. The thought of abandoning the attempt to get a meeting with Davis on this day seemed more and more a good idea as the South Bay sun scorched my Irish complexion. But, as I sat in the Palo Alto heat, it occurred to me that if I was willing to approach Davis in the wake of a decisive loss, he might have more respect for my willingness to do whatever it takes. A lynchpin in his success during the '70s in Oakland.

Early in the fourth quarter, I abandoned my seat in the stands and began my assent to the press box. The cool air provided by the shade of the concourse was a welcomed relief from my afternoon in the stands. The entrance to the press box at Stanford was right off the main concourse that rims the seats around the natural grass field. Two Stanford game-day workers were stationed at the bottom of the cement stairs that led up to the press box.

Earlier in the day, and probably right after halftime, these two older gentlemen were no doubt diligently checking for press credentials, assuring no unauthorized people gained access to an area that required a game credential. But now, late in the afternoon, they both appeared relaxed on the job, and when an attractive lady in yellow shorts asked where the nearest restroom was, they both turned her way to point her in the right direction. When they did, I slipped onto the bottom step leading to the press box and when they turned back I bounded onto the concourse and looked back at them, asking the one closest to me, if he had seen Glenn Dickey leave.

"Haven't seen him," he said while shaking his head no, while the gentleman behind him in the matching red jacket shook his head yes in agreement to not seeing him.

"Geeze," I said, "I thought we were leaving the press box together. Where the heck did he go?" I said to them, knowing that my charade while carrying a briefcase had them believing I had already been in the press box.

"Maybe he's still upstairs," I said while quickly moving up the stairway to the press box.

There was very little movement in the press box; about a third of the media positions were vacated by newsmen getting a jump on gaining access to the locker room for postgame quotes. Right inside the area fed by the concrete stairs were eight seating positions, with three of the chairs filled. There were three unoccupied chairs right in front of me, while down the press row sat Jim Otto, Al Davis, and Sam Bercovich. Two seats were unoccupied on Bercovich's right, and I sat down with one chair vacant between Otto and me.

I put my briefcase on the table in front of me, Otto nodded a hello without extending his hand, and Bercovich smiled a hello with an open hand wave while leaning forward in his chair.

Davis sat stoic between them, only once glancing my way that I caught in the minutes I was at the table. He was not happy, not offering good cheer in the waning moments of a thrashing of his beloved Silver and Black. Davis' jaw was pushed forward, and he was talking about what needed to be done almost under his breath while his soldiers on both sides focused on the field.

Finally, Davis spoke in a volume meant to be heard, and talked in that full New Jersey thug inflection while asking a young Raiders employee what was going on in the Denver/Dallas game.

"It was 13 to 13 last I heard," came the response to Davis from the rosy-cheeked young worker.

I was so excited to see what happened next. If I had given Davis a response like that to a request in the mid-seventies, I would have been taken to task about what was really acceptable and unacceptable behavior. This was where one of Davis' next generation of great workers was going to be groomed, learn the difference between sort of going for and doing whatever it fucking takes to win.

Davis was going to teach him that when he asked what is going on between the Cowboys and Broncos he was not interested in the last thing you knew. He wanted to know the details right now.

What was the fucking score; where were the teams on the field; how much time was left in the game; has either team suffered any significant injuries? Let's go, get the fucking details; I can almost hear Davis driving me to excellence, beginning with my run across the field on a fogging morning in Santa Rosa 20 years earlier.

But none of that came. No moment of correction to set context today. Instead, Davis just nodded while aimlessly tossing a piece of rolled-up paper on the counter in front of him.

I wasn't aware of my mouth being open after my jaw dropped until the young employee backed away from Davis and to his position against the press box wall. He was standing there for a moment before turning his eyes to me, which snapped my consciousness and I noticed that my stare included a wide-open mouth. I closed it and instinctively shook my head while still startled at Davis' lack of commitment.

Didn't he know what that kid needed to learn? Was he done with the effort it took to do the little things to be great? If this kid was a reflection of the Raiders, how were they doing?

When the final gun sounded, Davis grumbled to Otto, "At least we didn't get anybody hurt."

I glanced at the uninspired worker who was standing against the wall with one of his shirttails out and thought differently. I shifted my attention to the scoreboard, which showed the 49ers whitewashing the Raiders, 27–0. Then Davis caught my eye as he rose from his press box chair, acknowledging me with a nod and raising his eyebrows before an indistinguishable sound seeped from between his teeth.

For the first time, he looked old to me as he shuffled out of the press box with Bercovich holding the door and Otto following close behind.

Too old, at least on this day, to do what he taught me had to be done to win.

– – – – – –

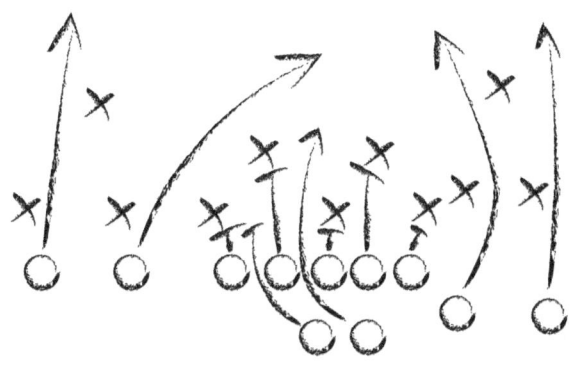

Acknowledgments

It started with Tom Grimes, moved along by Ron Wolf, and brought to fruition by Al Davis. Whenever something works, people are the reason. I was too young to fully grasp the lessons offered by Al LoCasale, but I benefited from his tutoring.

Ken LaRue was an adult friend, whereas Ken Bishop was a good friend. Tom Flores was the best at taking care of people. Likewise, other coaches who worked on John Madden's staff inspired me every day.

In the production of this book, I appreciate the immense contribution of John Paine, who edited the wealth of material I began with to the stories and life-defining events that made the final cut. More recently, my sincere thanks go to Michele DeFilippo, Ronda Rawlins and their crew at 1106 Design that brought the final product to market.

- - - - - -

About the Author

In 1973, Dennis Ranahan parlayed a summer internship and training camp job to a full-time position with the Oakland Raiders. His rise in the organization was tied to his relationship with the Raiders dynamic owner, Al Davis.

In 1981, Ranahan took his knowledge of the league, and what makes an athlete and team perform above or below their accepted level, to the task of delivering winning point spread decisions to clients. He named his company Qoxhi Picks, taking five "football" letters to create the name. "Q" for quarterback, "O" for offense, "X" for defense and "HI" to represent a motivational high, which is the key to his success as a handicapper.

Today, Ranahan is a weekly featured guest on KNBR radio in the San Francisco Bay Area and publishes insightful handicapping stories and point spread edges on his website: picksfootball.com. In 2001, Ranahan introduced an online tool that is designed to transform wagering on football to a lucrative business investment. The business Account Manager allows clients to declare an opening account balance and receive exact wager amounts on each Qoxhi selection to stay within any of the five money management strategies offered on the site. In the 23 seasons this investment tool has been available, 20 seasons have shown a profit with the Basic Strategy and in 43 years the weekly Top Pick has never had a losing campaign.

Ranahan makes his home in the East Bay with his wife of 49 years, Pam, and they have two children and five grandchildren.